Now About All These Women in the Swedish Film Industry

Now About All These Women in the Swedish Film Industry

Louise Wallenberg, Frantzeska Papadopoulou,
Maaret Koskinen, and Tytti Soila

BLOOMSBURY ACADEMIC
NEW YORK • LONDON • OXFORD • NEW DELHI • SYDNEY

BLOOMSBURY ACADEMIC
Bloomsbury Publishing Inc
1385 Broadway, New York, NY 10018, USA
50 Bedford Square, London, WC1B 3DP, UK
29 Earlsfort Terrace, Dublin 2, Ireland

BLOOMSBURY, BLOOMSBURY ACADEMIC and the Diana logo
are trademarks of Bloomsbury Publishing Plc

First published in the United States of America 2023
This paperback edition published 2024

Copyright © Louise Wallenberg, Frantzeska Papadopoulou,
Maaret Koskinen, and Tytti Soila, 2023

For legal purposes the Acknowledgments on p. x constitute
an extension of this copyright page.

Cover design by Eleanor Rose
Cover image: Malin Ek (as Gerd Osten) in *Mamma/Mother*,
Dir. Suzanne Osten, 1982, SFI. Photograph by Solweig Warner.
With the kind permission of Malin Ek and Solweig Warner.

This work is published open access subject to a Creative Commons Attribution-NonCommercial-NoDerivatives 4.0 International licence (CC BY-NC-ND 4.0, https://creativecommons.org/licenses/by-nc-nd/4.0/). You may re-use, distribute, and reproduce this work in any medium for non-commercial purposes, provided you give attribution to the copyright holder and the publisher and provide a link to the Creative Commons licence.

Bloomsbury Publishing Inc does not have any control over, or responsibility for, any third-party websites referred to or in this book. All internet addresses given in this book were correct at the time of going to press. The author and publisher regret any inconvenience caused if addresses have changed or sites have ceased to exist, but can accept no responsibility for any such changes.

A catalog record for this book is available from the Library of Congress

ISBN: HB: 978-1-5013-6621-5
PB: 979-8-7651-0085-1
ePDF: 978-1-5013-6619-2
eBook: 978-1-5013-6620-8

Typeset by Integra Software Services Pvt. Ltd.

To find out more about our authors and books visit www.bloomsbury.com
and sign up for our newsletters.

Contents

List of Figures	vi
Foreword *Anna Serner*	vii
Acknowledgments	x
Introduction *Louise Wallenberg*	1

Part One Frameworks: The Power of Institutions

1	The Sex of the Author: On Authorship *Frantzeska Papadopoulou*	31
2	Gendering Film Distribution *Frantzeska Papadopoulou*	49
3	In the Crossfire: Anna Serner and the Swedish Film Institute *Maaret Koskinen*	67

Part Two Histories, Herstories, and Representation

4	Women on Screen I: 1910s–1960s *Louise Wallenberg*	95
5	Women on Screen II: 1970s–2010s *Louise Wallenberg*	119

Part Three Routines, Practices, and Practitioners

6	Making a Living: On the Working Conditions and Salaries for Actors and Extras within Swedish Film Production 1930–1955 *Tytti Soila*	143
7	Bibi Lindström: "Easy to Work With" *Tytti Soila*	159
8	Lisa Langseth: "Make Sure That What's in Your Heart is Done, So it Doesn't Drown and Stay in the Heart" *Maaret Koskinen*	184

Afterthoughts *Louise Wallenberg*	196
Bibliography	200
Filmography	220
Biographies	224
Index	225

Figures

I.1 Film and theater actors organizing at the "Guldbagge" Awards in January 2018 — 11
1.1 Poster from *Tösen från Stormyrtorpet* — 41
3.1 Anna Serner on Twitter — 73
3.2 The Swedish Minister of Culture and the CEO of the Swedish Film Institute in Cannes — 84
4.1 Jenny Tschernichin-Larsson as suffragette leader and agitator and Lili Ziedner in *Den moderna suffragetten/The Modern Suffragette* (Mauritz Stiller, 1913) — 101
4.2 Sisterhood, intimacy, and friendship in the adaptation of Elin Wägner's *Norrtullsligan* (Per Lindgren, 1923) — 104
4.3 Young Ann-Marie getting her father Holger's (Gösta Ekman) and everyone else's attention in Gustaf Molander's melodrama *Intermezzo* from 1936 — 107
5.1 On the film set of Gunnel Lindblom's *Paradistorg* (*Summer Paradise*, 1976) — 124
5.2 Malin Ek as Suzanne Osten's mother Gerd in *Mamma/Mother* (Suzanne Osten, 1982) — 127
5.3 Mother (Malena Engström) "becoming horse" in Maria Hedman Hvitfeldt's *Min skägiga mamma* (*My Bearded Mum*, 2003) — 132
5.4 Director Mia Engberg and actor Olivier Loustau during a night shoot in Paris in *Lucky One* (2019) — 135
7.1 A sketch for studio floor plan of *Fadern* (Alf Sjöberg 1969) — 160
7.2 Paintings on the wall in the film *Flickorna från Gamla Sta'n* (1934) — 166
7.3 A sketch on the throne hall in *Karin Månsdotter* made on a graph sheet — 175
8.1 Lisa Langseth instructing Alicia Vikander in *Hotell* (2013) — 185

Foreword

Anna Serner
Former CEO of the Swedish Film Institute

Working with gender equality is a constant struggle with resistance, and the barriers are usually arguments that distract focus. By finding other problems that, according to the opponents of gender equality work, supposedly are more urgent, the work for equality has to be put on hold.

One of the barriers is the fact that a lot of stakeholders postpone change, arguing that they "first need to study things more thoroughly." The actual work has to wait to be correct. Sometimes that's true, but a lot of the time it's only a pretext to avoid the most painful part of managing change—to go from talking about the problem to doing something about it. My main message when talking about how to actually achieve gender equality is that you need to stop talking and start doing.

In the work to change the funding system at the Swedish Film Institute we have taken several measures, but two were of central importance. First of all, we started to count all our decisions throughout the year to be able to work proactively. Instead of seeing discrepancies at the end of the year, we could see our tendencies earlier in the year, which gave us clues as to where to take action and time to do so. For instance, this could involve launching a special program for women scriptwriters of bigger budget films, when we noticed that very few applications had women as writers.

The second key measure was to add new knowledge into the field—something like this book, but with a much more limited scope. Books like this are an important contribution to the knowledge of how gender equality in the film industry is developing today while also regarding it in a historical context. The academic depth in this book is important as there are too many opinions and too few facts in the area of gender equality.

At the Swedish Film Institute we decided to publish a special report every year. These reports do not have the same weight in academic merit, but they are all based on facts and are all translated into English, and as such they constitute a solid platform for raising awareness in the industry both in Sweden and internationally. The reports have had an intersectional approach on gender equality, studying different aspects of what results gender inequality has in the film industry. We have studied how the funding in terms of proportion reaches men and women differently, and what difference age and aspects of being racialized make.

It is too early to say whether our work has resulted in any sustainable change or not, but the fact is that during the past ten years the funding decisions have been made 50/50 to men and women, and Swedish film has never been of such high quality. This is confirmed by all the invitations to the international A-film festivals, true proof of high quality, and the invitations have been extended equally to both men and women filmmakers. The only part that has shown decreasing numbers are films with bigger budgets, namely more commercial films. This is also the area where our work has encountered the largest barriers and still show poor numbers in gender equality.

Despite the obvious rise in quality in Swedish art house films during the last decade, the barriers haven't disappeared but rather changed. When we started the work for reaching 50/50, the argument against proceeding was the risk of losing the quality of films if women received more of the funding. Men were getting a lot of media space to express their feelings of being misunderstood and discriminated against. Another argument was the audience. Producers voiced their concern that too much gender equality would take the focus away from how to get the Swedish audience to buy tickets in cinemas to see Swedish films. These are valid concerns for everyone, because who can argue that quality isn't important or that the revenues from cinema ticket sales aren't fundamental for the film business model? The correlation between more work opportunities for women filmmakers and a loss of audience for films made by men is of course very hard to prove. But when a portion of an industry is openly critical toward the public funding authority, it of course amounts to a lucrative media angle, and the media coverage gives these problems a lot of space but never questions the premise that the very cause of the problem was gender equality. So, when critics' opinions are not scrutinized, the criticism tends to become truth in the public awareness.

Over time, when our work has shown no sign of fading out (and when its scope was widened to include an intersectional approach) the arguments of resistance have taken on a more serious shape. The argument is now the threat to democracy. Acting to change unequal structures is accused of infringing the freedom of expression. The opponents to this change have been successful in making a barrier, which equates structure with content.

Everyone agrees on the importance of the freedom of expression, and that the content of art should not be interfered with. Working with the structures, however, as we have tried to do in the Swedish Film Institute, has nothing to do with the decisions that are made about the specific content of individual films. But the media-driven narrative has successfully changed the notion of that fact—and if a narrative stating that working with structures in an artistic industry is comparable to interfering with the artistic content becomes a "truth," then we have a serious problem.

When a governmental body such as the Swedish Film Institute has to back off from actions taken on, and communications about, structural issues, to not ruin the trust in its decisions concerning content, and ultimately to avoid that the very existence of the Swedish Film Institute is questioned, it is indeed a democratic problem. This would certainly make any governmental work for gender equality impossible, and the freedom of expression would remain in existence only for a chosen few.

And now—as of late December 2021—the barrier has proven to have had a real effect, for in the 2022 guidelines to the Swedish Film Institute there has been changes made in relation to the work with gender equality and diversity by the government. The prior guideline, clearly assigning work for gender equality and diversity (and children), has been withdrawn, even though the goals of a gender equal and diverse film industry is still valid. Thus, the official signal is that it isn't given the same weight any longer. The reason for this change is explained as being to ensure that the freedom of art is not interfered with. The opponents succeeded, the barrier worked.

Acknowledgments

The authors wish to express their gratitude to all the women film workers who have contributed with their experiences, memories, and time and without whom this book would not have been written. Special thanks also go to Krister Collin at the Swedish Film Institute who has kindly helped us access the many beautiful images that accompany most of the chapters. Finally, we would also like to thank our publisher Katie Gallof and editorial assistant Stephanie Grace-Petinos at Bloomsbury for their patience, help, and always positive attitude throughout the process of finalizing this book project.

This book is part of the three-year-long research project "Representing Women: Gendering Swedish Film Culture and Production" (2018–2021) that was generously funded by Riksbankens Jubileumsfond, contract no. P170079:1. We are also grateful to Riksbankens Jubileumsfond for financing this publication as Open Access, making it accessible to a larger audience.

Introduction

Louise Wallenberg

No women—no film. This may seem like a simplified overstatement, but it is not. To be sure, the film industries—worldwide—have been dominated by men, both in terms of the work carried out behind and in front of the camera, and men's dominance has stretched from the very incitement of film in the late nineteenth century (as an analog medium) up until today (when film has come to be understood as indeed miscellaneous through its various digitalized forms). Still, while being excluded from the making of film on many levels, women have always played crucial roles in this industry, and just like men they have been pivotal both on and off screen. Women have acted in front of the camera in secondary and supporting roles, and, at times, as main protagonists and as stars, although in many of these cases they have been ascribed sexist and stereotypical roles.[1] But the fact is that women have also served behind the camera in the various roles that make up the production or system of film. Women have often been script girls, costume designers, and make-up artists, yet they have also had more "above-the-line" positions such as directors, scriptwriters, and producers.[2] They have also acted as film critics, as film exhibitors, and as film educators—and, from the early 1970s onward, they have worked unitedly to organize film festivals, women's film organizations, and film screenings that deal with women's film and women's stories.[3] In recent years, women have also held positions as presidents or CEOs of large corporate film companies and as CEOs of national film institutes.[4] In the latter category, Anna Serner, former CEO of the Swedish Film Institute (2011–2021) and author of the foreword to our book, stands out: her work and demands for gender equity in the film industry—known under the slogan "50/50 by 2020"—has come to be inspirational to many other film nations worldwide.[5] The women are there, they have always been there, and yet their work and their contribution to film production and film culture have been thought of as "different" and marginal rather than central. Also, film scholars and historians have tended to focus on contributions made by male film workers, and their research has often been tainted by the notion of an artistic genius who has, by definition, been thought of as male.[6] This attitude has perhaps been most clearly expressed in terms of unequal financing for men and women: women's films and work have attracted less funding, this goes for salaries as well as for production and distribution costs.

Women's Presence and Representation

Our aim with this book is to investigate women's specific *presence* in Swedish film culture—both in past times and today—and to investigate their *representation*, that is, we look into how they have been portrayed on film and how they have tried to add to or change these images. As many studies have shown, women's presence in mainstream film has often been counteracted by men, when they have not been required as the erotic and subjugated Other (that is, as Image) on screen. In many ways, for women, the film industry has been a place where the democratic system does not work since the very right to be present is one of the most fundamental issues in a democracy and also one of the oldest and most pertinent demands in the women's movement.

The first half of this book's title—*Now About All These Women in the Swedish Film Industry*—is borrowed from Swedish auteur Ingmar Bergman's film *För att inte tala om alla dessa kvinnor* (1964), translated to *All These Women* and *Now About All These Women* for the international audience. This is a film that focuses almost solely on women of various ages (all of whom are played by some of Bergman's favorite actresses). The title, then, is meant as a reference to this specific film and the manner it treats women on screen, and also to the many women beyond it. In that vein, we also have chosen this title because it pinpoints our ambition to take a step ahead from just ascertaining the obstacles women have and have had, and to spotlight the very presence of women (and the excellent contributions they have accomplished) within so many levels of film cultural fields in Sweden. Accordingly, looking at the Swedish film industry as a specific case, our book aims to bring a variety of women film workers to the forefront. We highlight women's specific work in various sectors of the film industry and give testimony to their professional experiences, struggles, and joys. By doing so, *Now About All These Women in the Swedish Film Industry* is aligned with feminist production studies and with projects such as the Women Film Pioneer Project (headed by Jane Gaines at Columbia University) and Women in Nordic Film, all of which have as their aim to identify and flesh out women film workers and their contributions to film production and history.[7]

The notions of *presence* and *representation* are central to this book as the results of our study manifest themselves in the tension between the two: it is about the work created by women's physical presence in this particular industry, but also about their visual representation, that is, the very image of women created by women. While we have been inspired by production studies, we are still interested in how women are being portrayed on screen. This book, then, through its eight chapters—or case studies—looks both behind and in front of the camera. We cover some of the earliest instances where women have played crucial roles in the filmmaking process, with author and Nobel Prize winner Selma Lagerlöf; actor and director Anna Hofman-Uddgren; and author, journalist, and social critic Elin Wägner, as important examples. We discuss women's working conditions in the 1930s, 1940s, and 1950s, focusing on a few particular women and their work, namely art director Bibi Lindström and actor and director Gunnel Lindblom. Working for and in close relation to this industry, we turn our gaze to Anna Serner and offer an analysis of her "mission impossible" as the CEO of the Swedish Film Institute (SFI) in a time of strong gender equality policies.

As for women' representation on screen, we also investigate how women and femininity have been represented in Swedish film from the early 1910s up till today, looking at films made by both women and men. Alongside these readings, we also engage with women film workers' experiences of trying to create images and stories that serve to counter or deconstruct the stereotypical portrayals that populate most cinematic representation. In conjunction with these more ethnographic narratives, collected through interviews that we have conducted and through various kinds of publications in which they have spoken up, we also include an interview with one of the most significant film directors of her generation, Lisa Langseth (*Hotell* [2013], *Euphoria* [2017], *Kärlek och anarki* [Love and Anarchy; 2021–2022]), in which she offers her perspective on various aspects of Swedish film culture.

Using a wide range of different sources including archival material, laws, contracts, films, biographical materials, and interviews, *Now About All These Women in the Swedish Film Industry* tells the history of women in the Swedish film industry, laying bare the very roots for the more recent rise of gender equality efforts undertaken by the SFI and the emerging—and increasing—dominance of "quality films" made by women in the past ten years. Of importance to all our chapters is the "reading" of women's stories and experiences—told to us through autobiographies, interviews, or archival and legal documents. Through our mutual and separate readings, we strive to describe and understand the representation and the presence of women in the film industry both off and on screen. For, as Miranda Banks writes: "This field-based analysis of the lived experience of practitioners complicates the more text-based research of media scholars who have focused on the narrative worlds of media genres. This behind-the-scenes scholarship details how tensions behind the scenes are reflected—and even mirrored—in the finished [...] text."[8]

... and Capital and Power

The analyses in this book are supported by an eclectic theoretical framework that embraces various strands of critical theory, including a wide array of gender and feminist theory and feminist (and queer) film theory. Hence, the thoughts of scholars such as Luce Irigaray, Kaja Silverman, Teresa de Lauretis, and Richard Dyer—most of whom have been influenced by semiotics, psychoanalysis, and political theory in their thinking on gender and cultural criticism at large—are used as inspirations in some instances, yet in others, we also rely and take inspiration from non-feminist (or even "non-gendered") work by thinkers such as Pierre Bourdieu and Michel Foucault.

As for Bourdieu, we would like to stress that our aim is not to use his thoughts to explain certain societal conditions during certain historical periods, nor do we directly apply his sociological method. We do, however, take inspiration from established critical concepts such as *cultural field* and *cultural capital* when discussing women's presence in the film industry.[9] We also find his notion of *habitus* useful in our effort to make structures manifest in the confined cultural and social field of the film production industry in Sweden.

For our take on inequalities and struggles within the industry, power, resistance, and technologies, as theorized by Foucault and further developed by de Lauretis, are crucial.[10] As mentioned above, the concept of *representation* constitutes one of our main tools for analyses. Here, we rely on Dyer's early work on the matter of images—and on stereotypes.[11] The notion of *power* is tightly related to both *presence* and *representation* (and the lack thereof)—the power of being present and the power of having the possibility to represent the world and oneself on screen from one's own perspective. In this context it should be pointed out that whereas Foucault focused on an unidentified "group," our book expands and moves beyond such an ungendered notion by engaging with a specific group: *women*. This is an important point, for as Angela King has noted, Foucault's work was throughout curiously gender-neutral.[12] Being fully aware of the critique his work has faced, the main bulk of his work still continues to inspire feminist scholars, and even us.[13]

At the center of our investigation are both individual women's agency as power (which, in many of the cases we have investigated, constitutes a kind of *counterpower*) and the kind of power that manifests itself in a web-like formation—that is, as a "constitutive power." Investigating power in its twofoldness—as constitutive and as counterpower—matters, not least because the relationship between constitutive power and human agency still remains under-theorized.[14] Hence, rather than looking solely on human agency as the only source of power, we, following Amy Allen, set out to try and investigate the kind of constitutive power that works in both "trans-individual and relational ways."[15]

Early Film Culture in Sweden

The earliest expressions of a film culture in Sweden can be traced to the Southern parts of the country, where communication with Denmark and the UK and their more advanced production and distribution systems were easier to establish. However, as the formation of the film industry was stabilized in the 1920s and then became fully organized according to the industrial Hollywood model, "the studio system," during the 1930s, Stockholm soon became the center of gravity. The basis of this development was proximity to governmental authorities such as *Statens Biografbyrå* (the national film censorship organ), the Swedish broadcasting company, the many main theater institutions with access to their actors and other staff, as well as the larger financial establishments—which were all concentrated in the city. As a consequence, the production facilities were developed in terms of sizable localities such as Filmstaden (Film City), the studios of the country's largest film company, Svensk Filmindustri, in the north of the capital city. For a short period during the first half of the 1900s, the film industry would provide work for a number of craftsmen and women in the building sites and studios, laboratories, and fashion industry. The superstructure consisting of artists in many branches, as well as critics, journalists, and even politicians was in place, as were the audiences. A considerable number of different kinds of consumers lived in and around the capital city. One consequence of this concentration was a confined cinema culture with an intricate network of contacts and exchanges—a system that developed into a larger national social field where Stockholm, again, was one of the most noteworthy "hubs." As time has passed, a number of new "hubs" have developed in the country's larger cities such as Gothenburg and Malmoe. In addition, it is worth noting that the regional politics of the past decades has spread film production across the country.

In the early days of silent cinema those most interested in film as a medium (besides risk-capital investors) were the professional theater directors and actors who were fascinated by the (artistic) possibilities offered by the new medium. Traditionally, quite a few theater company directors were women and, not surprisingly, some of them were interested in directing films, as we will see below. Yet, the more the film production business developed according to the industrial model—demanding large monetary investments and expecting larger profits—the sooner women lost their fortuitous position for decision-making in the business. Some of them, however, were able to keep their standing, such as Karin Swanström (1873–1942), an influential leader of a touring theater company, who at the age of sixty was called to be the artistic leader of Svensk Filmindustri and successfully governed the production policies of the company throughout a decade from the 1930s.

Another woman of power was Pauline Brunius (1881–1954), who during her career was the director of different theaters, among them the Royal Dramatic Theatre. Meanwhile, she also directed eight films for several companies between 1920 and 1934—and wrote the script for most of them. Nearly twenty-five years passed after she gave up the film branch until another woman, this time the journalist Barbro Boman (1918–1980), would direct a feature film. For by then, the film industry had become infused by male dominance: within finance the large corporate investors were men, as well as at the studios—while there was no institutional education in the country. In effect, film production was led by men in a manner consistent with a kind of medieval guild system: the profession was learned *in situ*, and a master was most likely to have himself a male apprentice. Women, in their turn, took their place in front of the camera—or around it in supporting yet professional capacities. A structural change took place in the 1960s that opened up new opportunities for women: first, the introduction of television in 1957 meant new working opportunities for women as TV producers. Second, the establishment of the Film School (later the Dramatic Institute) on the initiative of the SFI in 1964 provided a center of learning with democratic application systems for both men and women.

Let us now turn to discuss the gender policy work carried out at the SFI and to a short description of SFI as an institution before discussing the impact that the #MeToo movement had on the Swedish film industry (and beyond).

Gender Equality Work

When Anna Serner presented SFI's action plan and goal with the slogan "50/50 by 2020" at the Cannes Film Festival in 2016, aiming at raising international awareness about gender equality in film (and highlighting Sweden's gender politics as progressive), she was only expressing an already established ambition shaping the equality policies advocated by the SFI.[16] In fact, efforts to try and make the Swedish film industry more equal were taken already back in 2000, when the government for the first time ever charged the SFI with tracking statistics on the gender of directors, scriptwriters, and producers. The then CEO of SFI, Åse Kleveland, went on to commission a report on gender equality and this was published in 2002.[17] In 2004, the SFI published a collection of interviews with experts, film commissioners, and film workers, and one of the points discussed was whether or not the Swedish film industry should rely on a quota to increase the number of women in filmmaking.[18] The collection revealed indeed divergent views on affirmative action such as using quotas: the Gender Equality Ombudsman was in favor, whereas some film practitioners, including one film commissioner, were highly against it. In 2006, a clause stating that Swedish film production should aim for at least a 40 percent share of the "underrepresented gender" in the key creative positions of director, producer, and scriptwriter was inserted in the Swedish film policy—known as the Film Agreement.[19] Yet, little happened, and when Serner came into her position as CEO in 2011, she was appalled. In an interview she said:

> It was a catastrophe ... We had to change it. I gave myself half a year to understand why and find out what the real obstacles for women were and then I presented an action plan. I had a very clear idea of what I wanted to do—I wanted to achieve 50/50 and I just hoped the industry would help me because I am not afraid of progress.[20]

The critique that had preceded her appointment continued to flow, not least from male-centered corners, yet Serner's tireless efforts to try and make the industry more gender equal were also applauded. And after just two years with Serner as CEO, the gender equality work actually seemed to make a difference: between 2013 and 2017, the average share of women was 38 percent directors, 34 percent scriptwriters, and 52 percent producers. The all-time high took place in 2017 with 40 percent women directors in all feature-length fiction film releases.[21] Films with production support from the SFI has generally done better in terms of gender equality than films without such support, and in 2016 the share of women directors in feature-length fiction films supported by the SFI peaked at 65 percent.

Reaching the 50/50 objective with women in the positions as directors, scriptwriters, and producers has generated positive attention to Swedish film and to Anna Serner in the international press. Still, Serner—and the SFI—continued to be under attack from critical voices in Sweden (as discussed in Chapter 3): women's increasing presence in the industry has clearly stirred hostile emotions, and the SFI was accused of conducting "identity politics" by a wide range of Swedish film professionals, including heads of regional film funding bodies.[22] When SFI in 2018—following the revelations that the #MeToo movement together with the national *#TystnadTagning* movement (with more than 700 women actors speaking up) had revealed—launched an education program for film producers to combat sexual harassment in the industry, editorials in major newspapers accused the institution of breaking the arm's-length principle, namely the norm that public agencies should not interfere with the content of cultural expressions.[23] Clearly, actions taken to try and improve gender equality in film—and to improve women's working conditions—have challenged the industry's status quo.

The Swedish Film Institute

Before describing the content of this book in more detail, let us first say something about the constitution of and the impetus behind the Swedish Film Institute, since understanding its position and role is paramount for understanding how the Swedish film industry works (and has worked). The institute was inaugurated in 1963, and it was financed both by state funding and by various professional bodies of the film industry (from 2017, it has been solely funded by the state).

The SFI was the outcome of a longer debate on how to bring the audience back to the movie theaters. And although Swedish politicians had debated film before, not least regarding censorship and the effect of cinemagoing on young audiences back in the 1910s and 1920s, the new Swedish film policy was the result of the increasing dominance of television. With fewer people flocking to the cinemas in the late 1950s, the sustainability of Swedish film production was being threatened.[24] The outspoken goal of the SFI was to support the production of new and qualitative films, to distribute and screen film to preserve and promote Swedish film heritage and to represent Swedish film on the international level.

It was entrepreneur and former film critic Harry Schein, who had suggested creating an agreement between stakeholders in the Swedish film industry to collectively amass funding for the production of Swedish film.[25] Schein became the institute's first CEO, and it needs to be pointed out that his success with the SFI was much indebted to his already close connections with the film industry and to the Social Democratic government. The Film Agreement (Filmavtalet) was an internationally unique construction, where the industry and the state contributed money to a fund handled by a foundation created for this purpose: the SFI.[26] Schein designed the Film Agreement in cooperation with Gunnar Sträng, the Swedish Minister of Finance, as a "cure" for the drop in film production, and it came into effect in 1963.[27] For Schein, public support was a route to increasing the making of what he termed "quality film" in Sweden, while decreasing the lowbrow popular comedies that dominated Swedish film production.

Inspired by the Academy Awards Ceremony and other international Film Awards, the SFI inaugurated its own gala, Guldbaggegalan, in 1964. As we write this book, only nine Best Director awards have gone to women, with Gabriela Pichler as the most recent winner for her *Äta sova dö* (*Eat Sleep Die*, 2012) and Marianne Ahrne the very first winner with *Långt borta och nära* (*Near and Far Away*, 1977).[28] And while nine awards in total may seem like a depressing number, it must be viewed in light of how many international awards women have received over the years: in the United States, Kathryn Bigelow became the first woman ever to win an Oscar for best direction in 2010 for *Hurt Locker*, and in 2021, Chloé Zhao received the second award for best director for her *Nomadland* (2020). And to date, Jane Campion and Julia Ducournau are the only two women to receive the Palme d'Or in Cannes, Campion for *The Piano* (1993) and Ducournau for *Titane* (2021).

Along with the instigation of the Film Agreement, the plan for public support involved a film school, which opened in September 1964. The Film School soon became an important institution and gateway for women to enter into film production, together with the Swedish national public television broadcaster, Sveriges Television (SVT), an institution that in the 1970s funded a significant number of documentary films made by women. Several of the women we have interviewed have highlighted that SVT was a "great school" which allowed them to make the films they wanted to make and gave them all the support they needed. Hence, for some women, television led the way into film, making their actual presence and representation more acceptable than before.

Money, Distribution—and *#TystnadTagning*

When investigating women's presence and power in this industry, one is tempted to turn to Machiavelli, since it becomes apparent that power in this creative context can only be at work if *present*. As in the Machiavellian scenario, non-visible, non-present, and non-noticeable power in the film industry would only fail. Yet, presence and power as discussed here refer not so much to the threatening power of a present power, but more to the strategies to fight the dominant power *and* to create space for one's own presence—and power. Yet, we wish to point out that the film industry is an institutional context, and as such, it is a web of "capillary power"—a web in which an elusive power exists. Although there is no specific ruler that exerts power, this web is formed by relations and positions that are structured by an executive power held by a few. Not surprisingly, *financing*—and the lack of finances for most film workers in creative positions—is crucial here. As one of the senior filmmakers interviewed for this book put it: "It is the dough that is the problem!"[29] And in a report published by the SFI in 2018, one finds that, statistically, women and men are quite equally represented in low-budget films, and that with bigger budgets the number of women involved—both in front and behind the camera—decreases. The more money involved, the less women are likely to feature as directors, writers, producers, or as the lead actor. That few women manage to take the step to high-budget projects is a catch-22 situation: the number of cinema visits is highly linked with the budgets of the films, and films with male directors, producers, and protagonists generally get wider distribution, which in turn means more cinemagoers.[30]

And while financial problems discriminate women film workers, they are not uniquely women's problems: for most film workers, getting funding for film projects is difficult. There is one problem, however, that to a large extent seems to be a womanly problem: sexual harassment and the constant risk for sexual assault. When the #MeToo movement went viral on October 17, 2017, following actor Alyssa Milano's petition for women to speak up about sexual harassment and assault in the North American film industry, Swedish women actors were quick to react.[31] In early November 2017, more than 700 women working in film and theater signed a petition entitled *#TystnadTagning*, giving voice to hundreds of experiences of having been harassed, threatened, and belittled sexually by male co-workers.[32] It should be pointed out that the impact of #MeToo in Sweden was somewhat incredible (especially if compared to its lesser impact in the other Nordic countries) and that a large number of different occupations and industries created additional hashtags in Sweden, all speaking up against sexual violence. In fact, by early March 2018, there were no less than sixty-five different hashtags and petitions.[33] The readiness and will to speak up and confront existent structures must be understood as a continuation of the many efforts and measures taken to try to make Sweden an equal nation in terms of social class and gender, starting already back in the 1930s when the Social Democratic Party came into power. Also, for women film workers, the efforts made to make the industry more equal since 2000, probably made their organizing via *#TystnadTagning* painless and almost natural: a broad feminist consensus and the will and need to improve the industry were already in place.

Figure I.1 Film and theater actors organizing at the "Guldbagge" Awards in January 2018. Photo: Jonas Ekströmer / TT.

What the #MeToo movement and *#TystnadTagning* have taught us is that the often sexualized, sexist, and misogynist representation of women on screen is parallel with the sexualization, sexism, and misogyny carried out toward women film workers off screen. And here is the double bind that women film workers find themselves caught in: how can they gain the same credibility and authority and hold the same positions as do their fellow men if they continue to be represented in these stereotypical, misogynist, and not least sexist terms? Representation on and off screen must to be altered, and women characters and film workers must be made equal to men, that is, they need to be represented as full subjects and as individuals, and they need to be treated as equal colleagues (Figure I.1).

Women on Screen, in Production, and in Organizations

While issues of women's presence and work in the screening industries have surfaced in film studies only in the last few decades, research on women's visual representation has always had a central position in film studies.[34] Feminist film theorists have investigated women's images ever since the early 1970s, when feminist writers began to discuss representations and myths of women and the feminine in film.[35] Since then, feminist film theory has developed in two different yet interconnected strands, both of which deal with representation: the first, continuing to explore the visual representation of women (and of Woman) that interested the pioneering scholars and, the second, investigating women's experiences and place in the film industry, including attempts made by women filmmakers to produce new images of women and women's subjectivity.[36]

The research strand focusing on visual representations of femininity has gone through different stages: from a focus on the image, to the textual spectator, and further to the empirical spectator. Initially, with the early works of Marjory Rosen and Molly Haskell, the focus was primarily on the stereotypical and often circumscribed representation of women on screen, and later, with inspiration from feminist, psychoanalytical, and Marxist theories, the focus shifted slightly to the female spectator as a textual category, a category that was understood to be denied any active desiring positions vis-à-vis film.[37] This first shift implied that feminist film theory went from the empirically concrete to the theoretically abstract, marking the spectator as a purely textual one while leaving no room for the real, empirical spectator, "munching her popcorn in front of the screen."[38] In the late 1980s, with the increasing influence from cultural studies, the focus began to shift toward the actual, empirical film spectator. Crucial to this process was Jackie Stacey's *Star Gazing*, published in 1994. Critically questioning the previous focus on textual spectatorship—and the abstract theorizing that had come to color feminist film studies, advocated for by scholars such as Mary Ann Doane and Giuliana Bruno, Stacey writes: "The reluctance to engage with questions of cinema audiences, for fear of dirtying ones hands with empirical material, has led to an inability to think about active female desire beyond the limits of masculine positionings."[39] Opening up for female subjecthood, identification, and desire, Stacey managed to change the "route" of this strand of feminist film theory. In tandem with a more cultural studies-influenced approach came a broadened perspective on gender and sexuality from masculinity studies (with an emphasis on male "spectacle") and from a burgeoning queer theory.[40] These two areas of study helped to open up the field even more, so as to include critical readings of representations of genders, identifications, and sexualities in the plural.

The second strand, which is concerned with women's experiences in the film industry has often, but not always, been combined with the image focus of the first research strand, since theorists have been interested in what kinds of images of women and their subjectivities are created by women filmmakers. For Sandy Flitterman-Lewis, for instance, the work of the French directors Germaine Dulac, Marie Epstein, and Agnès Varda represent attempts to create a feminine cinematic discourse. This strand of research also includes efforts to *rewrite film history*, analyzing the works of historical women filmmakers who have been marginalized by earlier generations of film critics and historians and criticizing the film historical canon from a feminist perspective.[41] The rewriting of history includes both looking at women directors and looking at all the other women who have participated in the making of film in below-the-line positions.[42] And while this book aims to make women's work and agency visible, we recognize that differences between women not only have to be acknowledged but also problematized in terms of privileges and power within the category of women.[43] This is also due to the fact that gender is registered in all public activities, while the registering of race/ethnicity, disabilities, and sexuality is forbidden. Although there are certain statistics at the national level, it is not allowed for schools or the SFI to keep such registers of people who attend or are awarded funding.

As noted above, feminist film scholarship has come to be influenced by production studies in recent decades—and our book is an example of how film studies can be both interdisciplinary and multi-methodological through relying on both theory-driven textual analysis, archival research, and ethnographic production studies.[44] Patrick Vonderau and colleagues describe how production studies constitutes a field that has as its aim to explore and investigate media and film as production *cultures*.[45] This means gathering empirical data about the lived realities of the people in various positions who are involved in media production, including their working conditions, daily routines, rituals, as well as existent hierarchies and relations between different professions. Production studies, then, focuses upon film and media as *cultural practices* of media production, and it does so from a variety of perspectives and with various methods. And since our focus is on women's presence and representation—and power—within the film industry, our book situates itself within the pertinent subfield of feminist production studies. This subfield engages in studying how "routines and rituals [...] the economic and political forces [...] shape roles, technologies, and the distribution of resources according to cultural and demographic differences," as stated by Vicki Mayer, Miranda Banks, and John Caldwell in their introduction to *Production Studies* from 2009.[46] The goal is to understand how "power operates locally through media production to reproduce social hierarchies and inequalities at the level of daily interaction."[47] An important contribution within this field has been the critique of the "auteurist" view: instead, it is argued that films are the result of collective work. Hence, production studies scholars emphasize the importance of studying the work that is carried out in the margins, that is, to pay attention to the work done "below-the-line."[48] In *Now about All these women in Swedish Film Industry*, we strive to include both experiences of and contributions by women who have worked, or still work, above and/or below the line.

Although production studies has originated from media and film studies, indicating a tour from text to production, it is closely aligned with social sciences in a certain regard. Because organization scholars too have turned to studying the screen industries as organizations, with a certain focus on the people working in these organizations. In organization studies and work life research, the early 2000s saw an increased interest in exploring the working conditions in the screening industries, alongside the growing interest for (women's) working conditions and experiences in what is often referred to as the creative industries.[49] Alongside these two fields of research, there is a third, and more recent, field that is dedicated to studying women's presence in screening industries with a specific focus on policy measures targeting gender (in)equality along with a focus on studying the impediments to gender equality in these industries. This strand of research comes out of feminist media and production studies, encompassing both the humanities and the social sciences, and one of its characteristics is that it looks into both the local and the global aspects of women's changing working conditions and experiences.[50]

Let us now present each of the eight chapters, all of which are situated within our three pillars of *presence, representation,* and *power*. They are divided into three sections: "Frameworks: The Power of Institutions"; "Histories, Herstories, and Representation"; and "Routines, Practices, and Practitioner." Together and separate they give both context and history to women and their work in the Swedish film industry.

Outline

In the first section, "Frameworks: The Power of Institutions," we start with a chapter that deals with authorship and film: "The Sex of the Author: On Authorship." Departing from the theoretical debate on the role of the *auteur* as the sole creator of a film work, as well as from the critique that the auteur has met (not least from feminist production studies claiming that film is always collective work), this chapter aims at investigating (1) the definition of the "author" from a copyright-law perspective; (2) how the role of the "author" has developed over the years because of changes in the industry, in policy, and in discourse; and (3) women's experiences with regards to the award, exercise, and management of their authorship rights as well their experiences of being an authority on the film set. This chapter follows the genesis of the term "author," the role it plays in the copyright system as well as in the theoretical framework of film studies. In this respect it also turns to the conditions under which "she" geniuses arose, and how these influenced the debate on authorship and how they claimed and exercised their rights in film production projects. The chapter adopts a double perspective, both a historical and a contemporary one.

The following chapter, "Gendering Film Distribution," looks into the different aspects of film distribution and the powerful role that distributors hold from the production to the final release of the film. Furthermore, the chapter investigates the structure of the film distribution industry and maps the role of women in positions of power in Swedish film distribution companies. To illustrate the impact of film distribution on women filmmakers and their power and presence, the chapter presents and analyses three cases of legal disputes. All three cases illustrate the role of women in film distribution, and while the first two share the same protagonist, Selma Lagerlöf, and concern film distribution disputes in the 1920s, 1930s, and 1940s, the third and fourth case concern contemporary film distribution disputes. The first dispute concerned the adaptation of *Herrgårdssägen* (*The Tale of a Manor*), a film that only after strong reactions from Lagerlöf would be distributed under the name *Gunnar Hedes Saga* (The Blizzard, 1923). The second case focuses on the dispute concerning the international production and distribution rights of the adaptation of *Gösta Berling's Saga* (The Story of Gösta Berling, 1924), a lengthy legal dispute stretching from 1919 to 1937 and involving the legal systems of both Sweden and Germany. The third case illustrates the distribution concerns of a documentary, *Mod att leva: en film till Pia* (The Courage to Live: A Film to Pia, 1983). In this very interesting case, the subject matter of the documentary, a young dying film director, Pia Kakossaios, participates in the filming of her last months of life. Once she died, her family attempted to block distribution.

The final case concerns a legal dispute between the SFI and Sandrews for the distribution of the film *Pelle Svanslös* (*Peter-No-Tail*, 1981). The case is illustrative of the legal implications of the long-term character of distribution contracts. This chapter sheds light on the complicated world of film distribution and the position women have, while by means of the three concrete legal disputes, the reader is offered a representative illustration of how film distribution influences the power held by women in the film industry as well as how and to what extent their presence is guaranteed.

The third chapter continues to investigate power positions within the industry, this time focusing on the role that the CEO of the SFI holds. "In the Crossfire: Anna Serner and the Swedish Film Institute" returns to this introduction to discuss Anna Serner, the SFI, and the impossible position of being its CEO. Departing from Serner's demand of a 50/50 gender quota (in regards to the specific film professions of director, producer, and scriptwriter), the chapter analyzes how Serner in the international context became a kind of "rock star," holding frequent keynotes as well as hosting panel debates at major institutions and film festivals, such as the New York Film Academy, Cannes, and Berlin. At the same time, in Sweden she became a highly controversial figure, not only—as could be expected—among commercial production companies and in the film business at large, but also—and quite paradoxically—among individuals and groups who one would expect to side with her position. This will be achieved in the context of current, ongoing debates in the media as well as in academia, but also from a unique insider perspective, as the author was a member of the SFI Board between 2011 and 2016.

The second section, "Histories, Herstories, and Representation," takes women's images on screen into account, and consists of two chronological chapters. The first chapter, "Women on Screen I: 1910s–1960s," offers an analysis of women's actual representation on screen by focusing on a number of films made by both men and women. Offering a presentation of how their representation has changed over a period six decades—in tandem with their changed role in society and, also, with women's presence in the film industry, or lack thereof—the chapter aims at sketching the first part of a two-part history of women's portrayal on the Swedish screen. The chapter departs from a more general discussion of how women have been represented on screen in both mainstream and non-mainstream film, and how the international (mostly Anglo-Saxon) scholarship has investigated and theorized women's roles on screen. From there, the chapter examines how women in Sweden have been represented in film up until the late 1960s and it does so through six different "case studies" based in visual analysis. The central issues addressed in this chapter include what women are allowed to be, to do, and to become on screen, as well as how they are positioned vis-à-vis male characters in terms of subjecthood (i.e., agency and voice) and objecthood (as in erotic objectification, i.e., lack of agency and voice).

The second chapter of this section, "Women on Screen II: 1970s–2010s," takes up where the first ended with an analysis of the representation of women in Swedish film, but now the visual analysis is combined with women film workers' stories and experiences from producing the films discussed. This chapter hence mixes visual and ethnographic methods in investigating women on screen. Based on semi-structured interviews with women working in the Swedish film industry carried out between 2018 and 2019, the chapter provides an analysis of women's agency, experiences, struggles, and resistances in regard to the representation of "femininity" on the screen. To conclude, the chapter discusses how representations of women created by female filmmakers may differ from the stereotypes found in (male) mainstream cinema. In addition, the political stance and messages conveyed by women filmmakers are discussed in relation to their very representation—on, as well as off, screen. Films focused upon belong to a variety of genres, and all of them are award-winning films. In chronological order, Gunnel Lindblom's drama *Paradistorg* (*Summer Paradise*, 1977); Suzanne Osten's semi-biographical drama *Mamma* (*Mother*, 1982); Christina Olofson's documentary *I rollerna tre* (*Lines from the Heart*, 1996); Maria Hedman Hvitfeldt's short children's film *Min skäggiga mamma* (*My Bearded Mum*, 2003); and Mia Engberg's poetic and experimental film *Lucky One* (2019), are discussed and analyzed in relation to their representation of women and, when plausible, in relation to the interviews carried out with the filmmakers.

Our third and final section, "Routines, Practices, and Practitioners," focuses on the lived realities and working conditions of women film workers, in the past and in the present. The section opens with "Making a Living: On Salaries and Working Conditions for Actors and Extras within Swedish Film Production 1930–1955." This chapter shows how the traditions and working conditions from the early theater practices were transferred into the film production business in Sweden more or less seamlessly: the hierarchy and the conditions remained roughly the same at least until the end of 1940s. The directors of theater companies—renowned artist—were now directing film, choosing their actors among those they considered able and reliable. The contract system based on seasonal periods was unfavorable and created dependency and uncertainty. Young aspiring actors were employed by learners' contracts for years and, for a long time, clothes and other accessories used in film recordings could do as a part of an actor's fee—a practice that was not different from the customary wages for rural servants and kitchen maids. The chapter presents unique archive material consisting of film contracts, costume lists, and correspondence between different parts in the production process.

The following chapter is on a specific film worker: the art director—or film architect as it was called in the first half of the twentieth century—Bibi Lindström. "Bibi Lindström: Easy to Work With" offers a case study focusing on one of Sweden's most prominent art directors, or *metteurs-en-scène*, and without whose work the films of Alf Sjöberg and Ingmar Bergman would definitely have looked very different. The chapter illustrates how Lindström built cinematic worlds, 149 to be exact, during her long career, including *Fröken Julie* (Miss Julie) by Alf Sjöberg (an award-winning film at Cannes in 1951) and *Gycklarnas afton* (Sawdust and Tinsel, 1953) by Ingmar Bergman—both for which Lindström did the mise-en-scène. In addition, by mapping the personal background of Lindström, her professional education and her network of contacts within the Stockholmian modernist elite, the chapter shows in what manner it has been possible for a woman to create a distinguished career path where no such paths existed.

Further, focusing on a number of works designed by Lindström, this chapter even sets out to discern a pronounced "Lindströmian" aesthetics, to present some principles for her working method as well as insights on her work day at the studios, and to present the people who became her friends and shared her days and years at the studios: *scriptas*, costume designers, carpenters not the least, editors, electricians, and the make-up choir.

The last chapter of this section, and of our book, focuses on a contemporary film director, who since early 2002 has had several national and international successes with her films, including *Hotell* (Hotel, 2013) and *Euphoria* (2017). In "Lisa Langseth: 'Make Sure That What's in Your Heart is Done, So it Doesn't Drown and Stay in the Heart,'" we offer an interview with Langseth, who delves into the new media landscape for filmmakers, as well as her previous films. As such, this chapter functions as a complement to the chapter on Anna Serner in our first section on power positions, in the way that it gives a perspective from a film practitioner's point of view not only on Swedish film policy but also on other aspects of Swedish film culture.

The book concludes with a short "Afterthought" in which we reflect on the status quo of the Swedish film industry after the pandemic, but also, after the swap of CEOs at the SFI in January 2022 and the fundamental change that was being made to its statutes, with the outspoken striving for gender equality in the industry being eliminated. After twenty years of gender equality policies, the SFI no longer includes gender equality as a desirable goal in its statutes, and this needs of course to be addressed.

***

It is our hope that this book will make a useful contribution to the already existent (and growing) research on women in film, in film studies, and beyond, and that it will inspire new scholarship on women's presence, representation, and power in the film industry in both national and transnational film contexts, in the past as well as in the present.

Acknowledgments

A heartfelt thank you goes to Tytti Soila and Maaret Koskinen who have given feedback and added indispensable sections to this introduction.

Notes

1. The academic investigation of the roles and stereotypes that have circumscribed the representation of women on screen has a long history. See, for example, Marjorie Rosen, *Popcorn Venus* (New York: Avon Books, 1973); Claire Johnston, "Women's Cinema as Counter-Cinema," in Claire Johnston (ed.), *Notes on Women* (London: SEFT, 1973), 24–31; Molly Haskell, *From Reverence to Rape* (New York: Holt, Rinehart and Winston, 1974); Laura Mulvey, "Visual Pleasure and Narrative Cinema," *Screen*, vol. 16, no. 3 (1975), 6–18; Ann E. Kaplan, *Women and Film: Both Sides of the Camera* (London: Routledge, 1983); Jane Gaines, "Women and Representation," *Jump Cut*, no. 29 (February 1984), 25–7; Tanya Modleski, *Women who Knew too Much (Hitchcock and Feminist Theory)* (New York: Methuen, 1988); and Barbara Creed, *The Monstrous Feminine: Film, Feminism, Psychoanalysis* (London: Routledge, 1993). The Anglo-American dominance is next to total, and feminist film theory and history is in need of a rewriting too, just as is mainstream (malestream) film theory and history. This is pointed out by film scholar Ingrid Ryberg in her forthcoming book *Swedish Film Feminism: Between Grassroots Movements and Cultural Policies* (London: Bloomsbury, forthcoming).
2. "Above-the-line" and "below-the-line" are industry terms used to distinguish between creative and crafts professions and are derived from "a particular worker's position in relation to a bold horizontal line on a standard production budget sheet between creative and technical costs." Creative work is understood to be artistic and inventive (as in "imaginative"), whereas technical work is understood to be pure craft (as in "hand work"). Hence, cinematographers, gaffers, editors, production designers, costume designers, etc., are professions considered to be below-the-line (and most of which are dominated by women). See Miranda Banks, "Gender Below-the-Line: Defining Feminist Production Studies," in Vicki Mayer, Miranda Banks, and John T. Caldwell (eds.), *Production Studies: Cultural Studies of Media Industries* (New York: Routledge, 2009), 89.
3. On women film exhibitors in the early days of cinema, see Ingrid Stigsdotter, "Women Film Exhibition Pioneers in Sweden: Agency, Invisibility and First Wave Feminism." *Nordic Women in Film*, April 2020, https://www.nordicwomeninfilm.com/women-film-exhibition-pioneers-in-sweden-agency-invisibility-and-first-wave-feminism/, accessed September 6, 2022.
4. For example, Sherry Lansing at Paramount Pictures and at 20th Century Fox; Stacey Snider at 20th Century Fox; Ann Sarnoff at Warner Bros. Studios; and Victoria Alonso at Marvel Studios.
5. Serner's work has also inspired film scholars who work on women in the film and screening industries. See, for example, Orianna Calderón-Sandoval, "Implementing

Gender Equality Policies in the Spanish Film Industry: Persistent Prejudices and the Potential of Feminist Awareness," *International Journal of Cultural Policy* (2021), https://doi.org/10.1080/10286632.2021.1978439. Recently, a perceived lack of women behind the film camera has gained political attention internationally (see, e.g., UNESCO [2016, https://en.unesco.org/creativity/policy-monitoring-platform/promotion-women-film-worldwide, accessed September 15, 2022]), regionally (see, e.g., Council of Europe, n.d. [https://www.coe.int/en/web/eurimages/gender-equality-documents, accessed September 15, 2022]), and nationally (see the report from the European Women's Audiovisual Network [EWA]: "Where Are the Women Directors?" [2015, https://www.ewawomen.com/wp-content/uploads/2018/09/Complete-report_compressed.pdf, accessed September 6, 2022]; and Susan Liddy, ed., *Women in the International Film Industry* [London: Palgrave, 2020]). In several countries where filmmaking is subsidized by the state, there have been efforts to increase the number of women working in film. In international media, Sweden has been hailed as the "most gender equal film nation." See, for example, Paul Byrnes, "How Sweden Hit its 50:50 Gender Target for Film Production in Record Time," *The Sydney Morning Herald*, May 24, 2015. www.smh.com.au/entertainment/movies/how-sweden-hit-its-5050-gender-target-for-film-production-in-record-time-20150519-gh489a.html#ixzz41CyTwsjc, accessed September 6, 2022. However, the most recent gender equality report from the Swedish Film Institute, *Han, hon och pengarna* (*The Money Issue: Gender Equality Report 2018*, https://www.filminstitutet.se/globalassets/_dokument/sfi-gender-equalityreport-2018--lowres.pdf, accessed September 6, 2022), shows that much remains to be done. Despite various policy initiatives and the implementation of gender equality measures during the past twenty years, women in the Swedish film industry still work with smaller budgets than their male colleagues, their films open in fewer cinemas, and have smaller budgets allocated to promotional campaigns. Further, in a larger context, gender equality policies within the film industry need to be viewed more critically and with a longer perspective: what we have seen in the last ten years may seem like a movement forward, but may, in fact be a *movement without progress*.

6 For problematizing readings of the genius as male and how this notion hinders gender equality in the industry, see Thomas Schatz, *The Genius of the System: Hollywood Filmmaking in the Studio Era* (New York: Pantheon Book, 1988); Stefania Marghitu, "'It's just art': Auteur Apologism in the Post-Weinstein Era," *Feminist Media Studies*, vol. 18, no. 3 (2018), 491–94, https://doi.org/10.1080/14680777.2018.1456158; R. Regev, "Hollywood Works: How Creativity Became Labour in the Studio System," *Enterprise and Society*, vol. 17, no. 3 (2016), 591–617, https://doi.org/10.1017/eso.2015.89; and Maria Jansson, Frantzeska Papadopoulou,

Ingrid Stigsdotter, and Louise Wallenberg, "'The Final Cut': Directors, Producers and the Gender Regime of the Swedish Film Industry," in Louise Wallenberg and Maria Jansson (eds.), "On and Off Screen: Women's Work in the Screen Industries," special section of *Gender, Work and Organization*, vol. 28, no. 6 (2021), 2010–25.

7   As for feminist productions studies, see the early work by Julie d'Acci, *Defining Women: Television and the Case of Cagney and Lacey* (Chapel Hill: University of North Carolina Press, 1994) and Elana Levine, "Toward a Paradigm for Media Production Research," *Critical Studies in Media Communication*, vol. 18, no. 1 (1998), 66–82. See also Banks, "Gender Below-the-Line"; Erin Hill, *Never Done: A History of Women's Work in Media Production* (New Brunswick, NJ: Rutgers University Press, 2016); Shelley Stamp, "Feminist Media Historiography and the Work Ahead," *Screening the Past*, vol. 40 (2015), http://www.screeningthepast.com/2015/08/feminist-media-historiography-and-the-work-ahead/, accessed September 6, 2022. In regards to projects, see the Women Film Pioneer Project, https://wfpp.cdrs.columbia.edu/pioneers/?sort=occupation, accessed September 6, 2022, a project providing ample evidence of women's contribution to film history as does the project Nordic Women in Film, 2018, https://www.svenskfilmdatabas.se/sv/nordic-women-in-film/, accessed September 6, 2022.

8   Banks, "Gender Below-the-Line," 89.

9   See, for example, Pierre Bourdieu, *Outline of a Theory of Practice* (Cambridge: Cambridge University Press, 1977); *The Field of Cultural Production* (New York: Columbia University Press, 1994); "The Forms of Capital," in J.G. Richardson (ed.), *Handbook of Theory and Research for the Sociology of Education* (New York: Greenwood Press, 1986), 241–58; and *The State Nobility: Élite Schools in the Field of Power* (Palo Alto, CA: Stanford University Press, 1998).

10 See Michel Foucault, *Discipline and Punish: The Birth of a Prison* (1975; London: Penguin, 1991) and *The History of Sexuality: The Will to Knowledge* (1976; London: Penguin, 1998); and Teresa de Lauretis, *Technologies of Gender: Essays on Theory, Film, and Fiction* (Bloomington: Indiana University Press, 1987).

11 Richard Dyer, *The Matter of Images: Essays on Representation* (London: Routledge, 1993).

12 Angela King, "The Prisoner of Gender: Foucault and the Disciplining of the Female Body," *Journal of International Women's Studies*, vol. 5, no. 2 (2004), 29–39.

13 See, for example, Biddy Martin, "Feminism, Criticism and Foucault," *New German Critique*, no. 27 (1982), 3–30; Sandra Bartky, *Femininity and Domination* (London: Routledge, 1990); Jana Sawicki, *Disciplining Foucault: Feminism, Power and the Body* (London: Routledge, 1991); Caroline Ramazanoglu (ed.), *Up Against Foucault: Explorations of some Tensions between Foucault and Feminism* (London: Routledge, 1993); and Amy Allen, *The Power of Feminist Theory* (London: Routledge, 1999).

14 Amy Allen, "Feminist Perspectives on Power," in E.N. Zalta (ed.), *The Stanford Encyclopedia of Philosophy* (Stanford, CA: Stanford University Press, 2014).
15 Allen quoted in Helene Ahlborg and Andrea J. Nightengale, "Theorizing Power in Political Ecology," *Journal of Political Ecology*, vol. 25 (2018), 384.
16 The year after, in 2017, the SFI together with WIFT Nordic presented "50/50 by 2020—Global Reach," a seminar at the Cannes Film Market focusing on the development of gender equality work outside of Sweden. And in 2018, the SFI arranged "Take Two: Next moves for #MeToo" at that same festival with Swedish Minister for Culture and Democracy Alice Bah Kuhnke and French Minister of Culture Françoise Nyssen, focusing on the work against sexual harassment and the misuse of power against women.
17 Vanja Hermele, *Män, män, män och en och annan kvinna* (Stockholm: Swedish Film Institute, 2002).
18 Vanja Hermele, *Hur svårt kan det vara? Filmbranschen, jämställdheten och demokratin* (Stockholm: Swedish Film Institute, 2004).
19 The Film Agreement was a policy originally created in 1963 to regulate and (part) finance the work of the Swedish Film Institute (inaugurated in 1964) based on an agreement between the Swedish state and representatives from the film and television industries in Sweden. This contractual agreement, which originally involved a 10 percent levy on cinema admission tickets going back into the production of Swedish film, through funding distributed by the Swedish Film Institute, was updated and renewed at regular intervals up until 2016, when it was replaced with a policy funded by the state. This will be introduced in further detail below.
20 Diana Lodderhouse, "International Disruptors: Outgoing Swedish Film Institute CEO Anna Serner on her Commitment to Gender Parity and Why 'the Old Industry needs to Change,'" *Deadline* (September 15, 2021), https://deadline.com/2021/09/international-disruptors-anna-serner-gender-parity-swedish-film-institute-1234833086/ (accessed October 7, 2021.
21 SFI, *Han, hon och pengarna/The Money Issue*.
22 For a thorough discussion of the attacks launched toward the equality politics of the SFI (and toward Serner), see Chapter 3, "In the Crossfire."
23 See, for example, Erik Helmersson, "Ledare: Normkritiken tar över kulturen och ingen vågar klaga" [Editorial: Norm-Critics Take Over Culture, and No One Dares to Complain], *Dagens Nyheter* (January 3, 2018).
24 The Swedish 1950s are strongly associated with the Social Democratic welfare project and what has become known as the "Swedish model." The Swedish economy boomed after the war with favorable economic conditions for individual consumption, and by the late 1950s, many Swedish households were able to

purchase a television set. Between 1958 and 1961, domestic film production dropped by almost half and for the first time since the introduction of sound, cinema ticket sales were decreasing, from 80 million tickets in 1956 to 40 million in 1963. See Olof Hedling, "Cinema in the Welfare State: Notes on Public Support. Regional Film Funds and Film Policy in Swedish Film," in Mette Hjort and Ursula Lindqvist (eds.), *The Blackwell Companion to Nordic Cinema* (London: Blackwell, 2016), 62–3.

25 Schein was an Austrian-born Swedish entrepreneur with Jewish roots who had come to Sweden as a child during the Second World War. There is a bulk of academic writings on Schein and his role in Swedish film, see, for example, Lars Ilshammar, Pelle Snickars, and Per Vesterlund (eds.), *Citizen Schein* (Stockholm: Kungliga biblioteket, 2010); Per Vesterlund, *Schein: en biografi* (Stockholm: Bonnier, 2018); Mats Hyvönen, Pelle Snickars, and Per Vesterlund (eds.), *Massmedieproblem* (Lund: Lunds Universiteet, 2015); and Maaret Koskinen and Louise Wallenberg (eds.), *Harry bit för bit* (Stockholm: Carlsson förlag, 2017).

26 "Vägval för filmen" (https://lagen.nu/sou/2009:73#PS1, accessed September 16, 2022).

27 There had been some film support efforts before 1963, but this year is usually seen as the beginning of Swedish film policy.

28 *Äta sova dö* (Eat Sleep Die, 2012) won the awards also for Best Film, Best Director, and Best Screenplay.

29 Interview conducted by Louise Wallenberg and Maria Jansson with director, producer, and scriptwriter Mai Wechselmann on December 21, 2018.

30 SFI, *Han, hon och pengarna/The Money Issue*.

31 We wish to point out that the very first #MeToo movement started back in 1997 on the social network MySpace by Tarana Burke who wanted to help girls who had fallen victim to sexual violence. Burke decided to name the movement "Me Too" as a way to express one's support without having to tell any details.

32 The petition *#TystnadTagning* was published in one of Sweden's biggest dailies, *Svenska Dagbladet*, on November 8, 2017.

33 SVT, "65 metoo-grupper lämnar kravlista till regeringen," March 6, 2018, available online: https://www.svt.se/nyheter/inrikes/65-metoo-grupper-lamnar-kravlista-till-regeringen, accessed September 6, 2022.

34 See Vicki Mayer, *Below the Line: Producers and Production Studies in the New Television Economy* (Durham, NC: Duke University Press, 2011); Vicki Mayer, Miranda Banks, and John T. Caldwell (eds.), *Production Studies: Cultural Studies of Media Industries* (New York: Routledge, 2009); Banks, "Gender Below-the-Line," 87–98; Miranda Banks, "Production Studies," *Feminist Media Histories*, vol. 4, no. 2

(2018), 157–61; Miranda Banks, Bridget Conor, and Vicki Mayer (eds.), *Production Studies, The Sequel!* (London: Routledge, 2016).

35 Rosen, *Popcorn Venus*; Haskell, *From Reverence to Rape*; and Mulvey, "Visual Pleasure and Narrative Cinema."

36 See, for example, Teresa de Lauretis, "Aesthetics and Feminist Theory: Rethinking Women's Cinema," in D. Carson, L. Dittmar, and J.R. Welsch (eds.), *Multiple Voices in Feminist Film Criticism* (1985; Minneapolis: University of Minnesota Press, 1994); Sandy Flitterman-Lewis, *To Desire Differently* (New York: Columbia University Press, 1996); and Brenda Austin-Smith and George Melnyk (eds.), *The Gendered Screen: Canadian Women Filmmakers* (Waterloo, ONT: Wilfrid Laurier University Press, 2010).

37 See, for example, Mulvey, "Narrative Cinema and Visual Pleasure"; Mary Ann Doane, "The Voice in the Cinema: The Articulation of Body and Space," *Yale French Studies*, vol. 60 (1980), 33–50; and Flitterman-Lewis, *To Desire Differently*.

38 Mary Ann, Untitled contribution to the "Spectatrix" special issue in *Camera Obscura*, vol. 21, no. 20 (1989), 142–43.

39 Jackie Stacey, *Star Gazing: Hollywood Cinema and Female Spectatorship* (London: Routledge, 1994).

40 See, for example, Steven Cohan and Ina R. Hark, *Screening the Male* (London: Routledge, 1993); and Patricia White, *Uninvited* (Bloomington: Indiana University Press, 1999).

41 See, for example, Claire Johnston, ed. *The Work of Dorothy Arzner: Towards a Feminist Cinema* (London: BFI, 1975); Giuliana Bruno, *Streetwalking on a Ruined Map: Cultural Theory and the City Films of Elvira Notari* (Princeton, NJ: Princeton University Press, 1992); Tytti Soila, *Att synliggöra det dolda: om fyra svenska kvinnors filmregi* (Stockholm: Brutus Östlings förlag Symposium, 2004); Alison McMahan, *Alice Guy Blaché: Lost Visionary of the Cinema* (New York: Continuum, 2002); Ingrid Stigsdotter (ed.), *Making the Invisible Visible: Reclaiming Women's Agency in Swedish Film History and Beyond* (Lund: Nordic Academic Press, 2019); and Stamp, "Feminist Media Historiography."

42 See, for example, Jane Gaines, *Pink-Slipped: What Happened to Women in the Silent Film Industries?* (Champaign: University of Illinois, 2018). It is, of course, of importance to still look at women directors (as auteurs) because, as Yvonne Tasker has pointed out, it is the director who through public and commercial discourse is made a film's most prominent public figure. See Yvonne Tasker, "Vision and Visibility: Women Filmmakers, Contemporary Authorship, and Feminist Film Studies," in Vicky Callahan (ed.), *Reclaiming the Archive: Feminism and Film History* (Detroit: Wayne State University Press, 2010), 213–30.

43 In Sweden, intersectionality was introduced in the 1990s as a way to raise questions about Sweden's history as a colonial state, to critically investigate Swedish gender equality policy, and to question the rhetoric of Sweden as a model in terms of gender equality. Soon, the notion of diversity (*mångfald*) was introduced and inserted into the Swedish Film Agreement in 2013. And in late December 2021, the Swedish government decided to delete the formulation in its "directives" regarding diversity and equality so as to secure an "arm's length" between free art, creativity, and political demands. See Serner's Foreword in this book. See also Elisabeth Andersson, "Regeringen stryker krav på mångfald," *Svenska Dagbladet*, December 28, 2021, https://www.svd.se/regeringen-stryker-krav-pa-mangfald (accessed September 6, 2022).

44 See Anne O'Brien, *Women, Inequality and Media Work* (London: Routledge, 2019); Liddy, *Women in the International Film Industry*; Maria Jansson and Louise Wallenberg, "Experiencing Male Dominance in Swedish Film Production"; Lisa French, "Gender Still Matters: Towards Sustainable Progress for Women in Australian Film and Television Industries," in Susan Liddy (ed.), *Women in the International Film Industry* (London: Palgrave Macmillan, 2020), 271–91; A.A. Ukata, "Women and Representations in Nollywood: Questions of Production and Direction," in Susan Liddy (ed.), *Women in the International Film Industry* (London: Palgrave Macmillan, 2020), 315–30; Maria Jansson, Frantzeska Papadopoulou, Ingrid Stigsdotter, and Louise Wallenberg, "Studying Women in Swedish Film Production: Methodological Considerations," *Journal of Scandinavian Cinema* vol. 10, no. 2 (2020), 207–14; Louise Wallenberg and Maria Jansson, "On and Off Screen: An Introduction," in Louise Wallenberg and Maria Jansson (eds.), "On and Off Screen: Women's Work in the Screen Industries," special issue of *Gender, Work and Organization*, vol. 28, no. 6 (2021), 2010–25; and Susan Liddy and Anne O'Brien (eds.), *Media Work, Mothers and Motherhood: Negotiating the International Audio-Visual Industry* (London: Routledge, 2021).

45 See ProductionStudies Research, https://productionstudies.net (accessed September 7, 2022).

46 Mayer, Banks, and Caldwell, *Production Studies*, 4.

47 Vicki Mayer, "Bringing the Social Back In: Studies of Production Cultures and Social Theory," in Vicki Mayer, Miranda Banks, and John T. Caldwell (eds.), *Production Studies: Cultural Studies of Media Industries* (New York: Routledge, 2009), 15.

48 See, for example, Banks, "Gender Below-the-Line"; Banks, "Production Studies"; Mayer, "Bringing the Social Back In"; Mayer, *Below the Line*; Mayer, Banks, and Caldwell, *Production Studies*; Banks, Conor, and Mayer, *Production Studies, The Sequel!*

49 See, for example, H. Blair, "'You're only as Good as Your Last Job': The Labour Process in the British Film Industry," *Work, Employment and Society*, vol. 15, no. 1 (2002), 149–69; Marja Soila-Wadman, "Kapitulationens estetik: organisering och ledarskap i filmprojekt" (Ph.D. dissertation, Stockholm University, 2003); G. Delmestri, F. Montanari, and A. Usai, "Reputation and Strength of Ties in Predicting Commercial Success and Artistic Merit of Independents in the Italian Feature Film Industry," *Journal of Management Studies*, vol. 45, no. 5 (2005), 975–1002; J.J. Ebbers and N.M. Wijnberg, "Latent Organizations in the Film Industry," *Human Relations*, vol. 62, no. 7 (2009), 987–1009; Bent Sörensen and K. Villadsen, "The Naked Manager: The Ethical Practice of an Anti-Establishment Boss," *Organization*, vol. 22, no. 2 (2014), 251–68; S.L. Smith, M. Choueiti, E. Scofield, and K. Pieper, *Gender Inequality in 500 Popular Films: Examining On-Screen Portrayals and behind the Scenes Employment Patterns in Motion Pictures Released between 2007–2012* (Los Angeles: Annenberg School for Communication & Journalism, University of Southern California, 2013); Deborah Jones and Judith K. Pringle, "Unmanageable Inequalities: Sexism in the Film industry," *The Sociological Review*, vol. 63, S1 (2015), 37–49; Emma Bell and A. Sinclair, "Re-envisaging Leadership through the Feminine Imaginary in Film and Television," in Chris Steyaert, Timon Beyes, and Martin Parker (eds.), *The Routledge Companion to Reinventing Management Education* (London: Routledge, 2016); N. Meziani and L. Cabantous, "Acting Intuition into Sense: How Film Crews Make Sense with Embodied Ways of Knowing," *Journal of Management Studies*, vol. 57, no. 7 (2020), 1384–419.

50 See, for example, Smith et al., *Gender Inequality in 500 Popular Films*; Natalie Wreyford, "The Real Cost of Childcare: Motherhood and Project-Based Creative Labour in the UK Film Industry," *Studies in the Maternal*, vol. 5, no. 2 (2013), 1–22; Anne O'Brien, "Producing Television and Reproducing Gender," *Television & New Media*, vol. 16, no. 3 (2015), 259–74; O'Brien, *Women, Inequality and Media Work*; L. Cham Wing-Fai, R. Gill, and K. Randle, "Getting in, Getting on, Getting out? Women as Career Scramblers in the UK Film and Television industries," *The Sociological Review*, vol. 63 (2015), 50–65; Maria Jansson, "Gender Equality in Swedish Film Policy: Radical Interpretations and 'unruly' Women," *European Journal of Women's Studies*, vol. 24, no. 4 (2017), 336–50, https://www.doi.org/10.1177/1350506817692387; Liddy, "In Her Own Voice: Reflections on the Irish Film Industry and beyond," *Gender and the Screenplay: Processes, Practices, Perspectives*, in "Networking Knowledge" Special Issue, vol. 10, no. 2 (2017), 19–31; Akata Mukherjee, "Representational Politics in Bollywood Sports Movies of the 21st Century: Empowering Women through Counter Cinema," *PostScriptum: An Interdisciplinary Journal of Literary Studies*, vol. 3 (2018), 65–80; O'Brien, *Women, Inequality and Media Work*; M.M. Lauzen, "Where Are the Film Directors

(Who Happen to be Women)?" *Quarterly Review of Film and Video*, vol. 29 (2019), 310–19, https://doi.org/10.1080/10509201003601167; Shelley Cobb, "What About the Men: Gender Inequality Data and the Rhetoric of Inclusion in the US and UK Film Industries," *Journal of British Cinema and Television*, vol. 17 (2020), 112–35; Jansson and Wallenberg, "Experiencing Male Dominance in Swedish Film Production"; Shelley Cobb and Linda R. Williams, "Gender Equality in British Film-making: Research, Targets, Change," in Susan Liddy (ed.), *Women in the International Film Industry* (London: Palgrave Macmillan, 2020), 97–110; T.S.S. Thorsen, "Gendered Representation in Danish Film," in Susan Liddy (ed.), *Women in the International Film Industry* (London: Palgrave Macmillan, 2020), 111–30; Ukata, "Women and Representations in Nollywood"; Jansson and Wallenberg, "On and Off Screen: An Introduction"; Jansson et al., "The Final Cut"; Liddy and O'Brien, *Media Work, Mothers and Motherhood*.

Part One

Frameworks: The Power of Institutions

1

The Sex of the Author

On Authorship

Frantzeska Papadopoulou

Authorship and film, or authorship in film, coalesce in exciting if also rather blurry ways. Interestingly enough, both "authorship" as a concept of legal significance, and film as a new technological (if not artistic) achievement received their first official international exposure in Paris, the former during the Congrès Littéraire International on June 17, 1878, and the latter in the public screening of the Lumière brothers' films in Paris on December 28, 1895.[1]

It is not at all difficult to imagine why the application of the term "authorship" in film production and consumption culture has been anything but frictionless. First, it took several decades for public opinion and then the legal system to recognize film as a form of art or, in general, an intellectual work subject to copyright protection. At the same time, film is as such a complicated subject matter in terms of its process of production, the importance of the active involvement of several contributors, and the difficulty to discern who in fact is the mastermind—the "genius"—behind the end result.[2] The multilevel and multiparty contribution, necessary for a film production is contradictory to crediting a sole author. These factors also explain why an "authorship" discourse, that of the *auteur theory*, emerges as late as the 1940s in film theory.[3] At the same time the *auteur* became central in the film context when the industry reached a certain maturity and there was an importance to claim its "fine art" status.

Authorship as such is a rather contemporary concept used to define the person that bares the sole responsibility and enjoys the benefits for the creation of an original work, initially literary works. Certainly, authorship constitutes evidence of origin, originality, a matter of branding, but also evidence of the legal control of works. Previously, the legal control of printed works was awarded to printers and publishers by means of royal privileges. It was not until the late 1800s that the "author" appeared as a unique individual, a genius that deserved to be compensated for his work. Gradually this "author" became an autonomous legal subject, one who should be elevated and compensated accordingly.[4]

In contemporary film studies, authorship has been awarded a number of different functions: that of origin, expression of personality, sociology of production, as a signature, as a reading strategy, as a site of discourses, or as a technique of the self.[5] It becomes thus a concept that is filled with content both with regard to the author's internal need for expression, as well as with regard to their communication with the public and other authors.

Further, authorship constitutes the theoretical foundation of modern intellectual property rights, the mere existence of copyright presupposes the identification of an author. At the same time, however, the concept has been an expression of a paternalistic and gender-biased discourse where the author, and thus also the owner of the intellectual property rights, is in fact a man, a "he."[6] There is very little feminist analysis of copyright law and thus also of the gender perspective of authorship as such.[7]

One could, of course, wonder why a discussion on authorship is relevant and how it actually contributes to address the core concepts of this book, namely the presence and power of women in the Swedish film industry. The reason should, however, be obvious. Authorship is today used as an all-encompassing term within a widespread area of cultural exchange, it signals property, control but also creativity, personality, the power to include and to exclude, and of course branding. The questions posed by this chapter are thus: (1) How does the presence of an author emerge in the field of film industries in Sweden, in regard to praxis, rights, and legislation? (2) What are the specific features of a feasible female author within the film industry? Is authorship equivalent to presence? (3) What are the means to create a "portrait" of an author in the film industry, and is it possible for an alleged female author to have control over her own "portrait"?

To address these questions, this chapter investigates the evolution of the concept of authorship from a specific theoretical point of view of the Auteur theory developed in the late 1940s by French film critics, its introduction to the world of film and the role it plays to the application of the copyright system. Subsequent to a theoretical and legislative overview of the terms author/auteur this chapter will proceed to look into how authorship has been comprehended and exercised by women who have aspired/aspire to the position of author/auteur in the film industry.

The Genesis of Authorship

Although Foucault's thought-provoking text "Qu'est-ce qu'un auteur?" was published in 1968, very little has been written about the origins of the term *auteur*. In his article, Foucault poses a series of interesting questions in relation to the genesis of the concept, namely:

> It would be worth examining how the author became individualized in a culture like ours, what status he has been given, at what moment studies of authenticity and attribution began, in what kind of system of valorization the author was involved, at what point we began to recount the lives of authors rather than of heroes, and how this fundamental category of "the-man-and-his-work criticism" began.[8]

What seems to be rather clear, however, is the fact that the term (at least in its contemporary use) is a new normative construction and one promoted by a group of literary authors that wished to find a legal basis that would allow them to actually make a living as a writer. It is in fact their struggle to acquire legal protection for the products of their labor that constituted the starting point for what came to be *the author* and by extension the *auteur*. In the Renaissance and post-Renaissance era of the early nineteenth century, the "author" was a craftsman, the "master of an art" who provided form to clay, color, notes, and words. These "craftsmen" provided their sponsors, mainly the royal court and the social elite, with literary and cultural expressions. It was also these sponsors that provided for the financial, political, and social protection necessary for these authors to live and thrive. The dependence of the authors on their sponsors most certainly had side-effects, since it also dictated very often also what was produced and how. The sponsors elevated certain authors and artists of extraordinary quality to such levels of those that have a divine source of inspiration, the glory of God, or a muse. The cultural hegemony of the cultural elite was gradually abandoned due to new political and economic circumstances, and in the late eighteenth century artistic creations and literature were increasingly accessible to a broader public. Authors and artists abandoned their protégé status and adopted that of public celebrities.

In this attempt to better serve the cause of linking authorship to a livelihood, late nineteenth-century theorists undermined the role of the craftsman and elevated the role of "genius" that is not of divine origin, and originates from the talents and personality of the "author" himself/herself. The central role of the personality, skills, and inspiration of the individual "author" led to the genesis of the "original genius." Undermining the role of the divine had a decisive impact on the internal relationship between the author and the work. Art and literature became the outcome of the "author's" genius, a commodity, and thus also the author's property. Although the role of royal and noble patronage was fading, authors found themselves in new dependency relations, this time exploited by printers and publishers who got richer and richer, while they (the authors) received a limited honorarium.[9]

It was under such circumstances that the first official international proclamation of the "author" was made, in 1878, the year of the Exposition Universelle in Paris, at the Congrès Littéraire International, initiated by the Societé des gens de lettres de France. Victor Hugo gave the inaugural speech and in it for the first time he constructed the modern international "author."[10] According to Hugo, if you deprive the author of his property then you deprive him of his independence. The "author" is a genius, possessing extraordinary qualities, an intellectual capital that should enjoy the extensive protection of the legislator. It was this speech that laid the theoretical ground for the Berne Convention (1886), the international treaty regulating copyright law and signed and ratified in principle by all the countries in the world.[11]

A discourse on the genius in film—the author—that strikingly recalls the origins of the literary author as "he" was presented in the speech of Hugo, arose some seventy years later in post-war France. The *director as auteur*—a term, concept, and value—gradually found its way to film critics and filmmakers in other countries in the late 1950s and 1960s. Two seminal texts contributed to launching the notion of the auteur—embedded, as it was, in a theory called *le politique des auteurs*—Alexandre Astruc's *Du Stylo à la caméra et de la caméra au stylo* (1948) and François Truffaut's *Une certaine tendence du cinéma français* (1954).[12]

In fact, some of the earliest attempts to theorize around the film medium approached filmmaking as an art form and emphasized the filmmaker as an artist comparable to a painter or a novelist.[13] Like the case of literary authors previously, the fact that there was no explicit proclamation of the role of the director as *auteur* does not per se also mean that the director's contribution would have been regarded as insignificant prior to the all-encompassing breakthrough of the concept. Indeed, silent film directors such as D.W. Griffiths in the United States, Carl Theodor Dreyer in Denmark, and Victor Sjöström in Sweden (to name just three examples) were renowned for their artistry and their individual and specific cinematic style.

In this respect, the *auteur* has been presented as the man who initiates the concept, writes the script (including the dialogue), directs, and finances his films. He is the one that has the sole responsibility for the artistic creation in a cinematographic work and the one to receive the sole credit.[14] However, Truffaut, together with other *Cahiers* critics, provided for a rather inclusive approach. To stress the artistic value of commercial genre productions as well, the French film critics supported their arguments by analyzing the works of Hollywood directors such as Howard Hawks and Alfred Hitchcock. To overcome the criteria asking for possession of the means of production and control of all phases in the production chain, the focus was put on the *style* of each director in a film. The style became the expression for the uniqueness and the artistic value of the final artistic product, the film. Thus, the notion of *auteur* came to signify not only filmmakers telling their own stories but also directors who succeeded in making personal films even when working from other people's scripts.[15]

Looking at the Swedish paradigm, the film industry had, for several decades, aspired to the status of art (as in opposition to the aura of lowbrow amusement) for their products. This was not only because of the importance to label "art as art" but as an effort to appeal to the culturally refined groups in society. Appealing to this stratum was in its turn expected to contribute to substantial increases in the box office income. Parallel to this, and toward the end of the 1940s, the government increased "amusement taxes" based on every paid ticket in different kinds of entertainment facilities, including movie theaters. On the other hand, theater performances and musical concerts, being considered as cultural forms, were exempted from the amusement tax. The film industry was presented with the pure economic interest of receiving similar tax reliefs to stage theaters. To achieve that, film had to be considered as an acknowledged fine art, as an expression of high culture. Fine art and high culture presuppose the existence of the alleviated author. Identifying the film director as an *auteur* was a priority under such conditions.

In the late 1940s, when *auteur theory* emerged, the film industry received both the self-confidence and the recognition of its artistic value and sought a way to individualize the director as the "author."[16] It seemed only natural that if film was to be recognized as a work of art, there should also be an "author." The ideal of the "author" who creates freely without any constraints from sponsors corresponds to the ideal of the "author" of the post-Renaissance era. It also perfectly matches the concept of the artist in use at the introduction of

Modernism in art and literature at the turn of the nineteenth century, where a piece of art was seen as the expression of a unique mind and an individual's view of life and values.[17]

Authorship in Film: Are the Ignition Points Timeless?

As previously shown in this chapter, authorship is a term loaded with different values, carrying different meanings and thus giving rise to a variety of legal implications. One important aspect in the discussion at hand is: what is meant by "authorship," and how does the film industry use the term? What are we really looking at when identifying authorship in film? Is it the level of creativity? Or is it a matter of ownership claim? Is it control of the creative process of film production, or is it control over the end result? Or is it a matter of being attributed the credits to a film? Is it merely a matter of branding? And can it be so that while using the same term "authorship in film" we weigh and value completely different aspects/meanings of the term?

At the beginning of the twentieth century, Sweden participated in the intellectual and legislative debates as to whether cinematographic works are dramatic works or photographs, and thus whether they would qualify for copyright protection to begin with. The law on the right to literary and music works of 1919, did not mention film as a protectable subject matter. The same year, however, the law on the protection of photographic works (FL) was adopted and was deemed as most appropriate to foster the protection of this new "subject-matter."[18] This law was considered to be of relevance for the film industry, since cinematographic works were initially considered a series of photographs. During this first period, discussions were concentrated on the status of copyright protected works used for the purposes of a film production (books, music), as well as to whether and under which conditions a film could be subject to copyright protection as such.[19] A review of the literature and the legislative works in this respect shows that film directors were granted a central position in the film protection debate. In the public inquiries both regarding the 1919 legislation and its 1931 revision, the contribution of the film director was expressly considered more important than that of the theatrical director in stage productions.[20] Nevertheless, in neither of these legislative works is the film director expressly awarded copyright protection for films. Knoph excludes in his work any possibility of protecting the film director as an author, yet at the same time he provides that the contribution of the film director is independent enough from the film and could thus be a basis for some form of protection. This was contrary to what the court decided with regards to a theatrical director in the Mazurka case.[21]

It is important to note here, however, that authorship in film was not officially recognized until the 1960 Swedish Copyright Act (URL). With the lack of an adequate legislative framework, the rights of directors, actors, and producers were safeguarded (when that was the case) by means of contractual agreements. What is noteworthy in this respect is the fact that although film productions fell outside the scope of the legislation, these agreements were still very laconic (very short in length and including only general terms). It seems that relations in the Swedish film industry at the time were to a large extent self-regulated by unwritten codes of conduct that were easy to follow and enforce considering the limited size of the industry at the time. The "author" in this respect was recognized as the author of the original literary work on the basis of which the film was produced.[22]

The 1960 Swedish Copyright Act has entailed a new era for the film industry by including in the copyright legislation a list of *sui generis* rights and so-called neighboring rights, several of which concern film, namely rights for performing artists, producers, and even photographers.[23] Neighboring rights, although placed strategically under the same legislation, enjoy a somewhat different legal status than that of copyright. Protection criteria differ, as does the duration of protection granted. Rights are not exclusively based on the creative expression of the right holder as the financial investment in the film also may determine the grant of the exclusive rights (44-47 §§ URL). In fact, these rights may protect a legal person (a company or organization) and do not require the existence of a human, an author/auteur, as is the case with traditional copyright. Furthermore, they reward economic investment and not creativity or originality.

According to Article 2.1 of Council Directive 93/98/EEC of October 29, 1993, harmonizing the term of protection of copyright and certain related rights, the author of the film as such was the principal director. While some other countries, such as the UK, have opted for a more hands-on clarification of the legal status of "authorship" in film, Sweden has chosen a more neutral position.[24] The copyright is awarded to the person/persons who have contributed with creativity and originality to the final artistic character of the work/the film. This leaves the question of "authorship" rather open and subject to an *in casu* evaluation.[25] In the Public Inquiry it is provided that the principal director of a film will also be the author of the film.[26] Following the same line is the law proposal 1994/95:151,[27] confirming the same view but not considering it necessary to specify this in the legislative text as such.[28]

The fact that copyright is in fact a two-faceted exclusive right containing both an economic right (2 § URL) and a moral right (3 § URL) brings an additional and not unimportant perspective to the discussion. Rights transferred by means of contract or assignment concern only the economic rights of copyright (the right to reproduction, distribution, etc.).[29] The moral rights are non-transferrable and remain with the original author of the work. This means that in theory the director, screenwriter, or any other joint-author to a film might claim moral rights and object to a certain form of exploitation of a film even after the transfer of their economic rights. (See, for instance, the case *Hajen som visste för mycket* in which the director of the film opposed it being disrupted by advertisements when broadcast by the Swedish television channel TV4, as this was considered a distraction from the atmosphere and historical character of the film.[30])

It is thus important to clarify that when using the term "authorship" from a legal perspective we refer in fact to a bundle of rights. The contemporary abstruseness of the legislation with regards to the copyright protection of film works is compensated by elaborate contractual agreements, concentrating the economic rights (be it traditional copyright or neighboring rights) in the hands of the producer/distributor. What authorship thus bestows on the film author above the economic rights of copying, distributing, and that of public performance, is the right to be named, the right to have the final say, the "final cut" on the artistic approach of the film, and the right to require that the film is distributed in ways that are not defamatory for the author.

In Search of the "She" Genius

Considering the above, the conceptual idea of the author/auteur has historically been a man, a "he." Victor Hugo, seventy-five years old at the time of his seminal speech quoted above, clearly identifies the male author. He also lived in a period of time when women had no legal rights after marriage, not even the acclaimed authors could in fact represent themselves and decide upon the management of their rights.[31] Looking into central principles and terminology of copyright law leaves no doubt of its gendered origins. The right of the author, according to copyright law, to have the name of the author attached to his work is named the "paternity right," as in fact the right of the father to protect the patrilineal line. The parental metaphors do not stop here, the author "creates," "originates," and acquires the rights to "reproduction," and when the identity of the author is unknown the work is an "orphan."[32] Regrettably, of course, both authorship as a political and legal term, and the concept of *auteur* in film theory were developed almost entirely by men who established the intellectual construction of a male author, the only one who could be a "genius." One woman with influence in the early discussion on authorship was the American film critic Pauline Kael, discussed below. One could of course attempt to understand (though not justify) why this was the case.

The notion of the auteur-director was created by male film critics, and the filmmakers that they canonized were also men. In 1963, a few years before Barthes and Foucault wrote their pieces on the (missing) author, Pauline Kael criticized "auteur theory" as "an attempt by adult males to justify staying within the small range of experience of their boyhood and adolescence."[33] After her, many feminist film theorists have rejected auteurist approaches to film, claiming that a focus on the director is inherently tied to a sexist cult of male personality. Yet, many feminist film scholars have also opted to use the idea of authorship to celebrate the work of women directors.[34]

Despite of the origins of author and auteur and their dependence on the male prototype, the "she" geniuses of the film industry are non-negligible. There is a long list of important contributions of women in the history of film production, be it as authors of literary works adapted to films, screenwriters, set decorators, directors, or producers.[35] It becomes also equally important to see how they praised and defended their acclaimed authorship (and the rights this bestowed them), as well as how this was welcomed by the state, the stakeholders of the film industry, and the audience.

On the basis of what was previously concluded as a core of authorship in film, namely the moral rights to the work, it is of interest to investigate how these rights were exercised by "she" geniuses of the film industry historically. An interesting illustration is that of state censorship emerging as a means to control the content and distribution of films in Sweden. The Nobel Prize-winning author Selma Lagerlöf was one of the female authors with the most notable resistance to the attempts of the censors to limit her creative freedom. In 1925, the Gustaf Molander film *Ingmarsarvet* (The Sons of Ingmar), based on the first part of Lagerlöf's trilogy *Jerusalem*, attracted the interest of state censorship. The distributor (SF) was in fact informed that certain scenes should be removed (in particular a scene with a woman drowning after a fight for a lifebuoy). The distributor replied that Lagerlöf was strongly against such interference in her creative work, since this would severely damage the artistic value of the film. In the letter informing of their final decision, the censors state clearly that they do not share Lagerlöf's opinion, but will, however, respect her wish.[36]

This decision is noteworthy since it illustrates how censorship and authorship collide in film, but also and above all, because Lagerlöf managed to defend her rights as the "author" and in fact impose her approach on the censors. At a period of time, where there was no established, self-evident author for the film work as such, the author of the literary work—that the film was based on—often became the frontal figure both to defend its intellectual and artistic sanctity as well as a brand name under which the film would be advertised.

In fact, this was not the first time the censors chose to abstain from interfering with Lagerlöf's authorship. Already in 1917, there were serious concerns for the film *Tösen från Stormyrtorpet* (The Lass From the Stormy Croft) (Figure 1.1) based on Lagerlöf's book with the same name, and whether it should be classified as white (prohibited for both adults and children) since it included the rape of a woman, a child born outside of wedlock, and a father who refused to take responsibility for his actions. However, the censors seemed unwilling to interfere with the work of Lagerlöf, recognizing her status and admitting some form of "sanctity" in her intellectual work.[37]

Lagerlöf's interaction with censorship provides an interesting historical illustration of the power and impact of female authorship in the early film industry. Contemporary stories of authorship expressed in the interviews conducted by Tytti Soila reveal that while the Copyright Act of 1960 provided for a more solid legal basis concerning rights on film works, authorship, as exercised and experienced by women in the film industry, has surprisingly been limited. These interviews had as a main focus the role of Mai Zetterling in the history of Swedish film. Zetterling's artistic work was admirable taking into consideration that Swedish film history could enumerate not more than three female film directors previous to her. In her interview, Stina Ekblad compares the creative space offered to Ingmar Bergman and to Mai Zetterling respectively and concludes that when Bergman used erotic scenes it was acceptable, while when a female director would do the same, it was perceived as less artistic and much more criticized.[38] According to Ekblad, a female director, such as Zetterling, had to be so much more in order to establish a career in the film industry, and at some point, this "much more" became "too much." Gunnel Lindblom discussed

Figure 1.1 The poster from *Tösen från Stormyrtorpet* is illustrative of the predominant position Selma Lagerlöf had as an "author" of the film.

the film *Flickorna* (The Girls, 1968), which she considers to this day to be a very important and powerful film raising issues of women's empowerment, but that met the criticism of the male audience, as well as of the women's rights organizations, most probably due to its female director.[39]

Director Marianne Ahrne provides that although she thinks that many of the commercially successful films made by male directors could have been made by women, women are in general more interested in preserving the integrity of their authorship. Women have a story they want to tell in their films.[40] This is also, according to Ahrne, the reason why most women make documentary films in Sweden, because in the production of those, the director has much more creative space and a much more active authorship. Equally characteristic is what she says about her films, among which she is able to see a distinction. Some of them being her "works," "works on life and death" (these seem to be the results of difficult and painful process), and as she herself says, "works made after taking a big risk."[41]

In her book *Ravinen*, film director Lisa Ohlin describes in diary form her work with the production of the film *De standhhaftige* (Walk with me, 2016).[42] In the detailed description of the working process with the specific film, Ohlin writes about her process of becoming a director, her love for film, and the difficulties she has encountered in her career due to the fact that she is a woman. Her creative freedom is limited by producers but also by photographers and other members of the production team that would normally be expected to execute her requests. The book describes all the turns that the lengthy production had to take: changes in the budget, in the cast as well as in the directions given by producers and distributors who had a clear view of what was needed for the film to become a success. All these comments and creative "contributions," gradually limited Ohlin's creative activity to the minimum.

The content of the book is not revolutionary as such, and the difficulties faced during the production of the specific film are not unique. It is, however, very interesting because it exposes to the broader public an industry-internal truth, namely the vital importance of being asked to make films—to become an author—that forces directors to remain silent, to avoid conflicts with someone that potentially can in the present or in the future influence their chances of future projects. A film director does not want to be considered difficult and picky, and thus they accept comments on the script, the scenery, the lighting, even the way the film is to be directed from producers, distributors, and other financers who should not have a decisive impact on the creative work of the film. While the scope of creativity that Ohlin as a director was able to exercise was extremely limited, she was the one held solely accountable for the commercial failure of the film. Thus, authorship that should be twofold, namely originating in the expression of the personality of the author, and at the same expressing the origin of the creative work, has in this case constituted sole grounds for accountability. While Ohlin had to accept and execute the directives of others, the result of the intellectual creation—the film—was her responsibility. Ohlin is clear on the difficulties she had to deal with during her career due to her sex. These included comments from male colleagues on her private and professional choices; the unwillingness of photographers to execute her orders, questioning her ability to direct; the sexual violence she was exposed to by a producer; and the defiance she had to deal with from the press when she chose to make a film about men (questioning what made her do a film about men, and whether she thought she was able to). It becomes obvious that the hurdles faced by authors in the film industry due to the particularities of the industry and economic restraints are accentuated when the author is a woman.

Apart from the economic restraints and the way producers restrict creativity and thus also indirectly authorship, there is another perspective of importance, inherent to film productions, that is, their collective and collaborative nature. The film as a creative work cannot potentially be attributed to the contribution of only one author (the director), there are several contributions that could be decisive for the final character of the film.

These contemporary voices make it clear, authorship of women in the film industry is framed and constrained. Whether it is budget limitations (women make films with lower budgets in general), the difficulties in taking the lead of the production team, or finally the constraints posed by distributors, women are not able to create freely. Their authorship is thus consequently limited, and its exercise timid.

Does Authorship Matter?

In conclusion, the cases presented here show that women's presence within the Swedish film industry has been tangible and even belligerent from very early on. They have been visible through concrete debates on issues of authorship and copyright, making a stand and claiming their rights.

The case of Selma Lagerlöf shows that for a woman, being successful in the debate concerning author/auteurship, a considerable amount of cultural capital has been necessary. Lagerlöf was an internationally acknowledged, Nobel Prize-winning author and member of the Swedish Academy. However, she clearly was a pathbreaker, and this study also shows that during the past decades the a number, awareness, and self-confidence of women within the (Swedish) film industry has increased exceedingly.

One needs to address one important question in this respect; namely, is the gender of the author important when investigating power, presence, and portrayal in film? And if so, why and to what extent? In fact, a decisive issue when discussing power, presence, and portrayal precedes any discussion of authorship; namely, the possibility to be given the chance to make a film in whatever position that may be. This possibility of actually being part of the creative process of making a film is what makes a woman an author. If you are excluded from film productions, then authorship is a very theoretical exercise. It seems, however, that even at times when women were still questioned with regard to their intellectual capacity, the exercise of their fundamental rights, and their right to a legal personality, a number of "she" geniuses emerged and occupied central positions in the film industry.

Today, authorship is framed by the strict constraints of the reality in which film productions take place; namely, the very few opportunities directors have to make a film, the strict budgets, and the extensive role and impact of other stakeholders such as producers, and distributors. The competition in the creative space of the author is high, the stakes are high, and thus the sanctity of aesthetics, creativity, and intellectual investment of the author (whoever that may be—the screenwriter, the director, the producer, the author of the original book, etc.) will, if necessary, be sacrificed to protect the commercial viability of the film or its broader distribution. Such a limited approach to authorship also means that women directors, producers, and authors in general are deprived of the power to choose what stories to tell, how to tell them, what to portray, and how. It means in the end that their power to control the result of their work is limited. All the compromises they are willing to make will without a doubt have an impact on the scope of their authorship. In this respect, it seems that these constraints are general and irrespective of gender.

Hence the sex of the author is vital. It is vital since the film industry is *de facto* an industry where women are still to this day underrepresented, it is vital because according to the statistics women work on films with lower budgets and because women, the "she" geniuses, have very often to deal with bigger hurdles in their exercise of authorship, exercising authority in the production team, or negotiating with the production company. It is also of central importance, since authorship has formed film politics and in particular gender politics and goals of the Swedish Film Institute. A lack of understanding of what authorship in film entails, what rights it includes, and to what extent these are framed by other objectives, such as budgets, corporate decisions, distribution policies, will without a doubt flaw any general conclusions that may be drawn about the success (or not) of gender goals in film politics. Women in film are aware and mindful of the value of their authorship. It seems also that this awareness is what sometimes forces them to take a step back, as constraints on their authorship are just too tight to make the whole process worth it.

Notes

1. Rune Waldekranz, *Filmens historia: De första hundra åren*, part 1 (Stockholm: Norstedts, 1986). See also S.B. Dobranski, "The Birth of the Author: the Origins of Early Modern Printed Authority," *DQR Studies in Literature*, vol. 43 (2008), 23–45; Abraham Drassinower, "Copyright, Authorship and the Public Domain: A Reply to Mark Rose and Niva Elkin-Koren," *Jurisprudence*, vol. 9, no. 1 (2018), 179–85. NB. I am aware that this fact is contested.
2. Marja Soila-Wadman, "Kapitulationens estetik. Organisering och ledarskap i filmprojekt" (Ph.D. dissertation, Företagsekonomiska institutionen, Stockholm University, 2003), 42.
3. For an elaboration on the evolution of the concept of "author," see Peter Jaszi, "Toward Theory of Copyright: The Metamorphoses of 'Authorship,'" *Duke Law Journal*, no. 2 (April 1991), 455–502; Benjamin Kaplan, *An Unhurried View on Copyright* (New York: Columbia University Press, 1967), 52–69; Martha Woodmansee, "The Genius and the Copyright: Economic and Legal Conditions of the Emergence of the 'Author,'" *Eighteenth-Century Studies*, vol. 17, no. 4 (1984), 425–58.
4. John Feather, *Publishing, Piracy and Politics: An Historical Study of Copyright in Britain* (London: Mansell, 1994); Rosemary J. Coombes, *The Cultural Life of Intellectual Properties: Authorship, Appropriation, and the Law* (Durham, NC: Duke University Press, 1998).
5. Janet Staiger, "Authorship Approaches," in David A. Gerstner and Janet Staiger (eds), *Authorship and Film* (London: Routledge, 2003), 27–57.
6. The historical presentation of the "author" will refer to the male author, the "he."
7. Andreas Huyssen, "Mass Culture as Woman: Modernism's Other," in *After the Great Divide: Modernism, Mass Culture, Postmodernism* (Basingstoke: Macmillan, 1988), 192; Seán Burke, "Feminism and the Authorial Subject," in *Authorship: From Plato to the Postmodern* (Edinburgh: Edinburgh University Press, 1995); Melissa Homestead, *American Women Authors and Literary Property* (New York: Cambridge University Press, 2005); Carys J. Craig, "Reconstructing the Author-Self: Some Feminist Lessons for Copyright Law," *Journal of Gender, Social Policy and the Law*, vol. 15, no. 2 (2007), 207–68; Ann Bartow, "Fair Use and the Fairer Sex: Gender, Feminism and Copyright Law," *Journal of Gender, Social Policy and the Law*, vol. 14, no. 3 (2016), 551–58.

8   Michel Foucault, "Vad är en författare?" in *Diskursernas kamp* (1969; Stockholm: Symposion, 2008), 141. See also Roland Barthes, "The Death of the Author," in *Image, Music, Text* (1968; London: Fontana, 1977); Seán Burke, *The Death and Return of the Author: Criticism and Subjectivity in Barthes, Foucault and Derrida* (Edinburgh: Edinburgh University Press, 1992); Per I. Gedin, *Litteraturen i verkligheten: Om bokmarknadens historia och framtid* (Stockholm: Rabén Prisma, 1997); Leif Dahlberg,"Rätt och litteratur," *Tidskrift för litteraturvetenskap*, vol. 32, no. 3 (2003), 3.

9   Bo Peterson, *Välja och sälja: Om bokförläggarens nya roll under 1800-talet, då landet industrialiserades, tågen började rulla, elektriciteten förändrade läsvanorna, skolan byggdes och bokläsarna blev allt fler* (Stockholm: Norstedts, 2003); Nancy Miller, "Changing the Subject: Authorship, Writing and the Reader," in Teresa de Lauretis (ed.), *Feminist Studies/Critical Studies* (London: Palgrave Macmillan, 1995); and Christopher, Buccafusco, "A Theory of Copyright Authorship," *Virginia Law Review*, vol. 102, no. 5 (2016), 1229–295.

10 Eva Hemmungs Wirtén, *No Trespassing: Authorship, Intellectual Property Rights, and the Boundaries of Globalization* (Toronto: University of Toronto Press 2004).

11 D.A. Brooks, *From Playhouse to Printing House: Drama and Authorship in Early Modern England* (Cambridge: Cambridge University Press, 2000); Sam Ricketson and Jane Ginsburg, *International Copyright and Neighbouring Rights: The Berne Convention and Beyond*, vol. 1 (Oxford: Oxford University Press, 2006); Gunnar Petri, *Författarrättens genombrott* (Stockholm: Atlantis, 2008), 28; and Janet Clare, "Shakespeare and Paradigms of Early Modern Authorship," *Journal of Early Modern Studies*, vol. 1, no. 1 (2012), 137–53.

12 Alexandre Astruc, *Du stylo à la caméra... et de la caméra au stylo. Écrits (1942–1984)* (1948; Paris: l'Archipel, 1992).

13 See, for instance, Ricciotto Canudo, "Naissance d'un Sixième Art: Essai sur le Cinématographe," translated as "The Birth of the Sixth Art," in Richard Abel (ed.), *French Film Theory and Criticism: A History/Anthology (1907–1930)*, vol. 1 (Princeton, NJ: Princeton University Press, 1988), 58–66; Menno ter Braak, *De absolute film* (Rotterdam: W. L. en J. Brusse, 1931).

14 François Truffaut, "Une certaine tendence du cinéma français," *Cahiers du cinéma* Cahiers du cinéma, vol. 6, no. 31 (January 1, 1954), 15. Our translation from the French original.

15 Miranda Banks, "Production Studies," *Feminist Media Histories*, vol. 4, no. 2 (2018), 157–61.

16 Waldekranz, *Filmens historia*; Tytti Soila, "The Phantom Carriage and the Concept of Melodrama," in Helena Forsås-Scott, Lisbeth Stenberg, and Bjarne Thorup Thomsen (eds.), *Re-mapping Lagerlöf* (Lund: Nordic Academic Press, 2014), 149–62.

17 Peter Luthersson, *Modernism och individualitet: en studie i den litterära modernismens kvalitativa egenart* (Stockholm: Symposium, 1986).
18 Martin Fredriksson, *Skapandets rätt* (Gothenburg: Daidalos, 2010).
19 Gösta Eberstein, *Den svenska författarrätten* (Stockholm: Norstedts, 1923); Ulf von Konow, *Författares och tonsättares rätt enligt gällande lagstiftning: Kommenterande utredning till Lag om rätt till litterära och konstnärliga verk den 30 maj 1919 med däri genom lag den 24 april 1931 gjorda ändringar och tillägg* (Stockholm: Natur och kultur, 1941); and Åke Lögdberg, *Auktorrätt och film* (Lund: Gleerup, 1957).
20 Elisabeth Liljedahl, *Stumfilmen i Sverige: Kritik och debatt – hur samtiden värderade den nya konstarten* (Stockholm: Svenska filminstitutet, 1975).
21 See the court case of the Supreme Court of Sweden, NJA 1943:101 s. 411. Ragnar Knoph, "Om ophavsmannens 'moralske' rett til sitt verk efter den nye lov om åndsverker," *Festskrift tillägnad Presidenten Juris doktor Herr Friherre Erik Marks von Würtemberg den 11 maj 1931*, 316; Lögdberg, *Auktorrätt och film*.
22 Lögdberg, *Auktorrätt och film*; Stig Strömholm, *Europeisk upphovsrätt: En översikt över lagstiftningen i Frankrike, Tyskland och England* (Stockholm: Norstedts, 1964); Strömholm, *Upphovsrättens verksbegrepp* (Stockholm: Norstedts, 1970); Strömholm, "Upphovsmans ideella rätt – Några huvudlinjer," *Tidskrift for rettsvitenskap*, vol. 88 (1975), 289–338; and Strömholm, "Upphovsrätten som nationell disciplin – exemplet droit moral," *Nordiskt immateriellt rättsskydd*, vol. 74 (2005), 650–63.
23 Latin for of its own kind, and used to describe a form of legal protection that exists outside typical legal protections—that is, something that is unique or different.
24 Brooks, *From Playhouse to Printing House*, 39; Pascal Kamina, *Film Copyright in the European Union* (Cambridge: Cambridge University Press, 2016), 47.
25 Jeffrey Knap, "What is a Co-Author?" *Representations*, vol. 89 (2005), 1–29. A case-to-case evaluation needs to be made in this regard.
26 See, *Upphovsmannarätt till litterära och konstnärliga verk* (SOU 1956: 25, 134).
27 Government Bill 1994/95:151, 25.
28 Kathy Bowrey, "Who's Writing Copyright History?" *European Intellectual Property Review*, vol. 18, no.6 (1996), 322–29; Strömholm, "Upphovsrätten som nationell disciplin"; Fredriksson, *Skapandets rätt*.
29 Kamina, *Film Copyright in the European Union*, 89.
30 The director of this film was Claes Eriksson (1989).
31 See Woodmansee, "The Genius and the Copyright"; Eva Heggestad, *Fången och fri:1880-talets svenska kvinnliga författare och hemmet, yrkeslivet och konstnärskapet* (Uppsala: Uppsala universitet, 1991).
32 Mark Rose, "Mothers and Authors: Johnson v. Calvert and the New Children of Our Imaginations," *Critical Inquiry*, vol. 22, no. 4 (1996), 613–33.
33 Pauline Kael, "Circles and Squares," *Film Quarterly*, vol. 16, no. 3 (1963), 12–26.

34 Annette Kuhn, *Queen of the B's: Ida Lupino behind the Camera* (Westport, CT: Greenwood Press, 1995); Tytti Soila, *Att synliggöra det dolda: om fyra svenska kvinnors filmregi* (Stockholm: Brutus Östlings förlag Symposium, 2004); Joan Simon (ed.), *Alice Guy Blaché: Cinema Pioneer* (New Haven, CT: Yale University Press, 2009).

35 Carol Rose, "Bargaining and Gender," *Harvard Law Journal & Public Policy*, vol. 18 (1995), 547–63; Rose, "Women and Property: Gaining and Losing Ground," *Virginia Law Review*, 78, no. 2 (1992), 421–59.

36 Gösta Werner, *Rött, vitt och gult: färgerna i censurens banér: den svenska filmcensurens bedömningar av Victor Sjöströms och Mauritz Stillers filmer 1912–1936* (Stockholm: Statens biografbyrå, 2002), 95.

37 Ibid., 82; Anna Nordlund, "Selma Lagerlöf in the Golden Age of Swedish Silent Cinema," in Helena Försås-Scott, Lisbeth Stenberg, and Bjarne Thorup Thomsen (eds.), *Re-mapping Lagerlöf* (Lund: Nordic Academic Press, 2014), 94–116; Soila, "The Phantom Carriage and the Concept of Melodrama."

38 Interview with Stina Ekblad, October 25, 2008, by Tytti Soila and Maaret Koskinen.

39 Interview with Gunnel Lindblom, April 26, 2011, by Tytti Soila.

40 Soila, *Att synliggöra det dolda*, 35–6.

41 Ibid., 36.

42 Lisa Ohlin, *Ravinen* (Stockholm: Type & Tell, 2018).

2

Gendering Film Distribution

Frantzeska Papadopoulou

Introduction

Film distribution is, without doubt, of key importance for film and filmmakers. In the absence of distribution channels the film will not reach its audience, the work of the director will remain unknown, and the producers (and other investors) will not be able to recuperate their investment. Thus, a starting point is that contributors to a film production will normally wish for the film to be distributed and that a series of efforts and compromises will be made toward this goal, very often already before even producing the film in question.[1]

In Sweden, the role of the distributor is even more crucial today than it has been in the past. Film productions in Sweden are in principle dependent on the financing of the Swedish Film Institute (SFI), and financing in its turn presupposes a distribution agreement. Thus, distribution becomes a prerequisite for making the film, and distributors become involved in the film's production from day one. This is naturally only one aspect of the layered and also very much complicated environment under which films reach their audiences. The choices that need to be made in relation to distribution include the content—namely the genre—the target group, the actors, the length, the posters, the film festivals, and windowing, to name just a few.[2] The digital era provides its own challenges to film distribution.[3] What makes matters even more complicated is that film is a hybrid subject matter, one that lies between being a (very expensive) commodity and a sophisticated art form. At the same time, stakeholders of the industry, private companies, and organizations are interconnected, and the same goes for the people representing them. Furthermore, while budgets required for a film production are non-negligible,[4] the uncertainty as to its commercial success and its reception by the public is very high. Securing the financing for a film production requires that several actors gather, negotiate, and financially and practically provide their support. This multiparty agreement does not only concern making the movie but most certainly also distributing it. Distribution-related considerations very often have an impact on the creative process of the film productions.

This chapter thus poses the following questions: What does the presence of women in the film distribution channels of contemporary Swedish film industry look like? How are the rights of female authors (directors, screenwriters, or authors of original books that are the subject matter of adaptations) addressed in the midst of distribution considerations—namely, what kind of power, if any, do the women execute in this segment of the process?

To address these questions, this chapter uses a breadth of materials and sources. On the one hand empirical material from the Swedish Authority for Company Registrations (Bolagsverket) has been collected, structured, and analyzed. The data concerns registered companies active in the field of film distribution in Sweden. In this respect, the collected data focuses on the gender of board members and managing directors juxtaposed with the size and importance of the company in question that in its turn is counted for in terms of annual turnover. Furthermore, with regard to materials, this chapter uses sources retrieved by means of archival research, as well as contractual agreements and materials submitted in court proceedings in Sweden as early as in the 1920s and as recently as in the 2020s.

Apart from the investigation of the positions held by women in film distribution companies, the chapter further analyzes three specific cases of film distribution. All three are situated in completely different historical settings, illustrating different challenges in the field of film distribution. All three cases have female protagonists and address a mixture of historical and modern distribution challenges.

The first case concerns matters pertaining to the distribution of adaptations of the books of Nobel Prize-winning author Selma Lagerlöf. In this first case, it is important to note how clear it is to see how the author is used, and sometimes even abused, for distribution purposes. It is equally interesting to see how Lagerlöf reacts to distribution challenges.

The second case concerns the distribution of a documentary film about a young filmmaker dying of cancer. The film was directed and produced by one of her friends and distribution met the resistance of her family. Finally, the third case concerns a contemporary distribution dispute in regard to an animated film, *Peter Svanslös* (Peter-No-Tail). This film illustrates the challenges of long-term distribution arrangements and the volatile character of the film industry in all its capriciousness, as well as the work of women as representatives (employees) of the distribution industry.

Gendering Film Distribution

When investigating power, presence, and portrayal of women in film distribution, it is of course of importance to start by identifying the women in the industry and the roles they play. Naturally, another vital aspect is all the different professional levels or production, that is, of the copyright holders, directors, authors of literary works, screenwriters of the films distributed. For a distribution company to proceed with the distribution of a film, a previous clearance of rights is a prerequisite. As has been discussed in a previous chapter of this book, however, the scope of flexibility and the actual power of authors are rather limited in the film context.[5]

The theoretical perspective that frames the discussion is twofold. On the one hand, it is interesting to investigate what it actually means that there are remarkably few women in decision-making positions in film distribution companies. On the other hand, taking into consideration the fact that film distribution is based upon complicated, lengthy, and long-term contractual relations, it is important to analyze women's role in the drafting, negotiation, and enforcement of contractual agreements concerning the distribution of films.

A central aspect of interest for the power, presence, and portrayal of women is women themselves and their positioning in the distribution industry: women owners of film distribution companies, members of the board, or managing directors. An empirical study conducted under the framework of this project has provided interesting data. A search in the Swedish Companies Registration Office (Bolagsverket) resulted in a list of 171 active companies that include among their activities that of film distribution. These companies present a very interesting divergence in turnovers (from 100,000 krona to hundreds of millions of krona). The numbers are revealing: out of the 171 companies, only seven have a woman as a managing director; out of these seven, five are also members of the board and one could thus possibly draw the conclusion that these are also owners or co-owners of the company in question. Yet, only 5 out of the 171 companies have 50 percent of women on their boards, 27 have only one board member that is a woman (in boards with several members), 45 companies have a woman as a deputy board member, while only 3 have only women on their board. Naturally, apart from the women that actually hold decision-making positions in the industry, women working in the industry as employees could constitute a sign of presence and power. It is still much more difficult to discern the scope of their mandate and the power they have in the strategic business choices of the company. The structure of the entire branch makes it easy to suspect that these would be limited.

The reason why identifying women as board members is of essence is the fact that the board of directors monitors the activities of a company. It decides upon the corporate strategy, appoints and supervises senior management, and has the responsibility for major issues of concern for the company and its future. Thus, the fact that women are, as it seems, excluded from the board of companies dealing with film distribution is important. It is a factor that must have an impact for the industry as a whole.[6]

The impact of gender diversity in boards, and in the overall performance of companies, has been the subject matter of extensive research focusing on different perspectives, branches, and countries.[7] Furthermore, there has been considerable research conducted in relation to which factors from the side of supply (i.e., women wanting to be part of boards) and the demand side (i.e., shareholders actually choosing women for their boards) influences the presence of women in company boards. On the side of supply previous research has identified a number of factors such as gender differences in values and attitudes,[8] identification with gender role expectations,[9] or conflicts with private and family life.[10]

With regard to hindrances concerning the demand side, research has shown that gender discrimination plays a central role. Gender discrimination may have different justifications such as false statistical grounds (statements such as "women often make mistakes") or taste (social and cultural factors linking leadership skills to masculinity). It could also be dependent on biases that are subconscious and that shareholders (or other recruiters) would never admit to.[11]

It falls outside the scope of this chapter to investigate whether and how the compositions of a company board actually influences the actual working conditions and all-round agency of the women film workers; namely, how women film workers are treated by companies where women hold the position of managing director or hold a majority on the board.[12] However, a non-negligible number of sources seem to show that the power of women in the film distribution industry is very limited.

Film distribution as such is based upon contractual agreements, and thus the gendered character of contract law needs to be considered.[13] Contract law has for a long time fallen outside the ambit of feminist scrutiny and impact. This might be due to the fact that it is an area of law that has been extensively promoted as a typically gender-neutral one.[14] The fact is that under closer scrutiny, contract law in Sweden as well as in the majority of other key jurisdictions, such as the United States, United Kingdom, Germany, and France, does not seem to have recognized women as equal contract parties until the late nineteenth century.[15]

Contract law in Sweden dates back to 1915, a time when women were not represented in the government or in the parliament. An illustration of the per se gendered character of contract law is that its cornerstone principle, the freedom of contract, was sex-based. This is because, to begin with, those free for signing a contract were only men.[16] This fundamental principle of contract law continues to be gendered. As Sandra Fredman argues, contemporary perspectives on contracts emphasize women's freedom of choice instead of recognizing the structural constraints on these choices and the impact social systems have on women's freedoms.[17] This chapter proposes to adopt a feminist relational approach to contract law in order to proceed to a reconceptualization of contracts, what they are, how they are structured, and in which ways they are negotiated and enforced.[18] A feminist relational approach focuses on relational aspects of business arrangements, which are characterized by values of mutuality and solidarity.[19] This approach stresses the need to examine the constellation of relationships surrounding decision-making processes and their evolution as decisions are executed.[20]

To scrutinize issues regarding film distribution from such a perspective, namely, where relations are at the center of business arrangements, would provide us with the tools for a critical analysis of the context, challenges, and effects of distribution arrangements—and even more importantly to pinpoint pitfalls and shortcomings.

Gendered Film Distribution Scenarios

Case 1: Distribution and the Role of the Author Behind the Film

Choosing Selma Lagerlöf as a paradigm of an author who was actively engaged in distribution matters but also regularly seen as an important distribution facilitator by the film industry comes as no surprise. Lagerlöf was both curious and interested in the new medium already from its first years of existence. In 1909 she was approached by Svensk Filmindustri (SF) and asked whether she would be willing to proceed with an adaptation of her novel *Nils Holgersson underbara resa genom Sverige*.[21] This film was never made, but Lagerlöf came to produce her first film with SF a few years later, in 1917, *Tösen från Stormyrtorpet* (*The Lass from the Stormy Croft*) with Victor Sjöström (in the US: Seastrom) as the director. This film became a commercial success that in its turn contributed to an increase in Lagerlöf's popularity as a literary author abroad and gave rise to several offers for other adaptations from international film production companies. The film critics were very positive, and after a series of negotiations regarding reimbursements for her, the SF acquired exclusive rights to the production and distribution of the film adaptations of Lagerlöf's works over five years. According to the said agreement, SF would produce a minimum of one film per year and hold the exclusive distribution rights in Sweden and abroad.[22]

The Author as a Distribution Facilitator

There is no doubt that business arrangements in the film industry were very much dependent on personal relations, and Lagerlöf's trust in Sjöström and his work is characteristic. After making a number of films together, Sjöström decided to leave for the United States in 1923 and proposed that he would be replaced by his colleague Mauritz Stiller. During his years in the United States, Sjöström produced one more film based on one of Lagerlöf's books, namely *Kejsarn av Portugallien* (*Tower of Lies*). In the short film *Ett besök hos Selma* (*On a visit at Selma's*, 1925) by Raoul de Mat, one can see Lagerlöf inspecting the film negatives. This short film is an interesting one both because of the fact that the short clip is the only remaining part of the entire film. Also, it is a visual testimony of the fact that Lagerlöf held this very important position in Sjöström's creative working process even after he had left Sweden.

The first film of the Lagerlöf-Stiller collaboration was *Herr Arnes pengar* (*The Treasure*, 1919), a relationship that worked to Lagerlöf's satisfaction. Stiller adopted the production process of Sjöström; namely, he produced a script that closely mapped Lagerlöf's text and had a thorough discussion of the details of the film production with the author. The film was a commercial success and was soon distributed to no fewer than forty-six countries. Although the critics were positive, Stiller was disappointed. He considered the film's close dependence on the book a weakness and under all the circumstances a considerable limitation to his scope of creativity.[23]

This is also the most probable reason why Stiller decided to change his working methods radically and turn from Lagerlöf's text in the next film, *Gunnar Hedes Saga* (*The Blizzard*, 1923). The deviations from Lagerlöf's book *Herrgårdssägen* (*The Tale of a Manor*) were so noteworthy that Lagerlöf refused to be related to it. This was a book Lagerlöf based on autobiographical elements and that was of great personal value to her. Her opposition to Stiller's choices was of such a nature that she threatened to block its distribution. She even raised issues of breach of contract. After lengthy negotiations, Lagerlöf conceded to a settlement entailing that the film would be distributed under another name and with the addition of a short prologue stating that the film uses only the "motifs" (originally: motive) from Lagerlöf's book. It seems that not only the author of the story was discontented with this development; the film itself was disliked by film critics precisely for deviating too much from the original novel and the way it had discarded Lagerlöf's air.

Lagerlöf's role as a distribution facilitator became relevant in SF's communications with the Swedish censorship authority in that her name and status had a decisive role in avoiding state intervention.[24] An example of the importance of the author's name and the cultural credit it presented becomes more than obvious when reviewing film posters of the time. Advertising films in this period was principally done by means of film posters.[25]

In the distribution campaign for the film adaptations of her novels, Lagerlöf is promoted as a central "author" of the film, and thus a central figure of the marketing campaign. This is the case of the first adaptation of *The Lass from the Stormy Croft*, and the way it is presented gives the impression that she has been attributed the authorship of the film as a whole. The same applies to the film *Körkarlen* (*The Phantom Carriage*, 1921). A noteworthy difference here is that the name of the director, Victor Sjöström, is now in larger print, slightly larger than that used for Lagerlöf's name. And while the name of the director receives a more and more predominant place, the name of the author, Lagerlöf, continues to be included even if its importance is gradually minimized. It is interesting to note this evolution, from *The Lass from the Stormy Croft* (1917) to *The Treasure* (1919) to *Ingemar's Inheritance* (1925), *Till Österland* (1926), and *Charlotte Löwensköld* (1930).

In this respect, it is even more interesting to note the poster of *Gösta Berlings Saga* (*The Story of Gösta Berling*) which premiered in 1924, the last project in which Lagerlöf cooperated with Stiller. In *Gösta Berling*, Lagerlöf's name is not included in the two posters available, indicating the breach between the author, film director, and the production company. This is also an indication of the public perception of Stiller, whose work at this point had gained such an artistic value that he was considered to be able to stand on his own to produce sales, and also as grounds for the status of the film as a work of art. Also, by the time *Gösta Berling* was distributed, cinema as a medium and art form was acknowledged enough to claim the credit of creativity and artistic contribution of its own. In fact, it seems that this film's promotion is based on a rising star, namely Greta Garbo. But it also demonstrates the fact that the furious Lagerlöf had rejected the story changes in Stiller's script.

International Management of Distribution Rights

Although the distribution contract signed with SF removed part of the burden (and also the freedom) from Lagerlöf, the extensive communication between Sjöström and Lagerlöf concerning the international distribution of adaptations of her books constitutes evidence of the important role she continued to play. Out of respect or some moral obligation, or maybe seeking her advice and confirmation, Sjöström felt that he had to inform Lagerlöf of his suggestions for a script. It does not seem likely or possible, however, that such a requirement of reporting back to the author of the literary original would have been included in an adaptation contract at that time.[26]

In one of his letters to Lagerlöf, Sjöström presented the adventure of the film *Körkarlen* in the UK. The film was screened during the same period both in Sweden and the UK, and Sjöström was called to London to approve of what came to be the UK version of the film before its public screening. Sjöström reports of his shock when he watched the film; the film was altered to the degree that Sjöström hardly recognized it. The UK distributor had claimed that this was necessary for the film to be adequate for audience conditions in the UK.[27] According to Sjöström the film had become a banal story of a drunk. He worked intensively to restore the film to its original version. In Lagerlöf's immediate answer to Sjöström's report, she expressed her gratitude for his intervention and confirmed that she had dealt with similar problems in the translations of her books. She noted in fact that this development (the fact that the film in its unchanged state was so successful in the UK) would constitute a strong argument in her negotiations with translators who wished to modify her books to make them more "attractive" to the UK public.[28]

In one of her letters to Sjöström, Lagerlöf wrote that she would also have to travel to the United States to control the distribution of the *The Lass* film. She had been informed that the film in question was distributed by a company that charged so much for the cinema tickets that the film remained out of reach for less well-off people.[29]

Lagerlöf as a paradigm is illustrative of the way authors were engaged in distribution decisions, but also of the way they were used for distribution purposes. Their importance faded away gradually as film became a respected cultural expression, and new stars were entrusted with the responsibility of "selling" the films; namely actors and actresses. Another factor was the contractual agreements that could either facilitate or block distribution. In this respect without a doubt relations had a central role.

Case 2: Does Portrayal Impact on the Power of Distribution?

The second case is about a documentary film, a genre that as such often is made under very different circumstances from feature films, called *Mod att leva: en film till Pia* (*The Courage to Live: A Film to Pia*, 1983). The film was directed by Ingela Romare, who also owned the production company Ingela Romare Film. The film was co-financed by the Swedish Film Institute and distributed by Folkets Bio.

The young film student Pia Kakossaios had just started her career when at the age of twenty-four she passed away from cancer. After receiving her final diagnosis, Pia decided, together with friends and colleagues, to contribute to a documentary film that describes the terminal phase of her disease to her death. The film shows the evolution of Pia's disease its course, her family—her mother, sisters, brother, and father—and meetings with her boyfriend. Pia is filmed while she reflects upon her condition, her imminent death, her hopes, and what she had wanted to do if the disease had not stopped her. While the film focuses on the period while Pia was terminally ill, there are photographs of her as a child and teenager, as well as film of her funeral in Greece at her mother's village. The last time Pia is filmed is while her father gives her a morphine injection, on May 6, 1979. Pia died some days later, on May 18, 1979.

The film was completed in late 1982. Shortly after its premiere, Pia's family (her parents and sisters) expressed their strong objections against the further distribution of the film and filed a police report in an attempt to block it. At the same time, they wrote an open letter that was published in the daily newspaper *Dagens Nyheter*. They claimed that the film was the result of fraudulent activity; that the family was not aware of the character, content, and style of the film; and that they were tricked into participating by its director, Romare.[30] The family accused the director of exploiting a family tragedy for her personal commercial interests and stated that they had allowed the filming to take place because, after Romare first visited her, Pia actually felt that she was recuperating her role as a film worker and became a part of Romare's team. However, according to the letter, the political message Pia wanted to send to the public was removed in the final cut, giving way to general sadness and sentimentalization. The family underlined that they never received the script of the film (that would according to their oral arrangement with Romare be subject to their prior authorization). This open letter was answered by a journalist called Sverker Tirén, who described the process with the production of the film and defended Romare as an objective professional director.[31]

Analyzing part of the debate reveals many layers, as the family's focus is on one main issue. First, the final version of the film was not what the family was expecting. In this respect, Romare's gender actually seems to be of major importance. She is accused of producing a "cliché of a sorrowful film that oversentimentalizes" the fate of a dying woman. The undertone seems clear; Romare is a woman, and naturally the film became an oversentimental expression, lacking rigorous political messages and strength. The family mentions that the film is planned to be shown in a film festival for women, where Romare would also give a lecture on the topic. When reading the letter one wonders whether a male director would be exposed to such critique.

In due course, the police report led to a formal investigation by prosecutor Erik Hasselrot, who in an interview stated that his conclusion after a preliminary investigation was that there were no legal hindrances for the continued distribution of the film, neither on the basis of alleged copyright infringement, nor could it be considered defamatory or offensive.[32]

There are several issues of interest from a film distribution perspective. On the basis of the information that is available in the case, one may assume that there was no written contract regulating the distribution of the film between Romare and Pia or her family. As it has been previously stated in this chapter, film distribution presupposes a clearance of rights, the author of the film has to have agreed to specific terms and conditions of distribution or alternatively to have transferred all rights to the producer, who in turn enters into a contractual arrangement with the distributor (in this case Folkets Bio). In this respect, it is important and relevant to specify who the author of the film is and to what degree there is a case of co-authorship. An important aspect in the discussion that needs to be addressed is the role of Pia herself in the authorship of the film. She had been part of the initial discussions, it seems almost that the film was her idea, and that she was continuously part of the process not only as the subject matter of the documentary but also as a film worker, as a co-author. In the film she is even shown holding a camera, and her depiction with the instruments of work is a clear indication of her active role in the production process. The level of creativity that Pia had invested in the film would be decisive for her identification as a co-author. The fact that Pia is not named anywhere in the credits of the film, constitutes merely an indication and not evidence that she is not a co-author.

Case 3: *Pelle Svanslös* (*Peter-No-Tail*): A Modern Distribution Saga

This is the case of an animated film—representing yet another genre—an adaptation of children's book *Pelle Svanslös på äventyr* (*Peter-No-Tail in an Adventure*) published in 1939 and *Pelle Svanslös på nya äventyr* (*Peter-No-Tail in New Adventures*) published in 1940, authored by Gösta Knutsson. The director of the film was Stig Lasseby, and the scriptwriter a TV producer called Leif Krantz. The thirteen animators involved in the production were all men, led by Jan Gissberg, who had responsibility for the animation design. This is thus nearly a men-only film production, yet when carefully looking at the credits, the small detailed and precision-demanding work—namely, the coloring of the film frames—was mostly done by women. Of the sixteen artists named in the credits twelve are female.

An interesting fact is also that, when the legal dispute arose between the two major producing partners, the Swedish Film Institute (SFI) and the production company Sandrews, women took part in quite different capacities, as they represented both parties. Their task was to negotiate, namely, to clarify the details of the thirty years of business transactions just before the case was turned in to the Patent and Market Court at the Stockholm District Court. The lawsuit concerned unsettled monetary claims of distribution of royalties by SFI that were due to a counterclaim by Sandrews. The latter claimed that it had not recuperated any of the production costs during the thirty-year period, and thus had a claim that exceeded that of SFI.

The two women involved were the managing director "XY" of Sandrews and the person responsible for access, rights, and distribution at SFI, "XX."

The negotiations concerning the disagreement that arose were made by email, starting on February 11, 2020. The correspondence consists of a total of thirty-two emails, the most recent dated April 23, 2020, which have been submitted to the court.

Reading the email communications submitted as an appendix to the lawsuit reveals an uncertainty on the terms and conditions upon which distribution is to take place and in particular on the way royalties will be reported and shared. One of the representatives admitted to having no direct access to the contract and that to retrieve it she would have to search in the archive. The other representative was not certain how the reporting of royalties had taken place and admitted to a lack of relevant documentation. Both seemed to want to create a relationship, by asking about each other's families, giving personal information, and keeping a pleasant, almost friendly, and collaborative tone. Unfortunately, despite these attempts, the gap between the parties as to the understanding of the distribution contracts (and of their practical application over the past forty years) was so big that the case is now subject to court proceedings. It is clear that these women have been called to "clean up" the messy business arrangements that have been negotiated and (for a number of years) enforced by men.

The SFI and Sandrews entered three different contractual agreements related to the production and distribution of the film in question. The first one was signed on December 12, 1979, in which major aspects of the production and exploitation of the film were regulated. Apart from the SFI and Sandrews there were two other parties to the production agreement, namely Team Film AB and Filmbolaget Treklövern. According to this contract, SFI and Sandrews would both have the right to distribute the film and on the basis of the distribution income each party would have the right to receive 30 percent as a distribution fee, as well as to gradually recuperate production costs. On July 24, 1990, the parties signed yet another agreement according to which Sandrews would have the exclusive right to distribute the film *Peter No-Tail* via video. Finally, by means of a third contract signed on May 9, 2016, the SFI handed over the distribution rights to Sandrews. In this same agreement it is provided that both Team Film AB and Filmbolaget Treklövern were liquidated and that their right to royalties would thus be shared by SFI and Sandrews.

In this case there are several issues that are worth consideration. First of all, the high level of complexity of the contractual arrangements upon which the distribution of a film proceeds. Several contractual agreements have been signed during a period of almost forty years. At the same time, the compensation of film production costs is dependent on the distribution. Further, the hows and whens of this compensation are dependent on the reports of the distributing companies. Distribution royalties are a long-term form of compensation per se and thus dependent on the possibilities for the production companies to wait. Statistics show that a considerable number of companies in the film industry end up in bankruptcy or liquidation and are thus removed from any deals/contractual agreements that have been made. Consequently, this means that the big players, in this case Sandrews and the SFI, end up sharing the distribution incomes.

This case is also illustrative of the ever-changing business landscape of film culture. In fact, during the past three months, the court has been trying to serve the defendant with the lawsuit. It has, however, shown itself that Sandrew Metronome Sverige AB (built after the fusion of the two companies Sandrews and Metronome) has changed name and legal representative, and the rights are currently represented by SF Studios Film Rights 1 AB. A lengthy and complicated commercial arrangement that is built to a large extent on trust, of course, has difficulty thriving if the parties are not sure about who they actually are doing business with.

Gendering Distribution in Sweden: The Potential of Feminist Relational Contract Theory

The three different cases discussed in this chapter not only stretch over a long period time, from the 1910s to today, but also consider different film distribution scenarios and film genres, while they also shed light on challenges in the power and presence of women in the industry. In the first case, the focus is adaptations of very popular original works, with a very strong author profile in the background. In the case of *Courage to Live*, the film is a documentary, and one in which the subject matter of observation is also potentially a co-author, while the final case, *Peter-No-Tail*, is a commercial animated film subject to very complex distribution arrangements.

These three cases are characteristic of the very core of film distribution chains, the fact that parties to distribution contracts negotiate contracts that are to survive a particularly long period of time, a time period during which a series of unpredictable incidents might happen, that may considerably change the conditions under which contractual arrangements are to operate. These cases are also indicative of the importance of having as a starting point a complete clearance of rights. Furthermore, what all three cases also stipulate clearly is the importance of relations both in the negotiations but above all in the enforcement of distribution contracts. Relations are power, but do they always guarantee presence of the women? This chapter has shown the very limited number of women in decision-making positions in the Swedish film distribution industry, and this is of course particularly interesting when relations are at the center of business arrangements. There is considerable literature showing that men will prefer to do business with men, and thus one could conclude that the role of women in film distribution will be marginalized.[33]

A feminist relational approach recognizes the fact that parties to business agreements may be both self-interested and interdependent, and that contract law must look into the changing attitudes (and needs) of parties and not focus solely on wealth-maximization. This is a theory distinguishable from other approaches in contract law, since it introduces an overtly feminist approach which allows one to appreciate (gendered) patterns of power and the lived realities of the parties to agreements. What the last case discussed in this chapter has shown is that the lack of such an approach as the one proposed here, will in the end lead to intricate misunderstandings between the parties. When distribution arrangements fail to look into the parties' needs and particularities, and when these are not nurtured as long-term relations that need to be constantly reviewed and if necessary fine-tuned they fail. In fact, the involvement of distributors in the film production contracts becomes a defect of the system, since it is perceived as yet another perspective, almost a necessary evil, and marks the start of a separate, complicated, and long-term relation.[34] In all three cases, it becomes obvious that when women are involved (irrespective of in which way) in film distribution contracts, relations and their role become central. There is an attempt to create relations when these are missing (third case), relations are important for distribution arrangements to persist or to be initiated (first and second cases). Naturally, problems in the execution of distribution agreements depend on the lack of functioning communication and relations between the parties (see all three cases). Traditional contract law theory disregards the role of relations and consequently also the gendered dimensions of power that steers them and is thus too limited to cover the complexities of distribution agreements. The relational contract theory allows a new analytical framework shedding light on the power, presence, and portrayal of women in the film distribution chain.[35]

Notes

1. Jeff Ulin, *The Business of Media Distribution: Monetizing Film, TV, and Video Content* (Burlington, MA: Focal Press, 2010), 43.
2. See Anders Parment, *Distributionsstrategier: kritiska val på konkurrensintensiva marknader* (Malmö: Liber, 2006), 57; Finola Kerrigan, *Film Marketing* (Oxford: Butterworth-Heinemann, 2009), 45; John Durie, Annika Pham, and Neil Watson, *Marketing and Selling Your Film around the World* (Los Angeles: Silman-James Press, 2000), 38–49.
3. Victoria Crisp, *Film Distribution in the Digital Age Pirates and Professionals* (Basingstoke: Palgrave Macmillan, 2015), 38–42.
4. The budget for Swedish film productions ranges from 1.5 million to over 30 million krona depending on the genre of the film.
5. See Chapter 1, "The Sex of the Author," in this book.
6. Patricia Gabaldon, Celia de Anca, Ruth Mateos de Cabo, and Ricardo Gimeno, "Searching for Women on Boards: An Analysis from the Supply and Demand Perspective," *Corporate Governance: An International Review*, vol. 24, no. 3 (2016), 377.
7. Frances Milliken and Luise Marins, "Searching for Common Threads: Understanding the Multiple Effects of Diversity in Organizational Groups," *The Academy of Management Review*, vol. 21, no. 2 (April 1996), 412–14. See also Toya Miller and Triana Del Carmen, "Demographic Diversity in the Boardroom: Mediators of the Board Diversity–Firm Performance Relationship," *Journal of Management Studies*, vol. 46 (2009), 777–80; Stephen Brammer, Andrew Millington, and Bruce Rayton, "The Contribution of Corporate Social Responsibility to Organizational Commitment," *International Journal of Human Resource Management*, vol. 18, no. 10 (2007), 1701–719; Siri Terjesen, Ruth Sealy, and Val Singh, "Women Directors on Corporate Boards: A Review and Research Agenda," *Corporate Governance: An International Review*, vol. 17 (2009), 320–37; Jeremy Galbreath, "Are There Gender-Related Influences on Corporate Sustainability? A Study of Women on Boards of Directors," *Journal of Management & Organization*, vol. 17, no. 1 (2011), 32; Tukur Garba and Bilkisu Aliyu Abubakar, "Corporate Board Diversity and Financial Performance of Insurance Companies in Nigeria: An Application of Panel Data Approach," *Asian Economic and Financial Review*, vol. 4, no. 2 (2014), 259; Maria Gardiner and Marika Tiggemann, "Gender Differences in Leadership Style, Job Stress and Mental Health in Male – and Female – Dominated Industries," *Journal of Occupational and Organizational Psychology*, vol. 72 (1999), 312–15.

8   Renee Adams and Patricia Funck, "Beyond the Glass Ceiling: Does Gender Matter?" *Management Science*, vol. 58 (2012), 219–22; Alice Eagly, "Achieving Relational Authenticity in Leadership: Does Gender Matter?" *Leadership Quarterly*, vol. 16, no. 3 (2005), 459–63; Samuel Baixauli-Soler, Maria Belda-Ruiz, and Gregorio Sanchez-Marin, "An Executive Hierarchy Analysis of Stock Options: Does Gender Matter?" *Review of Management Science*, vol. 11 (2017), 740–45.

9   Kimberley Eddleston, "Do You See What I See? Signaling Effects of Gender and Firm Characteristics on Financing Entrepreneurial Ventures," *Entrepreneurship: Theory and Practice*, vol. 40, no. 3 (2016), 489–514; Gary Powell and Anthony Butterfield, "Gender, Gender Identity and Aspirations to Top Management," *Women in Management Review*, vol. 18, nos 1–2 (2003), 88–90.

10 Caroline Straub, "A Comparative Analysis of the Use of Work-Life Balance Practices in Europe," *Women In Management Review*, vol. 22 (2007), 289–95; Gary Powell and Jeffrey Greenhaus, "Sex, Gender, and Decisions at the Family → Work Interface," *Journal of Management*, vol. 36, no. 4 (2010), 1011–039; Magnus Bygren and Michael Gähler, "Family Formation and Men's and Women's Attainment of Workplace Authority," *Social Forces*, vol. 90, no. 3 (2012), 795–816.

11 Justin Wolfers, "Diagnosing Discrimination: Stock Returns and CEO Gender," *Journal of the European Economic Association*, vol. 4 (2006), 531–41; Madeleine Heilman, "Description and Prescription: How Gender Stereotypes Prevent Women's Ascent up the Organizational Ladder," *Journal of Social Issues*, vol. 57, no. 4 (2001), 670; Ian Gregory-Smith, Brian Main, and Charles O'Reilly III, "Appointments, Pay and Performance in UK Boardrooms by Gender," *Economic Journal*, vol. 124, no. 574 (2014), F109–F128; Xin Huang, "In the Shadow of Suku (Speaking-Bitterness): Master Scripts and Women's Life Stories," *Frontiers of the History in China*, vol. 9, no. 4 (2014), 590; Jean Luca Pletzer, Romina Nikolova, Karina Karolina Kedzior, and Sven Constantin Voelpel, "Does Gender Matter? Female Representation on Corporate Boards and Firm Financial Performance – A Meta-Analysis," *PLoS ONE*, vol. 10, no. 6 (2015), 22.

12 Samira Paydar, "Boys Club Behind the Scenes: Using Title VII to Remedy Gender Discrimination," *Hollywood, Law School Student Scholarship* (2017), 870.

13 Ann Bartow, "Fair Use and the Fairer Sex: Gender, Feminism, and Copyright Law," *American University Journal of Gender, Social Policy and the Law*, vol. 14, no. 3 (2006), 555; Alice Belcher, "Feminist Perspective on Contract Theories from Law and Economics," *Feminist Legal Studies*, vol. 8 (2000), 34; Miller and Del Carmen, "Demographic Diversity in the Boardroom."

14 Belcher, "Feminist Perspective on Contract Theories from Law and Economics," 32; Emily Chaloner, "A Feminist Critique of Copyright Law," *I/S: A Journal of Law and Policy for the Information Society*, vol. 6, no. 2 (2010), 221–32; Cary Craig,

"Feminist Aesthetics and Copyright Law: Genius, Value and Gendered Visions of the Creative Self," in I. Calboli and S. Ragavan (eds.), *Diversity in Intellectual Property Law* (Cambridge: Cambridge University Press, 2015); Debora Halbert "Feminist Interpretations of Intellectual Property," *Journal of Gender, Social Policy and the Law*, vol. 14, no. 3 (2006), 431–44.

15 Patricia Tidwell and Peter Linzer, "The Flesh-Colored Band Aid-Contracts, Feminism and Norms," *Houston Law Review*, vol. 28 (1991), 791–800.

16 Catriona Mackenzie and Natalie Stoljar, "Autonomy Refigured," in Catriona Mackenzie, Natalie Stoljar, and Ian Macneil (eds.), *Relational Autonomy: Feminist Perspectives on Autonomy, Agency and the Social Self* (New York: Oxford University Press, 2000); Diana Meyers, "Intersectional Identity and the Authentic Self? Opposites Attract!" in Catriona Mackenzie, Natalie Stoljar, and Ian Macneil (eds.), *Relational Autonomy: Feminist Perspectives on Autonomy, Agency and the Social Self* (New York: Oxford University Press, 2000), 132; Morten Hviid, "Relational Contracts and Repeated Games," in D. Campbell and P. Vincent Jones (eds.), *Contract and Economic Organisation* (Aldershot: Dartmouth, 1996), 44.

17 Sandra Fredman, "The Legal Construction of Personal Work Relations and Gender," *Jerusalem Review of Legal Studies*, vol. 7, no. 1 (June 2013), 114.

18 John Wightman, "Intimate Relationships, Relational Contract Theory and the Reach of Contract," *Feminist Legal Studies University Law Review*, vol. 8 (2000), 93–131; Kate Galloway, "The Role of Pateman's Sexual Contract in Beneficial Interests in Property," *Feminist Legal Studies* (2019), 263–85; Peter Goodrich, "Gender and Contracts," in A. Bottomley (ed.), *Feminist Perspectives on the Foundational Subjects of Law* (London: Cavendish, 1996), 24–7; Marjorie Maguire Schultz, "The Gendered Curriculum: Of Contracts and Careers," *Iowa Law Review*, vol. 70 (1991), 55; Susan Moller Okin, "Feminism, the Individual, and Contract Theory," *Ethics*, vol. 100, no. 3 (1990), 658–62.

19 Ian Macneil, "Contracts: Adjustment of Long Term Economic Relations under Classical, Neoclassical and Relational Contract Law," *Northwestern University Law Review*, vol. 72, no. 6 (1978), 854.

20 Debora Threedy, "Feminists and Contract Doctrine," *Indiana Law Review*, vol. 32, no. 4 (1999), 1247–265; Tidwell and Linzer, "The Flesh-Colored Band Aid-Contracts, Feminism and Norms," 791–99; Sharon Thompson, "Towards a Feminist Relational Contract Theory of Prenuptial Agreements," in *Prenuptial Agreements and the Presumption of Free Choice: Issues of Power in Theory and Practice* (London: Hart Publishing, 2015), 129–44; Sharon Thompson, "Feminist Relational Contract Theory: A New Model for Family Property Agreements," *Journal of Law and Society*, vol. 45, no. 4 (2018), 617–19; Uma Narayan, "Minds of Their Own: Choices, Autonomy, Cultural Practices, and Other Women," in Louise M. Antony,

and Charlotte E. Witt (eds.), *A Mind of One's Own: Feminist Essays on Reason and Objectivity* (New York: Routledge 2002), 38–42.
21 Here SF, at the time the name of the company was Filmindustri AB Skandia.
22 Victor Sjöström, "Selma Lagerlöf och Filmen," in Sven Thulin (ed.), *Mårbacka och Övralid; minnen av Selma Lagerlöf och Verner von Heidenstam* (Uppsala: J. A. Lindblad, 1940), 175–88.
23 Gösta Werner, *Herr Arnes pengar; En filmvetenskaplig studie och dokumentation av Mauritz Stillers film efter Selma Lagerlöfs berättelse* (Stockholm: Norstedts, 1979), 42–6.
24 Gösta Werner, *Rött, vitt och gult: färgerna i censurens banér: den svenska filmcensurens bedömningar av Victor Sjöströms och Mauritz Stillers filmer 1912–1936* (Stockholm: Statens biografbyrå, 2002), 38.
25 Jan Olsson, *I offentlighetens ljus. Stumfilmens affischer, kritiker, stjärnor och musik* (Stockholm: Symposium 1990), 32.
26 Sjöström, "Selma Lagerlöf och Filmen."
27 Ibid.
28 Ibid.
29 Ibid.
30 Familjen Kakossaios, "Vår integritet hotas av filmen," *Dagens Nyheter*, February 9, 1983, 15.
31 Sverker Tirén, "Familjens angrepp kränker Romare," *Dagens Nyheter*, February 10, 1983, 20.
32 "Om rätten att säga nej," *Dagens Nyheter*, February 19, 1983, 42.
33 Wolfers, "Diagnosing Discrimination"; Heilman, "Description and Prescription"; Huang, "In the Shadow of Suku"; Gregory-Smith, Main, and O'Reilly, "Appointments, Pay and Performance"; Jean Luca Pletzer et al.,"Does Gender Matter?", 35.
34 Hviid, "Relational Contracts and Repeated Games"; Wightman, "Intimate Relationships", 100–120; Christine Liyanto, "The Discrete, the Relational, the Selfish, and the Societal: Elements Present in all Transactions," *Hastings Business Law Journal*, vol. 4 (2008), 318.
35 Thompson, "Feminist Relational Contract Theory," 617–45; Goodrich, "Gender and Contracts," 23.

3

In the Crossfire

Anna Serner and the Swedish Film Institute

Maaret Koskinen

Introduction

Let me start with a personal statement, as it is relevant to what is to follow. I had become a member of the Swedish Film Institute (SFI) in the spring of 2011, and in October of that year Anna Serner was installed as CEO. At the time I was professor at IMS, the Department of Media Studies of Stockholm University, while also regularly reviewing films in *Dagens Nyheter*, Sweden's largest ("broadsheet") daily, which I had done for exactly thirty years up until then. However, while it was possible to (ethically) combine those two activities, being a board member of the SFI at the same time as a critic was not, which meant that from that point on I had to abstain from reviewing films. For it goes without saying that it is untenable to take part in shaping production policies for Swedish film or, for that matter, allocating funds for foreign co-productions and distribution deals—while at the same time risk assessing the outcome of those very same activities, in the form of articles and film reviews. In a small film culture such as Sweden's, nepotism and corruption always risk lurking too close for comfort.

Notwithstanding personal considerations, potential frictions and conflicts will always characterize the immediate environment of a board such as that of SFI. After all, it consists of media and film people from all walks of life—administrators, heads of media corporations, journalists, actors, editors, or academics, such as myself. While conflicts are, and arguably should be, part of the territory—those built into checks and balances of any decent enterprise—what gradually, over time, became apparent were the inbuilt conflicts between, on one hand, the agenda of the SFI and/or its CEO Anna Serner, and on the other, those board members representing, for instance, film production companies or film directors, whose livelihoods are (actually or potentially) dependent on those very same companies, not to mention the various financial support systems for film production run by the SFI itself. Thus for instance, Tarik Saleh, director of *The Nile Hilton Incident* (2016) and critically acclaimed winner of the Grand Jury Award for best foreign film at the Sundance Film Festival, soon decided to abstain from his membership on the board, as his film projects inexorably presented him with potential conflicts of interest.

The SFI board, then, can in a way be regarded as a miniature universe of those conflicting forces at play in any given society, as defined by Pierre Bourdieu. In fact, the discussion below may in its entirety be framed by the meta-critical power inquiry of Bourdieu. For even if his notions can (rightly) be criticized as sometimes being too bound up with the particular circumstances of the generally elitist French (educational/cultural/political) system, still arguably his basic notions remain useful in considering power structures in any given contemporary society in the West.

This is particularly true with regard to Bourdieu's oft-cited concept of *cultural field*, that is, the notion of a field that presupposes specialists and institutions and hence acknowledged hierarchies of value.[1] Such a notion is certainly relevant in the context of state supported film culture and film production, which in Sweden was at the core of "Filmavtalet" (the Film Agreement) since its launch in 1963 to its demise in 2016. At the time this unique deal between the state and the private film industry essentially came about to get the Swedish film industry back on its feet after television had robbed the cinemas of half of their audiences. In other words, at the time Anna Serner was appointed CEO in 2011, the Film Agreement had remained in force for close to fifty years (albeit with amendments in line with a changing media landscape), until it was replaced by a fully state-financed support system in 2016, right in the middle of Serner's ten-year aegis at the SFI—something that we will have reason to return to below.[2]

In this context it should also be pointed out that the Film Agreement over its five decades of existence had been led by the notion—arguably, at times, even ideology—of "quality," which more often than not has been conflated with auteur film. In fact, though the notion of quality has gone through various changes and redefinitions over the years, the notion of the auteur has remained quite unscathed or unquestioned within the SFI. This is true also of Anna Serner's particular take on the two interrelated notions of quality and auteurship, particularly in relation to gender, which is why they too will be a focus in the discussion below.

Besides being theoretically framed by Bourdieu, empirically this chapter relies on a select number of sources. One is Anna Serner's blog, which she kept running for ten years between 2011 and 2021, and in which she considers and comments upon current issues, virtually as they occurred. If nothing else, reviewing some of her posts offers a chance to come closer to some form of immediacy, as compared, for instance, to retrospective interviews or her responses in debates in newspaper articles. Nonetheless, public debate in various media is my other main source, if for no other reason than that during her ten years as CEO of the SFI, Anna Serner remained a constant and at times controversial presence in the public arena in Sweden.

A final, albeit minor, source for this chapter is my own recollections, including the minutes I have saved from my six years on the SFI board. As such these can perhaps be best categorized under the heading of participatory observation, framed by an auto-ethnographic approach. At the same time, it goes without saying that more recent theoretical approaches could equally well (or better) frame or be applied to the empirical results presented here, for instance organization theory.[3]

Anna Serner: "Rock Star of the Film World"

I have a memory from a film festival in Seoul [in 2015], where a film of mine was screened. Anna was there speaking at a seminar, and afterwards we were invited to the [Swedish] embassy. Then I was struck by the tenacity and professionalism that she radiated, mingling and making new contacts in a way that would have wiped me out after only five minutes. It was clear that she had set herself a goal [...] In my opinion she was all for dialogue, and dared throw herself into debate [...] I am convinced that the dialogue she has started will continue making an impression.

(film director Sanna Lenken)[4]

Serner obviously wants to sound like an activist who challenges the powers that be. But she *is* both the power, *and* wields it. And she has failed with her primary goal. Not because it was bad *per se* but because she lacked a realistic plan.

(film critic and editor-in-chief Jon Asp)[5]

So the question is what role do we want? Should we force the market [the commercial film industry] into changing? Should we give them carrots? [...] Do we wish to be game distributor or pawn? I believe that we have a great responsibility in daring to be players and not only victims of the game.

(Anna Serner)[6]

As is clear from the first two quotes, assessments of Anna Serner's ten-year reign at the SFI are rather contradictory. However, regardless of one's view of her legacy, when she was appointed the time was ripe for implementing the particular stances and values that she stood for. For in Sweden, just as elsewhere, debates concerning representation and diversity in the arts had taken center stage, for instance with films such as Ruben Östlund's *Play* (2011), which was accused of racism, or discussions about which books to clean out from the library shelves and tuck away in the basement, due to "inappropriate" content. As festival curator and film critic Katarina Hedrén put it:

> At the time, ten years ago, she [Serner] was undoubtedly the right woman at the right place. She came to the Filmhouse in a time that not only allowed but demanded a trailblazer who envisioned bold goals and more distinct parameters for a film industry characterized by equal opportunity.[7]

After a tough start in her post, during which time Anna Serner managed to ride out her first storm concerning film piracy, she redefined divisions in the SFI. For instance, the division that in organizations usually is thought of as mere "business intelligence" now started leaning toward societal issues in presenting statistics in its monthly newsletter, which was emphasized by a project called "Augmented Society," the focus of which is self-explanatory. In addition, a division named "Filmrummet" was launched, that is, a "room" or "space" for film, with the goal of acting as a forum for debate and meetings between the various players in the field of film culture, which Serner—characteristically— kick-started by inviting Germaine Greer, one of the figures at the forefront of second-wave feminism in the 1970s. So, her agenda was clear from the start: a focus not only on contemporary societal issues but clearly also on increasing transparency and information flow, in the hopes of creating a dialogue between the various parties of film culture that most of the time find themselves on opposite sides of the field.

In line with this, and with furthering her own agenda, Serner arranged the launch of three reports focused on gender and representation in the Swedish film industry to amend what she perceived as a knowledge gap. This was timely also since the gender equality goal in the Film Agreement of 2013 had been sharpened. Therefore it was now time for production funding to be divided equally between women and men, with the aim that by the end of the Film Agreement period in 2016, the total sum of funding would have been distributed equally—50 percent to women and 50 percent to men, in the professional categories of director, scriptwriter, and producer. As part of reaching this goal SFI published the action plan *Towards a Gender Equal Film Production* (2013), where some of the steps and incentives that were to help reach these goals were presented. One of the incentives was *Moviement*, a program for mentoring women directors, and another example was the website *Nordic Women in Film*, which was released in April 2016, the main objective of which was to increase historical knowledge about, as well as increase visibility of, contemporary women film workers.[8]

But, as noted on the SFI homepage, while "this goal was very close to being reached […] there is still a lot left to do." Therefore, the Department of Culture gave the SFI the mission to lead the work on equality, and in July 2016 a new action plan was launched called *Goal 2020: Gender Equality in Film Production, both in Front of and Behind the Camera*. Strategically, the plan had already been presented internationally at a seminar in Cannes in 2016 under the slogan "50/50 by 2020," consisting of four steps: (1) women in key roles in more and larger productions, and a qualitative survey to be conducted into what films women get the opportunity to make, and why; (2) increased visibility and continued updates to the digital knowledge bank https://www.nordicwomeninfilm.com; (3) counting numbers, both behind and in front of the camera, for instance, through an annual gender equality report featuring qualitative analyses; and (4) increased knowledge about gender and diversity through, for instance, an annual film education seminar focusing on gender, targeted at teachers and film educators to reach children and young people.[9]

While these goals resulted in controversy at home (more of this below), Anna Serner's policies rendered her a virtual rock star status. Particularly between the years 2016 and 2018 her blog is literally a travelogue of invitations from all over the globe. Thus, after proudly noting the launch of the site Nordic Women in Film in 2016, she adds: "Now I'm leaving for the US to talk about our site and work for quality. I'm invited to five states and will meet up with diplomats as well as professors, students, and film producers. Sweden is a role model in the world, and the interest is massive." She enumerates a plethora of events, including well-attended lectures at colleges and universities in Minnesota,

Wisconsin, Illinois, Washington DC, Los Angeles, the New York Film Academy (Blog April 17 and 23, 2016). Later that year there were also business meetings, for instance, with the management of the production company Magnolia, who aside from the Swedish talent they had already signed (actor Joel Kinnaman, and directors Babak Najafi and Daniel Espinosa) were particularly interested in women directors, such as Amanda Kernell, director of *Sameblod* (*Sami Blood*, 2016). After this Serner was keynote speaker on equality at an event organized by, amongst others, the Sundance Institute and the Screen Actors Guild-American Federation of Television and Radio Artists (SAG-AFTRA)—while the morning after heading off to Montréal, Canada (Blog October 31, 2016).

And so on. The year after, 2017, it is clear that Anna Serner is a central figure, if not instigator, of an international movement. For, after visiting Australian Women in Film and Television (WIFT), it was time for Cannes and the above mentioned "50/50 by 2020"—"our modest subtitle being 'Global Reach,'" she humorously notes in her blog. At this seminar, which was "packed," Canada, Ireland, and Norway presented their strategies to reach the goal, which was wrapped up by Serner managing to create a work group within Efads (European Film Agencies, including all film institutes of Europe) to work toward implementing a common ground. "Many countries wanted to participate, from UK, France, Germany, and Spain to Serbia and Poland," she wrote (Blog May 22, 2017).

In the fall of 2017, it was time for the Toronto International Film Festival (TIFF), at which she had been invited to a number of closed workshops, meeting with executive management of the TIFF on strategies for equality and diversity (Figure 3.1). In addition, she had been invited as a so-called MOGUL-speaker ("after two years of being on panels only, it is a great honour," she noted in her blog), and she was also interviewed by *Screen*, in an article "which stressed our goal that women should get equal access to the big budgets." And then, that term cropped up: "One never ceases to be surprised about the *rock status* of equality!," she exclaims in her blog—although, somewhat coquettishly, failing to add that the word "star" clearly pointed to her personally (Blog September 9 and 11, 2017). Finally, the year 2018 can be seen as a culmination of sorts of her efforts, for via a tour of lectures and panels in, amongst others, North and Central America, Serner again reached Cannes, which proved a slam dunk for her intensive lobbying. Here the festival director Thierry Frémaux, with his entourage of managers, as well as the whole jury headed by its Chair Cate Blanchett, signed a declaration that the Cannes festival from now on would contribute to the goal "50/50 by 2020" by, firstly, starting with continuous statistics chartering equality, which

Figure 3.1 Anna Serner on Twitter. Photo: Cameron Bailey/Toronto International Film Festival.

should be made available, secondly, being transparent regarding the members of all the selecting groups, and, thirdly, that 50/50 be part of the management of all sections. Hence, it was not without reason that Anna Serner in her blog proudly concluded that "50/50 by 2020, which we launched in Cannes in 2016 now is a global movement." At the same time, the success was pushed along by the #MeToo movement, the momentum of which did not escape Serner. For during the same festival she arranging a seminar called "Take Two – Next Moves After Metoo," which she did at the behest of the Minister of Culture, Alice Bah Kuhnke, together with her French counterpart Françoise Nyssen (Blog April 17 and May 17, 2018).

Culture Clashes: State Authority Meets Academia

As this "travelogue" shows, internationally Anna Serner was not merely one in a bunch. On the contrary, she acted as leader of a movement with global reach. While this is certainly worth stressing (after all, it is film history still in the making), the intention here is not to sketch a hagiography but rather give a background against which many problems still remain—even in a Scandinavian, supposedly more egalitarian, environment. Indeed, this environment in itself comes with internal and institutional specificities, some of which Anna Serner certainly encountered and tried to grapple with along the way. True enough, at home, while she was traveling, discontent was brewing—sometimes precisely for the same reasons that she was popular abroad.

In fact, Anna Serner's tenure raised a heated debate around a number of issues, which are worth delving into in more detail in hindsight, and, since they are part of larger systemic issues. Let us start with Serner's insistence from early on of producing and disseminating knowledge, the results of which would allow her to set in motion her goals and agenda. As mentioned, during her tenure three reports focusing on gender and representation in the Swedish film industry were published. The first two, however, were criticized for being too quantitative in their approach, and it was only by the third report, published as late as 2019/2020, that a more qualitative approach was implemented. Here the focus widened from gender to discrimination in general, for instance, on racial grounds as well as age.[10]

But this internal tug-of-war between quantity and quality had already started with the so-called Bechdel test, introduced by WIFT in November 2013 (the definition of which was whether there is a film where two women talk to each other about something other than men). Here, specifically, the complicated issue of counting and (the value of) mere numbers is illustrated. In discussing the phenomenon in her blog, Anna Serner notes, firstly, that she personally somewhat "undeservedly" was given focus regarding this test, when all she had said was that she thought "it was a good idea"—but which was enough to open up the floodgates to interviews from abroad, in (to mention but a few) the Danish *Politikken*; on Australian radio as well as BBC radio; articles in both *USA Today* and *The New York Times*; and in South Africa, as well as an overflowing Twitter account. Abroad, she writes, everyone has been "curious, positive, and shocked" over the fact that 90 percent of all films did not pass the test (Blog November 14, 2013).

In Sweden, however, the discussion focused on the quantity versus quality issue. In her blog Serner cites two film critics, Hynek Pallas and Jan Holmberg, both of whom are also academics with doctorates in film studies, who stressed that it is not possible to measure quality with the help of the Bechdel test. But more importantly, they both thought that Serner's positive attitude, given her role as CEO of SFI, could become problematic when allocating production funds. To this charge, she gives an inordinately long answer, defending her stance at the same time as pointing out that the SFI as an institution in no way supports this test financially, but only morally, as an initiative that focuses on stereotypes in film. "The test," she writes, "makes no more than the point that it wants to make – to ask whether it is reasonable that so many films don't pass the test … I think that by encouraging debate about stereotypes we [the SFI] makes more good than bad" (Blog November 14, 2013).

Personally, I think that Anna Serner, at least in the beginning of her tenure, sometimes got close to the risk of letting mere numbers uncritically glide into an unquestioned aspect of quality. At the same time, she was quick to test her assumptions, and doing so in open debate, of which she was very quick to learn. But still, and as we will see, similar issues haunted Serner throughout her ten years as CEO. With the Bechdel issue, however, she got out of it rather elegantly—at the same time as she achieved a splash introduction on the international arena, something that served her very well in the future. In this context, it should also be emphasized that a controversy like this at least in part can be explained by culture collisions in line with Bourdieu's field theory. For it should be noted that, as opposed to, for instance, the British Film Institute (BFI), SFI has never been a research institution, aligned with scholarly university departments. Clearly, given Serner's commendable ambition to disseminate new knowledge, so that the SFI could develop and go forward in a complex contemporary world, it would seem the cultural climate in her own organization (traditionally intent on gathering statistics with not much analysis) at times led to hindrances in furthering her agenda, some of which kept reoccurring.

Another specific case, pointing in a similar direction, is the fact that more often than not the SFI has turned to the market, for instance private consulting firms rather than university departments, to gather and analyze information. One such incident that ended up haunting Anna Serner (as we will see further on) to the end of her aegis, was the recruitment of a private consulting firm called Miklo for the purpose of mapping out representation in thirty features produced in 2014.[11] It created a heated public debate—rightly so, for as several critics pointed out, the writers of this report had absolutely no knowledge of film as a medium and narrative art, which resulted in extremely wobbly and biased conclusions. As critic Hynek Pallas put it, "It is the most unserious study of film content that I've had the dubious pleasure of reading":

> I have, as opposed to many others, no problem with the fact that this [study] is made. But I do think that there's a problem when one makes analyses of this sort without being interested in the medium studied. From the start the writers of the study stress that they won't enter "the artistic aspects of the films". Okay? But you still claim that this is "a qualitative study". How? [...] For instance, what does it mean that a character gets more screen time in close up, or is filmed from a particular angle, or is lit in different ways? One can go on and on like this, in attempting to unravel the astonishingly shallow analyses of this report.

And he adds: "I think it's odd that a report of this kind doesn't contain one single reference to previous work on such issues – that's what we have research for."[12] It goes without saying that I, as a board member representing academia, felt obliged to become involved as well—not however in public but, to the best of my ability, in the boardroom. Here I pointed out, firstly, that it was not optimal that decisions as to which experts to recruit were taken internally by the SFI, which meant that the board was routinely faced with *fait accompli* decisions. But more importantly I pointed out the (embarrassingly) obvious—that there was a Film Studies department (my own) on the same floor as the SFI in the Filmhouse, as well as many other institutions of learning throughout the country, to which the SFI not only could but should have turned to for expertise. In fact, knowing that the aforementioned Hynek Pallas had written a dissertation on whiteness in Swedish film, I had already at some earlier point suggested that he be a guest speaker at one of the SFI internal seminars, to present the most recent research to the board.[13] This suggestion was not well received, to put it diplomatically. In short, it seemed that the SFI at the time still regarded our university department—its students, teachers, and researchers—mostly as customers and renters of premises, rather than as experts and a potential resource of systematic knowledge. Not, however, necessarily out if spite but—again—because of the borders that for decades had existed between institutions across the film cultural field in Sweden.[14]

The Issue of Quality and the System of Film Commissioners

But besides issues of an organizational and/or academic nature, one of the most controversial aspects of Anna Serner's term that accrued most public attention and debate was the definition of "quality." Here it goes without saying that in this context the system of film commissioners within the SFI is key, as it involves their ability to define quality before a production is given funds and the go ahead. But so is also the question of governance, including the charges of excessive control of cultural policy that have been directed against Serner. These interrelated aspects will be discussed below.

When discussing the question of quality, it is hard to ignore Harry Schein, who founded the SFI (in close allegiance with the Social Democratic government at the time), and his (in)famous definition of film quality:

> Expressive and formal innovation, the degree of the film's [thematic] concern or urgency, the intensity or novelty in its view of reality or critical view of society, the degree of psychological insight and level of spirituality, playful imagination or visionary strength, epic, dramatic and lyrical values, technical skill in the script, direction and acting and other cinematic factors.[15]

In contemporary SFI parlance this had (understandably so) boiled down to three terms—concern or urgency, originality, and craftsmanship. Not surprisingly, given Anna Serner's agenda, she was from the beginning, but particularly later on, criticized for putting too much emphasis on the first word—the degree of concern or urgency. As Hynek Pallas pointed out in a 2018 debate article, Schein's term "has been discussed for years, in both film education and among critics, as well as in the context of film policy goals. Dopey? No doubt. But the very vagueness was in itself stimulating in relation to the central issue of quality," and he adds that "when Harry Schein hatched his definition of quality at the same time that he launched the Film Agreement in 1963, the brilliant thing wasn't the inclusion of a term like concern or urgency, but that it could be interpreted freely." But, Pallas adds, "now we don't even discuss it anymore … Quality has been a thing to measure. Quality is equal to culture having become instrumental."[16]

Given the previous debates around counting, measurements, quantities, and amateurish reports, it is not surprising that by 2018 Serner was accused of "politicizing" and "instrumentalizing" culture. In fact, by that point it seemed that no one was particularly interested in trying to listen to her reasoning, which for all intents and purposes is quite interesting, in a historical as well as principled light. For instance, if one reads her blog it is obvious that she did not push art house film, minor cinema, or for that matter gender issues at every corner, and at all costs. Instead, she has insisted on the importance of the broad audience film all along—which to some may seem to contradict supporting diversity and the voices of marginalized groups. For instance, in the beginning of her tenure, while the Film Agreement was still in force, she writes in her blog (September 11, 2012): "The road we've chosen is diversity and quality – but also respect for the fact that quality is a very flexible concept. I [...] have a film agreement to adhere to, which clearly indicates that we should support quality and breadth." But, she adds, the so-called "broad audience films need to become better (get longer time for scriptwriting and production) and reach more [audiences]." In line with this, she was also very critical of the Film Agreement's regulation regarding the so-called "Automatstödet." This automatic preliminary funding, allotted in advance to a select number of films with a high box office potential, certainly benefits the commercial film, she writes, "but not on the expense of art house film but *on the expense of other commercial film which should have a requirement to deliver vis-a-vis the film agreement's goals of quality, diversity, and equality*" (Blog April 21, 2013, my emphasis).

This is interesting since here she is alluding to that elusive "popular quality film" or "commercial art house film," or what in academia has been called the "middle brow film"[17]—which is why, as Serner puts it, SFI should aim at "identifying those arthouse films with higher budgets and a longer time for production that could attract a really wide audience," while "at the same time scoring high in critical reception and success at festivals"—the latter two being the main factors in measuring quality after a film's premiere (Blog March 6, 2015). Later, after the Film Agreement was gone, she continued arguing for these qualities, breadth and access, but now with a gender edge. "For the sake of film," she writes in her blog, "all voices should get the same chance to get our money. Because quality comes from making the most of all talent, and the more talents, the more breadth, and a greater chance at distinction [...] The work we do now with equality will create both breadth and distinction," she writes, adding that during the last four years Sweden has had the most films in the official programs of the best festivals than ever before – and that more than half of these had women directors (Blog April 29, 2017).

Looking at the facts one cannot but agree. For, as pointed out by Maria Jansson and Louise Wallenberg, the goal of 50/50 was realized in reality and "reached a peak in 2016, when film productions supported by public funding reached the goal of at least 50% women in all [the] positions" of director, scriptwriter, and producer.[18] In addition, while it is still so that quantitatively less films have been written, directed, and produced by women than by men in the last decade in Sweden, still many of the films made by women have been rated as being among the best, based not only on subjective quality criteria, for instance by critics, but by concrete, objective measures as well, such as participation in prestige festivals. To mention some examples: *Apflickorna* (*She Monkeys*, 2011) by Lisa Aschan; *Äta sova dö* (*Eat, Sleep, Die*, 2012) and *Amatörer* (*Amateurs*, 2018) by Gabriela Pichler; *Hotell* (2013), and the Netflix series *Kärlek & anarki* (*Love & Anarchy*, 2020) by Lisa Langseth; *Belleville Baby* (2013) by Mia Engberg; *Återträffen* (*The Reunion*, 2013) and *X & Y* (2018) by Anna Odell; *Sameblod* (*Sami Blood*, 2017) and *Charter* (2020) by Amanda Kernell; and *Pleasure* (2021) by Ninja Thyberg, which was selected for the major official program of the Cannes Film Festival in 2021.

As Serner put it in her blog, "I've said it before, but I say it again. It's the *filmmakers* who make the films, but we must be doing something right [...] It can't be only coincidence [...] we have worked hard at setting goals, being clear and defining quality" (Blog August 22, 2017). Clearly, then, for Serner there was no contradiction between diversity, equality, and quality. Rather, her take on quality and equality sometimes almost seems to conflate and include audience film, that is, those films that are given bigger budgets. This is, in my estimation, the route Serner has adhered to and attempted to steer all along, which is important for considering her special take of the notion of quality within the boundaries that the given system has allowed.

As is also clear from the entries in Anna Serner's blog, she regarded her responsibility as CEO as creating an infrastructure for producing films, while the allocation of money to the individual films is the responsibility of the commissioners, whose job it is to discern quality before the fact. Nonetheless, for all the transparent blog entries regarding implementing her values within the given SFI system, gradually Serner became the object of outright conspiracy theories, particularly in the latter part of her term. For instance, although she had her eyes (as she should) on production infrastructure, not on the *content* of the individual films themselves, which SFI helped finance, this is precisely what she was accused of, with next to semi-tyrannical control—her prime tool being the commissioners.

This was the case when, in 2018, Jon Asp, film critic and editor-in-chief for the online journal *POV.se*, in an article citing the guidelines to the commissioners—that while it is the role of each commissioner to "suggest production support to valuable feature film projects," the final decision was still to be "taken by the CEO"—insinuated that Anna Serner overstepped her boundaries by overriding the decisions taken by the film commissioners.[19] In her answer to this article, Serner pointed out that this procedure is purely a formal one:

> As CEO I have very little say in the decisions of the film commissioners. My role is rather to take responsibility for and support their work [...] We've had the system with commissioners since 1992. It's not a perfect system, which can and should be under scrutiny. Our surveys in the film industry show that a majority prefer this over a system of committees. Both have drawbacks, but nowhere else in the world another system has been invented. So for now we depend on the commissioners and their competence. I have full confidence in their judgement and that our system works well, but I still welcome discussion. Because it's all about selection, and it's a hard task having to discard 95 percent of all applications.

She added: "As far as I know, no CEO has said no to a commissioner's choice in saying yes to the five per cent who do get support." At the same time she did add something that implies a degree of misgiving on her part about the commissioner system. "My role in the process," she wrote, is "to ensure that these experienced professionals have something else than gut feeling before taking a decision"—thus, it seems, implying that arbitrariness and subjectivity may indeed have been at play, at least historically. But, she continues, by "demanding [written] assessments we have been able to find new types of films that show potential for quality [...] made by both women and men."[20] The fact is that already in the spring of 2013 Anna Serner had recruited a think tank consisting of representatives from the film industry (among them director Lisa Langseth) to discuss this issue and later also initiated an independent evaluation of the system of commissioners, which she also mentions in her blog. The system "needs to be evaluated and developed," she wrote, and should be done so "in dialogue with the film industry" (Blog December 9, 2014). In addition, in early in 2016 a director for the commissioners' section was recruited, for instance, to support internal cooperation among the commissioners, thus freeing up space to discuss the qualitative aspects of scripts and project developments.[21]

As for myself I can vouch for the fact that the board at each meeting was presented with the commissioners' written assessments and their arguments for allocating moneys. However, what did concern me at times was the fact that these assessments (in my estimation) often could be poorly written—which in turn made me wonder how and from where the commissioners were recruited. The fact is that they (still) almost exclusively consist of film practitioners—editors, sound technicians, actors, directors, etc. The fact that commissioners are chosen narrowly from the film industry in my view amounts to a structural problem (aside from their running the risk of being, or becoming, biased, given our small national film culture). In line with this, I suggested to the board that the area from which to choose commissioners should be broadened, for instance, to people with university degrees in film and even include film critics—that is, individuals who are used to assessing quality (albeit of finished films rather than potential films in the form of scripts and prospects). After all, where is it taken as an undisputed fact that an editor or a cinematographer is necessarily the best to assess quality in the work of others? In short, in this context there was, and still is, a need to broaden the possible choices in recruiting from the field of film culture at large. Again the silence that met this proposal was next to deafening.

In addition, there was another structural flaw with regard to the system of commissioners, and although it was, and still is, endemic in Swedish political culture at large, Anna Serner was blamed for it as well. It is the fact that the "quarantine" time between working in and for a tax-funded institution (such as the SFI) and moving to private business (such as the film industry) is absurdly short.[22] Thus, when in 2018 several film commissioners quit to move to other putatively more attractive jobs (likely due to the work overload brought on by the transition in 2017 from the Film Agreement to a fully state-funded film production), critic Jon Asp wrote that the quarantine duration "from a state donor to private beneficiary is only three months—in which other industry is this possible?" It is a perfectly logical question, given that the knowledge that a film commissioner holds is a very coveted commodity for the film industry. But arguably, it is equally absurd that this political and endemic problem in Swedish society as a whole was turned into yet another proof of Serner's alleged power hunger. In the charged words of Jon Asp: "It is remarkable how much power one finds among a very few decision makers […] while the increasingly offensive call for the 50/50 vision […] descends like a smoke screen over the control from the top. As long as the focus is on equality it is easy to deflect attention from less headline-friendly wrong-doings."[23] This is no doubt as close as you can get to a conspiracy theory—the argument being that here a feminist vision of equality is deployed, the putative controversiality of which is but a cloak for an even more insidious aim.

Cultural Governance—or Inordinate Control?

In regard to the issue of power and control, and the alleged instrumentalization and even politization of film production in its wake, what has not been noted as much—at least not abroad—is the role in this process of (then) Minister of Culture Alice Bah Kuhnke. Indeed, in hindsight there is arguably even a degree of underestimation of her role in supporting Anna Serner's agenda. Because undoubtedly it was no less than a win-win for Serner when the new Social Democratic government elected in 2014 appointed Bah Kuhnke. At this point, with the success Serner already had reached in implementing her agenda, she now clearly must have realized that there was an opening for her to take it even further. For now a potentially political infrastructure was in place, firstly in the form of a government that had created a ministry of culture that added the word "democracy" in its name (Ministry of Culture and Democracy). As Serner herself phrased it in her blog: "Great positive news that the sports area has been stricken in favour of democracy. Culture and democracy are intimately related, and there are many possibilities in this merger" (Blog October 3, 2014). In addition, when the Film Agreement soon was declared defunct by Bah Kuhnke (no doubt with much strategic lobbying by Serner), it opened up for a whole new flexibility, unhampered by the administrative patchwork of regulations that had been added to the Agreement through the years.

At the same time it is interesting that while Anna Serner showed great skill in engaging with both politicians and private film industry, her relation with media seemed much more problematic. For instance, there is an outburst in her blog that speaks loudly of her impatience with journalists as well as assorted cultural aesthetes:

> I think that the area of culture is no different from other political areas. Cultural politics costs money, affects society on many levels, both practically and immaterially. It earns its place within the tax-financed budget […] and that's

why I'm strongly against the view that culture shouldn't have to explain itself […] We should be able to ask more of ourselves than, when confronted with the question "why culture?", just flippantly answer "because!" "Because" doesn't create much understanding among the taxpaying citizen. Still that's the only thing I hear from the cultural critics.

Adding: "I think that if more people from the cultural world would make an effort to explain the raison d'être of culture in a state budget, then one could reach a better understanding outside of one's own narrow cultural sphere, which would increase the chance of culture becoming an integrated part in all kinds of other societal issues" (Blog November 11, 2014).

Anna Serner made her position clear, in no uncertain terms. This is of course why her wholehearted cooperation with Alice Bah Kuhnke raised some eyebrows (Figure 3.2). For instance, when assessing this cooperation in hindsight, cultural critic Maria Schottenius wrote that the SFI vision "50/50 by 20/20," which Serner and Bah Kuhnke presented in tandem at international film festivals, was no less than a "joint operation," and thus "a thorn in the eye of everyone who wanted to safeguard an arm's length" between pure politics (that is, the ministry) and a state authority such as the SFI, which should behave neutrally vis-à-vis the political powers that be.[24]

Arguably, then, at times Serner did seem to teeter too close to the political sphere, at the risk of politicizing (film) culture, using it as a mere means toward implementing certain ideological gals. At least this was certainly the perception when at Cannes 2018, Serner threatened to give all of the SFI selective aid and market support for 2020 to women only. As she wrote in her blog: "If we don't see a change we will consider allocating all of the market support for 2020 to women. So now we have a year and a half to see IF it's necessary, and in that case HOW it should be done." Not surprisingly this created a proper uproar—which was the point, as this was a conscious move to spread light on a long-lasting issue. For, as Serner further noted in her blog, in answering a critic in *Dagens Nyheter*: "Because I agree with Helena Lindblad, of course it would be problematic, both artistically and practically. But perhaps it's more problematic if we do nothing" (Blog May 15, 2018).

But perhaps the most severe crisis occurred when SFI, after #MeToo in 2018, offered a course on gender to producers who applied for financial support from the SFI. Not surprisingly, at the yearly so-called Almedal week, Anna Serner was attacked in a panel discussion by right-wing journalist Johan Hakelius,

Figure 3.2 The Swedish Minister of Culture and the CEO of the Swedish Film Institute in Cannes—a clandestine "joint operation"? Photo: Janne Göransson, SFI.

who accused her of turning this gender course to a prerequisite for receiving any production funds at all.[25] In hindsight this is rather ironic, given that now such courses are self-evident as a tool for all personnel in production companies and shoots, to keep track of a healthy work environment stipulated by unions. In addition, at this point in time Swedish film production companies have established such courses themselves.

In addition, at this same panel discussion, Hakelius attacked Serner for having insisted on publishing the SFI equality reports—and again she had to defend the strategy of counting. Here she simply repeated (for the umpteenth time) the self-evident; namely, that the SFI mission to find quality films should be led by equality and diversity—which has been decided in the parliament and may be read in the government bill on film of 2015/16:132.[26] Later, in her blog she sarcastically added that Johan Hakelius seems to believe that "it's dangerous to count": "Hakelius basic criticism, then, is that if we produce knowledge we steer or direct the filmmakers. I understand his view so that we are allowed to produce knowledge on all other phenomena (like genres, which production companies get our money, how many people see films etc), but that knowledge specifically on ethnicity, gender, and HBTQ is dangerous for democracy and the freedom of art." Besides, she added, if there was any truth in her being overly "steering," one should be able to see this in the current film repertoire. But, she writes: "It's very easy to see on the screens that [financing] don't come with certain demands, or even what kind of films are being made" (Blog August 17, 2018).

Serner's view was amply supported by film critic Charlotte Wiberg, who in an article actually did an overview of the statistics for the film production of 2018. Considering, Wiberg wrote, the accusations that have been directed against Serner regarding "politization, coerced gender balance, and the yoke of diversity," it would be interesting to take a closer look. For instance, she asks, how is the gender balance? Well, she answers, it looks like it always has, given that less than a fifth (four) of the Swedish film premieres of the fall of 2018 has a woman director, while three of the twenty-seven directors come from another background than Nordic. "That's the reality," Wiberg concludes. "The image of Serner as a dictatorial boss ousting white men stands in an absurd contrast to the actual fact." In addition, she notes the self-evident that "it will take an in-depth analysis of the panoply of films as well as terms and conditions in order to establish whether and how film policy works – but the increase in quality in the last decade ought to show that it is not mutually exclusive to work simultaneously with quality while also reaching artistic success."[27]

In my own estimation, Anna Serner never crossed any red lines with regard to politization, pure and simple. It is telling that when she defends the Culture Minister in her blog, noting that "Alice Bah Kuhnke gets much criticism for her alleged politization of culture, for instance as far as I understand for us as cultural institutions having a diversity and democracy mission," she makes sure to add, in sarcastic parenthesis: "(Something that we have had through all governments, Social Democrats, the previous coalition of the middle/right, and now with the

Social democrats and the Green Party. *This was not considered a problem until we started taking the mission seriously.*)" (Blog October 13, 2016, my emphasis).

At the same time there remains the ironic fact, discussed elsewhere in this book (see for instance the interview with film director Lisa Langseth), that toward the end of Anna Serner's tenure, she was accused of being too tight not only with politicians but also with their counterpart, that is, the film industry and its agendas. This became abundantly clear in the open letter that some of the most noted contemporary Swedish film directors, many of them women, published in *Dagens Nyheter* as late as February 2021.[28] Given the increasingly dominant position of the streaming channels, they write, the question of the role of the SFI in the future is a key issue. Should it, as has been proposed in the debate, finance less but bigger project, with the aim of competing commercially on the international market? The directors advise against this idea, arguing instead for the opposite. Let this new market take care of the fully commercial projects ("simply because they do it well"), while the money of the SFI should be directed toward "personal films based on original ideas, developed by headstrong scriptwriters and directors." However, they add, this is not the same as advocating art film, but films that travel to festivals abroad, mentioning for instance Ninja Thyberg's film *Pleasure* shown at the Sundance Film Festival among others. They also mention the Danish film *Druk* (*Another Round*, 2020), which, they point out, is both internationally awarded and an enormously successful audience film—thus unwittingly and ironically pointing out precisely the kind of "popular quality film" or "commercial art house film" that the SFI under Anna Serner's leadership had been on the lookout for all along.

The reason for their mentioning this film is that in Denmark, they argue, "it is the scriptwriters and directors who are in charge." Therefore, they ask in conclusion, who is to be at the helm of "leading Swedish film into the future"? "Is it future strategists who do not make films themselves," or is it "the top executives in the largest production companies?" If nothing else, this letter represents a kind of oblique summing up of how SFI, and possibly, through guilt by association, Anna Serner as well, was publically perceived—that is, as a mix between a bureaucracy in alliance with the film industry—just two months before Serner announced, in April 2021, that she intended to step down as CEO.

Regardless, at this point there had accrued a number of issues—as the film directors rightly point out in their open letter—in the new media landscape.

For of course the question is—what about the future? How should we tackle transnational forces, such as streaming? Will this make film, as we know it, obsolete, and therefore the very idea of an institution like the SFI obsolete as well? As Peter Fornstam, the CEO of cinema chain Svenska Bio, points out, now that Anna Serner has stepped down, it is no longer only a question as to who is to succeed her, but rather "what the Department of Culture first has to ask itself is what the future role of the SFI should be." Because, he argues, the risk is that its traditional role will be strongly reduced, as the conditions will increasingly be set by multinational agents who have no interest in national or local regulations, wishes, or—for that matter—cultural policy.[29]

Anna Serner's Legacy

I think that Anna has been the best [CEO] so far. As everyone knows, she has strongly pursued questions of representation and equality, which has been, and still is, totally necessary. I think that the criticism she has endured for this is misogynistic.

(filmmaker Göran H. Olsson)[30]

Anna Serner's announcement gave cause for both friends and foes to try to give an assessment of what she had achieved. Critic Helena Lindblad at *Dagens Nyheter*, who had been ambivalent at best, had already started her summing up in an article published in September 2020, significantly called "SFI.s Anna Serner should broaden her repertoire or leave her CEO chair." Even so, here Lindblad chooses to enumerate the positive, asking firstly "Was '50/50 by 2020' still a good vision?" Yes, she answered, "generally there has over time developed a better gender balance behind the camera, which many of us have called for. Specifically when it comes to films that have received production funds the percentage is impressive." This, she continued, "is a laborious effort that previous female CEOs at the SFI had started and that Anna Serner clarified and pursued powerfully and courageously." Other good things can be mentioned, Lindblad added, "that may not make headlines but are just as important"—that now there is in Sweden a dominance of women producers, as well as managers at SVT (Swedish public service television), C-More/TV4, and regional film production funds such as Film i Väst, and that both Swedish and foreign festivals now have more equal programming.[31]

In a later article, after Anna Serner in fact had announced her retirement, Lindblad again chooses to enumerate the positive, but this time focusing on the international angle.[32] Swedish film, she writes, "has reached the world in a way that has not happened since the days of Ingmar Bergman, and has a much more self-evident place in the large film festivals." Anna Serner herself seems to agree, as it is precisely the international angle that she emphasizes in her very last blog entry. In summing up her ten years at SFI, she writes that she is particularly proud of the fact that Swedish film during the last ten years has been strengthened internationally. "When I started at the SFI everyone was concerned about the fact that Swedish features were not selected for the official programming at the so called A-festivals," she writes, adding that "today instead we are spoiled with both participation and prizes all over the world," mentioning particularly the "amazing" year 2017 which saw Tarik Saleh's prize at the Sundance Film Festival for *The Nile Hilton Incident*, Amanda Kernell's LUX prize with *Sami Blood*, and Ruben Östlund's Golden Palm for *The Square* in Cannes (Blog April 27, 2021). Again Helena Lindblad concurs in summing up Serner's achievements. Anna Serner's vision on equality and diversity in the film industry, she writes, "is in line with what is happening internationally," mentioning that the Oscar jury's work in this regard (for instance #OscarSoWhite) "has given great results," concluding: "I feel great respect for Serner's solid work, which has given waves all over the world."

While I, in turn, have no vested interest in taking sides with all of Anna Serner's positions, I still—after having scoured the reception of her in the Swedish press and film journals—have to say that it is not difficult to conclude that such an appreciation was a long time coming. Perhaps the most reasonable and dispassionately sobering assessment can be found in Anna Serner's own last blog entry: "We haven't reached the realization of our vision, but surely toppled a mountain or two."

Notes

1   Pierre Bourdieu, *The Field of Cultural Production* (1972; Cambridge: Polity Press, 1993).
2   One of the main reasons for debunking the Film Agreement was the unwillingness of broadband operators to contribute to the system financially, even though they

benefited from having access to windows showing, for instance, Swedish film, which is content that had not cost them anything at all to produce.
3   See for instance Fiona Mackay, "Nested Newness, Institutional Innovation, and the Gendered Limits of Change," *Politics and Gender*, vol. 10, no. 4 (2014), 549–71, https://doi.org/10.1017/S1743923X14000415.
4   Sanna Lenken, "Jag hoppas mer pengar hamnar hos de modiga, inte hos jättarna" [I Hope that More Money Is Awarded to the Brave, Not the Giants], *FLM*, June 11, 2021. In a survey section called "After Serner" in online film journal *FLM*, https://flm.nu/?s=Efter+Serner, accessed January 6, 2022. All translations in this chapter are by the author, unless specified otherwise.
5   Jon Asp, "Publiktapp, politisering och locket på" [Loss of Audiences, Pollicization, and a Cover Up], *POV*, no. 72, October 29, 2020, https://www.povfilm.se/72/publiktapp-politisering-och-locket-pa-banar-vag-for-existentiell-kris-i-svensk/, accessed January 6, 2022.
6   Anna Serner's blog, September 19, 2014, https://annasernersfi.wordpress.com, accessed January 6, 2022. From here on, blog posts and dates will be noted in the text.
7   Katarina Hedrén, "Ingen kan sudda ut visionen om jämställdhet" [No One Can Erase the Vision of Equality], *FLM*, June 11, 2021, https://flm.nu/?s=Efter+Serner, accessed January 6, 2022.
8   Swedish Film Institute, *406 Days: It's About Time: Gender Equality Report for 2022/2022* (Stockholm: Swedish Film Institute, 2022), https://www.filminstitutet.se/en/about-us/swedish-film-institute/gender-equality/, accessed January 6, 2022. Another outcome was a book, Ingrid Stigsdotter, ed., *Making the Invisible Visible: Reclaiming Women's Agency in Swedish Film History and Beyond* (Lund: Nordic Academic Press, 2019).
9   Swedish Film Institute, *Goal 2020: Gender Action Plan* (Stockholm: Swedish Film Institute, 2016), https://www.filminstitutet.se/globalassets/_dokument/handlingsplaner/actionplan_genderequality_eng_final.pdf, accessed January 6, 2022.
10 Anna Adeniji and Ylva Habel, *Which Women? Gender Equality Report 2019/2020* (Stockholm: Swedish Film Institute, 2020), https://issuu.com/svenskafilminstitutet/docs/gender-equality-report_19_20_english, accessed September 16, 2022.
11 Miklo, "Svensk films representation av Sverige" [The Representation of Sweden in Swedish Film] (Stockholm: Swedish Film Institute, 2015).
12 Hynek Pallas, "Reducera inte filmkonsten till politik" [Don't Reduce the Art of Film to Politics], *Expressen*, June 18, 2015.
13 Hynek Pallas, "Vithet i svensk spelfilm 1989–2010" (Whiteness in Swedish Feature Film 1989–2010) (Ph.D. dissertation, Filmkonst, Gothenburg, 2011). For the

abstract in English, see: http://www.diva-portal.org/smash/record.jsf?pid=diva2%3A435285&dswid=-7177, accessed September 4, 2022.

14 Another example of the historically wobbly recruitment strategies occurred before Anna Serner's tenure, when the so-called regionalization of film was being discussed around the turn of the millennium, due to newly allocated EU funds. In this case the SFI chose to recruit experts from the discipline of human geography for a report, which predictably became one-sidedly financial, for instance focusing on how municipalities could make PR for themselves through film, in the hopes of increasing tourism—rather than focus on films and film culture in and for themselves. For an overview, spanning over the inauguration of EU funds up until the end of the period with Film Agreement policy, see Erik Hedling, Olof Hedling, and Mats Jönsson, eds., *Regional Aesthetics: Locating Swedish Media* (Stockholm: KB/Mediehistoriskt arkiv 15, 2010), esp. 60–77; and Olof Hedling, "Cinema in the Welfare State: Notes on Public Support. Regional Film Funds and Film Policy in Swedish Film," in Mette Hjort and Ursula Lindqvist (eds.), *The Blackwell Companion to Nordic Cinema* (London: Blackwell, 2016).

15 Swedish Film Institute, "Harry Scheins kvalitetsbegrepp" [Harry Schein's Concept of Quality], February 1, 2007, https://www.filminstitutet.se/sv/nyheter/2007/harry-scheins-kvalitetsbegrepp/, accessed January 6, 2022.

16 Hynek Pallas, "Svensk film politiseras – men var är debatten?" [Swedish Film Is Being Politicized – But Where's the Debate?], *Expressen*, August 14, 2018, https://www.expressen.se/kultur/ide/svensk-film-politiseras-men-var-ar-debatten/, accessed January 6, 2022.

17 See Mark Betz, "High and Low and in Between," *Screen*, vol. 54, no. 4 (2013), 495–513, https://doi.org/10.1093/screen/hjt044, as well as the concept "middle-brow" in Tim Bergfelder, "Popular European Cinema in the 2000s: Cinephilia, Genre and Heritage," in Mary Harrod, Mariana Liz, and Alissa Timoshkina (eds.), *The Europeanness of European Cinema* (London: I.B. Tauris, 2015), 44–5. Both concern films that occupy "an ambivalent or hybrid position" in "the intersection between art-house and mainstream."

18 Maria Jansson and Louise Wallenberg, "Experiencing Male Domination in Swedish Film Production," in Susan Liddy (ed.), *Women in the International Film Industry* (London: Palgrave Macmillan, 2020), 163, https://doi.org/10.1007/978-3-030-39070-9_10.

19 Jon Asp, "Enväldiga beslut om vem som får göra film" [Autocratic Decisions on Who Is Allowed to Make Films], *Aftonbladet*, July 17, 2018, https://www.aftonbladet.se/kultur/a/WLAn2K/envaldiga-beslut-om-vem-som-far-gora-film, accessed January 6, 2022.

20 Anna Serner, "Så ser vi bortom hudfärg och gör svensk film bättre" [This Is How We Look beyond Skin Color and Make Swedish Film Better], *Expressen*, August 16, 2018.

21 In "Stöd till utveckling och produktion av svensk film. En nulägesbeskrivning" [Support for Development and Production of Swedish Film. A Description of the Current State], November 1, 2016, 15 (unpublished), it is noted that the system of commissioners has been studied in an independent report by Tomas Lundkvist, *Svenska Filminstitutets konsulentsystem: En reflekterande studie* [The SFI's Commisssioner System: A Reflexive Study] (Stockholm: The Media Mentors, 2016), and that a conclusion that can be drawn from it that the majority of the film industry stands behind it. Also see: Swedish Film Institute, "Stöd till utveckling och produktion av svensk film. En nulägesbeskrivning" [Support for Development and Production of Swedish Film. A Description of the Current State], 2016, https://www.filminstitutet.se/globalassets/filmpolitiska-dokument/stod_till_utveckling_och_produktion_av_svensk_film.pdf, accessed January 6, 2022.

22 In Sweden there are still no rules as in many other countries regulating how soon a politician can take a paid position in the private sector, sometimes even transferring directly from being a Minister to working as a consultant with organizations that previously it was his or her job to regulate. As Peter Wolodarski, editor-in-chief for Sweden's largest daily, once phrased it, that while there is no reason to suspect, for example, lobbying or political consultants per se, as they are part of democracy, "this odd *laissez faire* represents a naïve attitude regarding Swedish incorruptibility, including that which is defined narrowly as involving favouring friends and family." See Peter Wolodarski, "Sverige förenar naivitet med självgodhet" [Sweden Combines Naivety with Complacency], *Dagens Nyheter*, May 5, 2013.

23 Asp, "Enväldiga beslut om vem som får göra film."

24 Maria Schottenius, "Vem ska hålla vakt vid luftslottet där konstnärlig frihet bor?" [Who Is to Guard at Castles in the Air Where Artistic Freedom Resides?], *Dagens Nyheter*, June 16, 2021.

25 The so-called Almedalen Week in Visby on the Baltic island of Gotland, which takes place in July each year. It started in the 1960s with the speeches held there by Prime Minister Olof Palme, an event which (before the Covid-19 pandemic) had grown into a highly influential as well as internationally noted get-together between all the political parties, lobbyists, and, not least, media. See, for example, "Almedalen Week: At Sweden's One-of-a-Kind Festival, All Political Parties Gather in One Place," Democracy Now! July 2, 2014, https://www.democracynow.org/2014/7/2/dn_at_almedalen_week_at_swedens, accessed September 4, 2022; "Almedalen Week," Wikipedia, August 1, 2022, http://en.wikipedia.org/wiki/Almedalen_Week, accessed September 6, 2022.

26 See film clip in Mattias Knutson, "Anna Serners utbrott: 'Det du säger är vulgärt!'" [Anna Serner's Outburst: "What You Say Is Vulgar"], *Expressen*, July 4, 2018, https://www.expressen.se/kultur/film--tv/anna-serners-utbrott-det-du-sager-

ar-vulgart/, accessed September 4, 2022. In this debate Serner is referring to the government bill on film *Mer film till fler – en sammanhållen filmpolitik* 2015/16:132, https://www.riksdagen.se/sv/dokument-lagar/dokument/proposition/mer-film-till-fler—en-sammanhallen-filmpolitik_H303132, accessed January 6, 2022.

27 Carlotte Wiberg, "Filmhösten avslöjar att jämställdheten inte har gått för långt" [This Film Fall Reveals that Equality Has Not Gone too Far], *FLM* August 17, 2018.

28 This open letter was signed by Amanda Kernell, Daniel Espinosa, Fanni Metelius, Fijona Jonuzi, Goran Kapetanović, Göran Hugo Olsson, Henrik Schyffert, Ivica Zubak, Johannes Nyholm, Lisa Aschan, Lisa Langseth, Lovisa Sirén, Mia Engberg, Mikael Marcimain, Pernilla August, Peter Grönlund, Peter Modestij, Rojda Sekersöz, Ronnie Sandahl, Sanna Lenken, Sofia Norlin, Tarik Saleh, and Tomas Alfredson. See "Svenska toppregissörer i upprop: Låt skattepengarna utveckla svensk films särart!" [Appeal by Swedish Top Directors: Let Tax Money Develop the Specificity of Swedish Film!], *Dagens Nyheter*, February 11, 2021, https://www.dn.se/kultur/svenska-toppregissorer-i-upprop-lat-skattepengarna-utveckla-svensk-films-sarart/, accessed January 6, 2022.

29 Peter Fornstam, "Staten hade inte räknat med den globala konkurrensen" [The State Had Not Counted on Global Competition], *FLM*, June 3, 2021, https://flm.nu/?s=Efter+Serner, accessed January 6, 2022.

30 Göran H. Olsson, "Ingen VD på SFI har gjort någon större skillnad" [No CEO at the SFI Has Made Much Difference], *FLM*, May 31, 2021, https://flm.nu/?s=Efter+Serner, accessed January 6, 2022.

31 Helena Lindblad, "Filminstitutets Anna Serner bör bredda sin repertoar eller lämna vd-stolen" [Anna Serner Should Broaden Her Repertoire or Leave Her CEO Chair], *Dagens Nyheter*, September 17, 2020.

32 Helena Lindblad, "Nu behövs en efterträdare som kan återupprätta det brustna förtroendet med publiken" [What Is Needed Now Is a Successor Who Can Restore the Broken Trust with the Audience], *Dagens Nyheter*, April 27, 2021.

Part Two

Histories, Herstories, and Representation

4

Women on Screen I

1910s–1960s

Louise Wallenberg

Introduction

So far, we have discussed issues concerning women film workers' presence, visibility, and ownership—or lack thereof—in Swedish film culture, looking at the cultural and national context, ownership issues, and specific "film events," in the first fifty years of Swedish cinema. While the previous chapters investigated issues of gender and authorship and questions regarding salaries and working conditions for women in the film industry, this chapter is more film focused. Turning the gaze to women *on* screen, that is, how women have been represented in (Swedish) film, I will analyze a variety of images of women by focusing on a small number of films made between the early 1900s and the late 1960s, some of which were made by men (but relying on novels or scripts written by women) and others that were made by women. One crucial impetus for this chapter (and for the entire book), then, is the urge to address the "paradoxical relation between women as historically specific individuals [i.e., women working in the film industry] and Woman as an imaginary cultural representation."[1]

Departing from a short discussion of how women have been represented on screen in both mainstream and non-mainstream film, and discussing the international (mostly Anglo-Saxon) scholarship that has investigated women's roles on and off screen, the chapter then turns its gaze toward the Swedish context, which is a context that is both specific and, in parts, universal. Images of how women are represented differ slightly between different film nations, and most women film workers, no matter where they are, have to fight the same struggles to get their representations "up there" and then *out* there. The central issues addressed include what women are allowed to be, to do, and to become on screen, as well as how they are positioned vis-à-vis other women characters (as well as male characters) in terms of subjecthood and objecthood. The trajectory is rather long, as I start off with a discussion of representations in silent cinema, and then move through the twentieth century, discussing representations from each decade leading up to the 1960s. For women filmmakers, this decade must be understood as defining our seminal moment, no matter how convoluted it may have been, since this is when the professional training of film workers was made possible—for both genders.

Woman as Image—Women in Plural

When it comes to representation, women have a rotten deal. Since the early days of cinema, they have been forced into a delimited number of stereotypes, leaving little room for deviation, for complexity.[2] The most dominating female archetypes on screen, first molded in early genre cinema and then amplified in all variations of narrative film throughout the twentieth century, are closely connected to the three roles that Luce Irigaray finds possible (and desirable) in patriarchal society: woman as virgin, prostitute, and mother.[3] While these archetypes are indeed static in themselves, they may however start out as one and, through pressures that are both intrinsic and extrinsic, develop or transform into another. But whereas virgin characters on screen may turn into prostitutes or mothers, and prostitutes may become mothers—mothers seldom become prostitutes. Male characters—constituting more flexible "social roles"[4]—have a much better deal since they may move between different positions (and "beings") with much more ease.[5] And whereas women characters are there as secondary figures who are supportive, comforting, and/or sexually attractive and available, male characters are given the lead to drive the story forward. Men on screen act as full and active subjects, and women as their supportive, passive objects.[6]

It comes as no surprise that it is the very representation of women on screen that has occupied most feminist film theory, from its outset in the 1970s onward. "Woman as image" has been the object for critical inquiries and readings, and these readings have often departed from the notion that film both *mirrors* existent gender roles and behaviors, and *works* to construct and conserve these roles. Film, together with other visual media, functions as a gender technology working to instruct its spectators how to "be" and behave in their gender.[7] And since film, as part of a heteronormative and patriarchal system, is in many ways a "male" medium, governed by men since its inception in the late nineteenth century, the rotten deal that women get does not only regard how they are represented: besides being represented in stereotypical and circumscribed ways, almost always drifting toward sexualization (and violation), they often experience how their possibilities to work in the industry are circumscribed. From the early days of feminist film theory, throughout the 1980s and 1990s, and up until our own era, the image of Woman in film has been debated, analyzed, and discussed through the use of different kinds of theoretical frameworks (e.g., feminist philosophy and theory, psychoanalysis, Marxist theory, and queer theory).[8] Underlining these various theoretical perspectives on how this clichéd and tiresome image can be analyzed, understood, and deconstructed are the tendencies in how gender and sex have been (and still are) conceived, which often has meant (and means) a certain movement between a more or less constructionist or essentialist standpoint.

Linking these different epochs and their varying theoretical strands and standpoints, however, is the mutual understanding that the mainstream, patriarchal, heteronormative, and one-sided image of how women are represented is the problem—and that this problem has to do with the very fact that men dominate the industry. In 1984, Italian-American scholar Teresa de Lauretis advocated for a movement away from "Woman as Image" to a more varied and plural representation of women as a diverse group, with differing experiences, stories, problems, and desires. Hence, to refuse the domineering "Woman as Image" in men's cinematic production, and instead try to embrace a more open and flexible representation of "women" in plural. While "Woman" can only refer to a fixed type, its pluralistic other, women, refers to an immensely diverse group consisting of a variety of subjects holding different experiences and occupying different positions and identities. Many feminist filmmakers and film theorists have shared this urge and have worked to dismantle the dominant image by introducing images that are plural, diverse, and yet inclusive.[9] This creative period saw the production of films such as *Born in Flames* (Lizzie Borden, 1982), *A Question of Silence* (Marleen Gorris, 1982), and *She Must Be Seeing Things* (Sheila McLaughlin, 1987), all of which were critically acclaimed and discussed at film festivals, in text books, and in classrooms. Here, the early work of filmmakers such as Barbara Hammer, Lizzie Borden, Sally Potter, Gunnel Lindblom, Agnès Varda, Anja Breien, Trinh T. Minh-ha, and Chantal Ackermann are also worth mentioning. And while the scholarship was heavily dominated by Anglo-Saxon perspectives, the making of feminist film was much more internationally spread, and Sweden constitutes an interesting example, in terms of both filmmaking and feminist film movements. In the 1960s, before the incitement of a feminist film scholarship, Mai Zetterling made no fewer than three pro-feminist feature films—*Älskande par* (*Loving Couples*, 1964), *Nattlek* (*Night Game*, 1966), and *Flickorna* (*The Girls*, 1968)—and the 1970s saw a string of feminist films being produced for the screen, as well as a joint feminist movement through the organization Svenska kvinnors filmförbund (SKFF; Swedish Women Filmmakers' Association). It is frustrating that, despite this broad and lively awakening, the one-dimensional image of women as "Woman" still dominates film production, Swedish or other, five decades later.

In fact, many of the women directors that we have interviewed have expressed the difficulty in getting their visions through when it comes to representing gender, and especially the female gender. There seems to be a set formula or principle for how women can and should look and act on screen, that is, how they can be represented on screen—and if deviating from this rigid formula, there is clearly trouble ahead. Women on screen are circumscribed as being "reliable" and this reliability is formed by a long tradition of men artists either idealizing or degrading women. But we also learn from our interviews that women characters are expected to be "likeable," as in sexually attractive and available. Within the universe of cinematic representation (as in most narrative forms), being reliable and likeable entails keeping within the gender specific roles designated to women throughout (film) history. These roles have generally included the girlfriend, the wife, the mother, and once in a while, the femme fatale or the hag—all of whom are reflections or versions of Irigaray's three archetypes. These are all supporting characters or positions, that is, roles that only serve to support the male lead and his development as a full subject—while also serving to "heteronormalize" him.[10]

Before discussing our chosen films, starting with a couple of early cinematic representations, it should be pointed out that it is not just the image that has occupied feminist film theory and practice—so has the *voice*. Kaja Silverman has shown how (classic) cinema is not only obsessed with the female image (as erotic object) but also with the sound that is produced by the female voice.[11] Women's voices—on screen—are invariably tied to their bodily presentation or spectacle, and they are so through crying, screaming, and panting. Yet, they have little, if any, authoritative voice in the narrative and their speech is characterized as "unreliable, thwarted, or acquiescent."[12] Silverman, in her now thirty-year-old treatise, finds in experimental feminist film practice a striving for freeing the female voice from its otherwise dominant referencing to its body. By detaching the voice from the body, the old imagery of the female body as an erotic, passive object can be challenged and destroyed, leaving space for new images and voices to be visualized and expressed. In Mai Zetterling's film *Flickorna* (*The Girls*) from 1968, to be discussed at the end of this chapter, women's voices and narration are at the center, as the three girls try to challenge the patriarchal system into which they have been forced. Instead of seeing their chatting as nonsensical and unfocused, one is led to understand their acoustic expressions as counter-discursive: their sayings are feminist utterances that have political implications for their (quest for) equality and freedom.[13]

1910s: Early Representations

As in most national and international cinemas, representations of women have been present and abundant since the very inception of Swedish cinema in the late nineteenth century. As it developed into a narrative medium, in tandem with French and, somewhat later, American cinema, women characters were given central positions—although in the circumscribed (and objectified) roles described above. The first decades of Swedish narrative cinema relied on existent literary works by famous novelists such as Selma Lagerlöf and Hjalmar Bergman, but also on actors coming from theater, that is, professional performers who were already known to the wider audience. Here, Anna Hofman-Uddgren needs to be mentioned: out of the six films that she made between 1910 and 1911, two were based on literary works by August Strindberg, *Fröken Julie* and *Fadren*. Hofman-Uddgren is usually credited as the first Swedish woman to direct a film, although her work has attracted little attention. Like many other venturing into film, she had a background in theater and vaudeville, and her first pioneering practice was that of organizing early film screenings, bringing film programs into her variety shows in theaters. It was cinema owner Nils Petter Nilsson, who managed six cinemas in Stockholm at this time, who commissioned her to direct six films, including Strindberg's *Fröken Julie* and *Fadren*, both filmed in 1912, and *Systrarna*, also filmed in 1912, and which was based on a script by social critic and suffragette Elin Wägner. The first three films were *Stockholmsfrestelser* (*Stockholm Temptations*), *Blott en dröm* (*Only a Dream*), and *Stockholmsdamernas älskling* (*The Darling of the Stockholm Ladies*), all of which premiered in 1911, and which were constructed around the attractions of Stockholm as a city. At the time of their reception, they were clearly discussed and reviewed in the Swedish press, yet there was little mention of the director: instead, it was the scriptwriter,

Gustaf Uddgren (Anna's husband), who was credited as the creator behind the films. Only one of Hofman-Uddgren's short films—*Fadren*—has survived, and her productive, albeit short, intervention into the Swedish film industry has been overlooked by most film historians. As film historians Marina Dahlquist and Ingrid Stigsdotter have noted, her case is telling for how women have been treated by and in film (history): whereas the work by directors Viktor Sjöström and Mauritz Stiller from the late 1910s and early 1920s have been continuously re-released and celebrated as masterpieces of silent cinema, Hofman-Uddgren and her contemporaries Pauline Brunius and Karin Swanström have received little attention.[14] These three pioneering Swedish women had confirmed directorial credits in the silent era, yet the little research that their work has generated reveals that the priorities of Swedish film historical scholarship has been painstakingly male-centered.

Women actors, on the other hand, received attention by the press, and they have also found their way into Swedish film history scholarship. In fact, during the era of what has become known as the golden age of Swedish cinema, occurring between 1917 and 1924, actors Hilda Borgström, Lili Ziedner, Lili Beck, Stina Berg, and Mary Johnson and somewhat later, Karin Molander and Tora Teje, became synonymous with the Swedish screen—next to a few male actors such as Richard Lund and Lars Hanson, and to filmmakers Victor Sjöström, Mauritz Stiller, and Georg af Klercker.[15] Some of these leading female actors also played protagonist roles, hence breaking with the male dominance that quickly was being established. Early examples of women protagonists are Hilda Borgström's role Ingeborg Holm in Victor Sjöström's social drama of the same name from 1913, and Lili Ziedner's roles in Mauritz Stiller's early short comedies from 1913: *Mannekängen* (*The Mannequin*) (which was never completed) and *Den moderna suffragetten* (*The Modern Suffragette*), which unfortunately is lost (Figure 4.1).[16]

Stiller's later full feature comedies are also worthy of mention since he gave his female actors agency and lots of space to maneuver next to his male leads: in his romantic comedies *Tomas Graals bästa film* (*Tomas Graal's Best Film*, 1917), *Tomas Graals bästa barn* (*Tomas Graal's Best Child*, 1918), and *Eroticon* (1920), Karin Molander plays one of the protagonists, and in the latter, she does so next to the great stage actor Tora Teje. It is also interesting to note that even if most of these Stiller films (from *Den moderna suffragetten* to *Eroticon*) depict modern women who try to put an end to their ascribed position as wife and mother only to end up going back to being docile and loving partners, they clearly express a desire to break free from conventional marital relations and traditional gender

Figure 4.1 Jenny Tschernichin-Larsson as suffragette leader and agitator and Lili Ziedner (situated in the front row, wearing white gloves) in *Den moderna suffragetten/The Modern Suffragette* (Mauritz Stiller, 1913).

roles.[17] In this manner, Stiller's early comedies are indeed pro-feminist as they engage with public discourses and notions about women's societal positioning and personal subjecthood and freedom in a society that is (still) strongly formed by patriarchal values.

While Stiller's humorous portraits of modern women who try to break free offer refreshing and complex images of women on the brink to self-sovereignty and subjecthood, it is probably Hilda Borgström's portrayal of Ingeborg Holm in 1913 that to most spectators has come to symbolize the representation of women on the Swedish screen in the 1910s. *Ingeborg Holm* is a contemporary drama that depicts how poverty destroys families, and as such, it was used as a plea for a reformed social system—causing a vivid social debate, the film actually contributed to changing the Poverty Law in 1918. The film was based on a play by Nils Krok from 1906, and it is a stirring drama about a middle-class woman who, on losing her husband to tuberculosis and, shortly after, losing their newly established business (a grocery store), ends up in the poor house. Considered unfit as a parent, her three children are taken away from her and placed in foster care. These disastrous events and conditions contribute to her mental illness; director Sjöström uses long takes to depict her mental state, one formed by what must be understood as emotional deterritorialization. This is Ingeborg's (and Hilda's) film, and it is one of the earliest motion pictures to focus solely on a woman and her story. Far gone into her social abasement and her madness, one believes that there can be no happy ending, yet, Sjöström suddenly changes Ingeborg's course, and there is redemption as her son Erik returns to see his mother after having spent years at sea, and she slowly comes out of her mental imprisonment and remembers him.

1920s: New Women and Happy Endings

As we have seen, two of Hofman-Uddgren's six films from 1911 were based on short stories by social critic, journalist, and suffragette Elin Wägner: *Hon fick platsen* and *Systrar*, both of which dealt with women at work. In 1923, a film adaptation of Wägner's acclaimed 1908 novel *Norrtullsligan* (*The Norrtull Gang*), based on her serials entitled "The chronicles of Norrtullsligan" published in the daily *Dagens Nyheter* in 1907, premiered—drawing a large audience to the movie theaters and receiving a lot of critical attention.

Norrtullsligan is about four young friends who share a two-room flat while trying to handle work life, friendship, being single, and love—and men's sexual advances and patronizing attitudes.[18] Like many of her other stories, *Norrtullsligan* describes women's changing position as Swedish society is becoming modernized (and a Sweden that slowly is moving toward becoming one of the most socially equal nations worldwide). Wägner sold the film rights of her novel to Karin Swanström, then head of the newly started Bonnierfilm, and later, chief producer and artistic leader at Svensk Filmindustri. The script was written by novelist Hjalmar Bergman, and it was directed by his brother-in-law Per Lindberg.

The film presents the four young women as "new women," that is, as liberated and as sovereign—and as the film opens, one is first led to believe that they together constitute a band of bandits or outlaws (this first interpretation is also due to the title of the film). It soon turns out that they are just hard-working women, struggling with their own set of problems, but with support and care from one another. The main character, "Pegg," is played by the great Tora Teje, and another leading role, "Baby," is played by up-and-coming star Inga Tidblad.

Lili Ziedner—who played the modern suffragette in Stiller's film from 1913—appears in a scene as an agitating suffragette and most possibly also a lesbian, surrounded by other (lesbian) women (and hence, recalling the scene in Stiller's film). *Norrtullsligan* is clearly pro-feminist, engaging with issues concerning women's economic and social standing (and freedom), and openly deals with questions regarding freedom contra marriage, and sex contra love. It is interesting to note that in the Swedish dailies, the film was marketed as *flickornas film*, "the girls' film." And also, that the name of the author of the literary work is attached to the film, so that it is presented as "Elin Wägner's Norrtullsligan" rather than highlighting the name of the film director.[19]

The four characters are presented as street smart, witty, loving, and loyal—and as having an advanced feminist awareness, which most probably is attained from the sexist resistance they encounter daily at work, but also, from more personal experiences of being a woman in a male-dominated society. For example, Pegg is constantly shown caring for her much younger "brother," and as the story progresses, it is being hinted that he is in fact her son, and that she must have had him in her early teens (after being abandoned by the child's father).

While Wägner's novel does not offer a happy ending for the four protagonists, the film does: according to the heteronormative standard that stipulates most film, it ends with romantic fulfillment, and so, our heroines end up in romantic relationships leading to marriage—and to the dissolution of their "band." This end is to be expected, since this is a mainstream film with a popular reach, but it is surely frustrating, not least because of the joyful representations of personal freedom and the sisterly closeness that have foregone the ending. Also, the frivolous and for that time brave depictions of pre-feminist (and lesbian) women make the square straight, ending a true disappointment. Some of the critics at the time also found the ending frustrating. One critic in the evening paper *Aftonbladet* wrote: "Is it absolutely necessary to have such a banal ending to a film with such solid acting? Because of it, this art form will end up being discredited by its more demanding spectators. It is also surprising that Bonnierfilm, departing from such an important literary novel, goes on to change the story."[20]

Three years later, Karin Swanström took on the directing role of another pro-feminist film when filming author Hjalmar Bergman's novel *Flickan i frack* (*The Girl in Tails*) published in 1925. Like *Norrtullsligan* (Figure 4.2), this film deals with women's situation in the Swedish 1920s, the decade that had given women the right to vote (1921) and the right to take up the same occupations as men (1923).

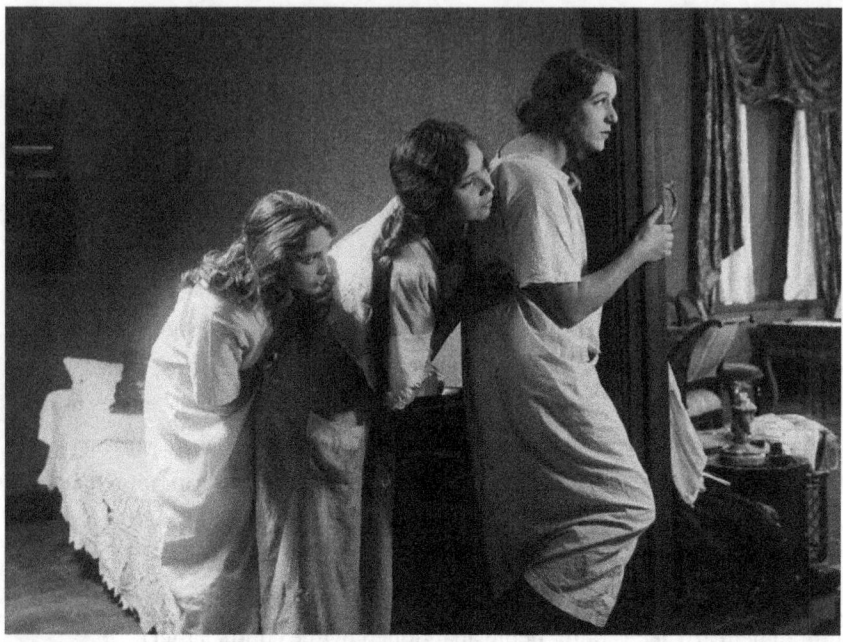

Figure 4.2 Sisterhood, intimacy, and friendship in the adaptation of Elin Wägner's *Norrtullsligan* (Per Lindgren, 1923).

Actor Magda Holm's character Katja is surrounded by stupid and/or misogynistic men (her own father and brother included), and the film depicts women to be smarter and more well behaved than men. After the pivotal scene, when Katja has appeared at the student ball in tails, and smoked cigars and drunk alcohol—to the huge dismay of the other guests—she takes refuge at a mansion inhabited by a group of lesbian intellectuals, led by a fearful feminist (played by Lotten Olsson). It is startling that these early representations of engaged pre-feminist women took their inspiration from existent notions of what lesbian women were supposed to be and look like. Inspired by sexologist descriptions that were spread at the turn of the century and which came to influence popular culture, lesbian women were seen as mannish, that is, as "male souls caught in women's bodies" with their internal masculinity pouring out from underneath.[21] While these cinematic images were constructed to make the audience laugh and must be understood as both homophobic and misogynist, they were also powerful in the way they so explicitly pointed at other ways, other possibilities, to be a woman.

Two years before Swanström's film, the Swedish film industry had gone into a relapse, and the reasons for this were many. Like many other countries,

Sweden experienced an overall economic setback in the early 1920s. In addition, the film industry had, based on its success, made some over investments that did not tally with a fading audience interest for going to the cinema. Another reason was that some of Swedish cinema's most prominent film workers, including Sjöström, Stiller, and Lars Hanson, were lured abroad to Germany and/or Hollywood. Hence, there was a drainage of talent and cinematic competence—but some film workers stayed, Karin Swanström being one of them (and she would take up a leading position as both chief producer and artistic leader at Svensk Filmindustri in the early 1930s, a position she kept until the early 1940s). It was, however, only in the early 1930s that Swedish cinema would rise to popularity and prosperity again: with the introduction of the talkie, and with a new (and older) generation of actors coming out of vaudeville, Swedish cinema turned highly popular within its national borders, focusing on local, contemporary, and well-known themes, "types," and genres.

1930s: Lovable Stereotypes—and Cinematic Emphases on Reproduction

It was in particular the comedy genre with slap stick ingredients, next to a few melodramas, that would prove to be very popular with the domestic audience.[22] Hence, the 1930s offered a clear break with earlier Swedish cinema, known mostly for its technically advanced adaptations from more "serious" literature, or for its elegant, gender-focused, upper-class comedies. In the 1930s, the present was at center, and at its core was the newly constructed "Folk Home"— an imaginary home that was to reflect a new, modern Sweden that was equal, inclusive, content, and thriving. It is interesting to note that while 1930s Hollywood cinema—and its most prominent stars—were popular with the Swedish audience, as with most other national audiences, the Swedish audience cherished its own stars. And it was not only the young and beautiful who reached star positions. In fact, among the most admired stars in the 1930s were the already mentioned Dagmar Ebbesen (a middle-aged and indeed full-bodied actor who most often played the part of the "satkärring," i.e., the unfriendly bitch), Thor Modéen (also full-bodied and middle-aged and often playing the role of the naïve, unrefined but well-meaning uncle), and Edvard Persson (an overweight actor playing the slow, well-meaning southerner).[23] Ebbesen often ended up playing one single stereotype, always type-cast in relation to her not so flattering looks (just like another favorite star of the 1930s, Julia Cæsar, who like Ebbesen, Modéen, and Persson, was also discussed in the previous chapter). In *Kvinnors ansikten* (1991), Tytti Soila describes how 1930s' Swedish cinema served the audience twelve steady female stereotypes in close relation with the dominant patriarchal ideology at the time—while also leaving space for an opposing and resistant female discourse and representation. And Ylva Habel, some ten years later, followed Soila's thread in her "Modern Media, Modern Audiences," analyzing how Swedish cinema was governed by the emergent Social Democratic discourse that emphasized a solidaric, equal, and "class-less-ness" society while also (in the midst of an explicit propaganda for the nation and its citizens to increase its reproduction) pinpointing ethnic Swedish-ness, as well as whiteness, as desirable.[24] This (paradoxical) discourse was perhaps most clearly depicted in Gustaf Edgren's *Valborgsmässoafton* (*Walpurgis Night*) from 1935, in which a blond and innocent-looking Ingrid Bergman plays an ideal woman who is made for marital bliss and childbearing.[25]

Another star who was favored by the audience in the 1930s was the esoteric Gösta Ekman, who came from theater and who had started filming in the early 1910s (playing the young lover) and who had a successful, albeit short, career at the UFA Studios in Berlin in the mid-1920s (playing the lead in F.W. Murnau's *Faust* in 1926). Ekman returned to Sweden with a cocaine addiction that would, together with his heavy workload, lead to his premature death in 1938.[26] Ekman was different from the other Swedish stars during this era: he was handsome, at times effeminate, and still—some twenty years after his breakthrough, and with an appearance that gave away his unhealthy living—playing lover roles. In 1936, he starred in Gustaf Molander's melodrama *Intermezzo* against Inga Tidblad (who played "Baby" in *Norrtullsligan*) and a young Ingrid Bergman. Here, Ekman played Holger Brandt, a middle-aged, world-known violin virtuoso, who is torn between three women (all of whom embody the archetypes outlined by Irigaray): his dedicated and faithful wife Margit (Tidblad); his mistress, the talented piano player Anita (Bergman); and his young daughter Ann-Marie (Britt Hagman), who simply adores her father. While this is a story about infidelity and passion, of (male) fear of aging and of redemption, it is also a film about the resilient love and care for one's child. In the end, it is the longing and love for Ann-Marie and the realization that his duty is to her (and possibly, to his wife and son) that forces Holger to break up with Anita and return home, and to restore the family happiness (Figure 4.3).

Figure 4.3 Young Ann-Marie getting her father Holger's (Gösta Ekman) and everyone else's attention in Gustaf Molander's melodrama *Intermezzo* from 1936.

The film positions Ann-Marie as both narrative and visual center: she stands for pure and unselfish love, and her essence is what will guide Holger to do the right thing. Visually she is positioned and constructed as the light, or the epicenter, in relation to which all adults turn. Dressed in white, with blond curls gathered together by a large white bow, and with the lighting directed toward her, she is the very center and the (only) way forward. Just like *Walpurgis Night*, *Intermezzo* functions as a forceful representation of the current political discourse with a binding focus on the nuclear family and the importance of reproduction.

1940s and 1950s: Women as Image—Still

Swedish film in the 1940s was characterized by the continuous production of dark dramas and lightweight romantic comedies that were rather mediocre—although there are a couple films that stand out, for example, Hasse Ekman's

Flicka med hyacinter (*Girl with Hyacinths*, 1949), a suspense drama about unhappy (lesbian) love, and Arne Sucksdorff's *Människor i stad* (*City People*, 1947), a poetic and impressionistic documentary about Stockholm and its inhabitants (and winner of the Academy Award for best short in 1949).[27] This was also the decade when women directors were conspicuous with their absence: there was only *one* film made by a woman during this decade, namely *Bröllopsnatten* by Danish Bodil Ipsen (1947). The following decade saw an improvement with a doubling in numbers: besides Mimi Pollack's *Rätten att älska*, two-time director Barbro Boman made *Det är aldrig för sent* (1956), based on her own script. While women's presence behind the camera was next to non-existent, they continued to be noticeable on screen. Mai Zetterling was one actor who lit up the screen, and she is of interest to us because after filming in the UK and in Hollywood in the late 1940s and the 1950s, she started making feature films. Her breakthrough as an actor came in 1944 with *Hets* (*Torment*), a drama directed by Alf Sjöberg with a script by Ingmar Bergman, and then, in 1946, she starred in *Driver dagg faller regn*, which was filmed by Gustaf Edgren and based on a novel by Margit Söderholm. And then, in 1948, she starred in Bergman's fourth feature, the romantic drama *Musik i mörker* (*Music in Darkness*), which was based on a script by female novelist and scriptwriter Dagmar Edqvist.

In the 1950s, Bergman proved crucial for Swedish film production and its reputation with award-winning films such as *Summer with Monika*, *Seventh Seal*, *Smiles of a Summer Night*, *Wild Strawberries*, and *Virgin Spring*. But so did the many women characters in his films and, more so, the women who played them: Eva Dahlbeck, Harriet Andersson, Ingrid Thulin, and Bibi Andersson soon became the new faces of Swedish femininity, and these women were modern, self-sufficient, and forceful. In Bergman's films, women take the lead since they are always more complex and interesting than their male counterparts (who were, in Bergman's own words, "children with adult genitals"). Women, in Bergman's films, talk and reflect over their being in the world—situated as they are as women in a patriarchal setting that strives to hold them back. In a film such as *Nära livet* (*Brink of Life*, 1958), based on a novel by Ulla Isaksson, women's voices and women's discourse is at the center—as is their silence, as exemplified by the character Cissi (Ingrid Thulin) who, when cared for at the maternity clinic after an abortion, starts to express herself for the first time. The film is portraying a female dominion *par excellence*, and it is one in which women dare to speak up and to share their most inner feelings and experiences.

And while many of Bergman's films from the 1950s focus on the situation of women in a modern and patriarchal society, this focus only became more central to his films of the 1960s, with *Tystnaden* (*The Silence*, 1963) and *Persona* (1966) as prime examples. And while woman as both image and as narrative motor is absolutely key here, and as Bergman and his women leads became synonymous with Swedish film in the 1950s, it must also be emphasized that many of the women working with Bergman *behind* the camera also proved to be of uttermost importance. Ulla Isaksson, a novelist and scriptwriter on whose work some of his films are based; Katinka Faragó, first script girl and later production leader and producer; Marik Vos, costume designer; Bibi Lindström, set designer; and Ulla Ryghe, editor, were all crucial to the success that his films would gain, not least internationally. Of these five, Faragó is worth a specific mention: they worked together for three decades and made no less than twenty-five film and TV productions together. Their first collaboration took place in 1955 (when Faragó was in her teens) for *Kvinnodröm* (*Dreams*) and their last collaboration was on *De två saliga* (*The Blessed Ones*, 1986), the latter was based on a script by Ulla Isaksson. Faragó and Bergman were, next to a few actors (Liv Ullmann, Harriet Andersson, and Erland Josephson), each other's longest lasting collaborator.

1960s: Mai Zetterling Paving the Way

The 1960s proved to be a decade in which Sweden became famous for its equality and gender politics, and for its sexual liberation—the utmost outcomes of three decades of a successful Social Democracy. And Bergman's films, still focusing on women, came to function as a kind of display window for this politics. But there were other directors who also offered cinematic representations of this new gender politics in Swedish cinema: out of these, Mai Zetterling came to the fore, making no fewer than four feature films before the end of the decade.

The 1960s—with its various political and feminist movements inflecting Swedish society, and with the inauguration of the Film School at the SFI—proved to be a time when a window was being opened for women to enter the film industry (again). Young talents were enrolled in the Film School, and later, in the 1970s, many of them started to work for Sveriges Television (SVT; Swedish public television) under what were rather free and generous terms.[28] In the first generation of film school educated filmmakers we find Ingela Romare,

Mai Wechselmann, and Marianne Ahrne, all three predominantly making documentary films, but there are others who did not go through film school and who still managed to make a name for themselves, such as Christina Olofson and actor turned director Mai Zetterling.

Zetterling is interesting, not least for her insistence on focusing on women's stories and portraying these women in ways that clearly broke with existent cinematic gender norms.[29] All of them, although not favorably met by the critics when they premiered, have come to reach a certain critical acclaim, not least in feminist circles and in feminist film scholarship.[30] These four films—*Älskande par* (*Loving Couples*, 1964), *Nattlek* (1966), *Doktor Glas* (1968), and *Flickorna* (*The Girls*, 1968)—were big productions, and Zetterling managed to enroll some of Swedish cinema's most famous actors, many of whom were part of Ingmar Bergman's "stable."

The Girls deals with issues that are feminist and socially political, and it is experimental both in terms of narration and cinematography. The film focuses on three women friends and actors who tour Sweden to perform *Lysistrata*, and all of whom are discontented with their private life: Gunilla (Gunnel Lindblom) has a string of needy kids and is married ("to what must be the world's most boring man by far"), Liz (Bibi Andersson) is married to a man who constantly cheats on her and who dislikes her having a career of her own, and Marianne (Harriet Andersson) has a child with an elderly, married man, which makes her the "other" woman. Zetterling uses different narrative levels to tell the story and she mixes "reality" scenes with beautifully constructed daydream scenes that invite the spectator to share the girls' inner thoughts and struggles. These dreamlike (yet extraordinarily sharp and clear) scenes are highlighted in a chiaroscuro that serves to heighten the three women's internal monologues.

The film critics were harsh and showed no understanding for the film and its qualities—in fact, Zetterling's experimental language was questioned and critiqued for *not* being innovative and for merely copying Bergman and Fellini: "[*The Girls*] is like old unrefined cotton [*fetvadd*] that is lying there, decomposing after Bergman and Fellini."[31] And further, that she was a "common" director, and not a proper filmmaker, since she was merely a translator, not a creator.[32] One critic launched out with a far cry from his man cave, calling it "congested menstruations."[33] Yet, *The Girls* is an exceptional film that uses humor, self-reflexivity, and an avant-garde film language to discuss sexual difference, patriarchy, and female subordination, and in doing so, it is in itself a kind of social critique. The "girls" are struggling to become free, yet find themselves caught in their own fear of changing the status quo. They are torn between freedom and security, between the unknown and boredom, between obedience and power. And the film expands and embraces a critique of patriarchy *at large* since these women are never taken seriously by men, be it their director, the male journalist, or their husbands and/or lovers. They are, in men's eyes, only "girls," hence refusing them both power and subjecthood. It is of course no coincidence that Zetterling chose acting as her vocation: as a former actor, she was most probably aware of the gap between acting as in *actively doing* and acting as in *performing*. The dilemma, or the double bind, that women actors find themselves caught in when trying to move from being image to becoming agent, from object to subject, is ironically addressed in *The Girls*, and the film constitutes a counter critique to how the critics had chosen to purposely misread Zetterling's previous two films. While her critique is subtle, it is still explicit; yet the critics (again) chose to interpret her work as naïve, mimicking others, and undeveloped. Yet, a couple of years after its premier, *The Girls* had reached a canonical status as a feminist masterpiece, and Zetterling was hailed as one of the most important feminist filmmakers internationally of her time. She also came to play a central role in what was to become an international feminist film culture and movement, starting in 1975 with "Film Women International."[34]

The Girls was made at a time when many Swedish film productions were tainted by a leftist, or even radical, impetus, depicting the poor and the abused, and pointing out society as a dominant perpetrator.[35] Victims—whether immigrants (as in *Jag heter Stelios*), young working-class mothers (as in *Jänken*), or felons (as in *Ni ljuger*)—were given center stage. Yet, it was issues regarding social and economic class that were put forward, and issues of ethnicity, gender, and sexuality were made less important. One may therefore suspect that some of the critique that Zetterling's film received was shaped by the fact that it was considered too women-focused (and also, too focused on middle-class women). In *The Girls*, Swedish society (and its class system) is not the main problem, *partriarchy* is.

And here, for Zetterling, speech and representation are both central to countering patriarchy. And letting the girls speak (for her), she anticipates Julia Lesage's statement that "The self-conscious act of telling one's story as a woman in a politicized yet personal way gives [...] women's conversation [...] a new social force as a tool for liberation."[36]

Conclusion

In all of the films discussed above, from the early 1920s to the late 1960s, the representation of women who deviate from mainstream representations is at the center. All films depict women who, in different ways and through somewhat different strategies, struggle to create their own place in a society that is male-dominated. From the "band" of best friends in *Norrtullsligan*, via the daughter, the mother, and the mistress (clearly impersonating the three archetypes) in *Intermezzo*, and the intimate (yet contested) relations between childbearing women in *Nära livet*, to the feisty colleagues and friends in *Flickorna* (The Girls), women are pluralistic as well as individualistic. They are young, they are middle-aged, they are modern, "new" women, they are socially aware, they are political, they are working class, middle class, they are sexually liberated, or they are single with no desire to enter a (hetero)sexual relationship—but they all demand that they be taken seriously and that they be listened to.

In fact, language (and voice), next to image, is a central issue in all of these films. Even in *Norrtullsligan*, a silent film, language holds a central role in connection to women's liberation and subjecthood: the film depicts the feminist event as one clearly structured by speech and vocal agitation. The women's thoughts and voices come through in the intertitles, many of which are taken directly from Wägner's witty novel and which clearly explains and expresses the very situation that they find themselves in. In *Intermezzo*, it is not so much the image of the young Ann-Marie that lures Holger back—it is her voice. It is telling that while his wife sadly expresses her feelings to him, loud and clear, he does not seem to hear her. But when separated from his family, he can hear his young daughter, and it is her voice that pulls him back. And in Bergman's 1950s as well as 1960s films, women talk and talk and they do have a lot to say—they see through the fakeness of it all and they see clearly their own position as women, while the men can only produce insignificant statements, as if detached from relationships and from themselves, and hence, from life.[37]

In *Flickorna* (The Girls), the three actors own and control language on stage—but it is one written by someone else, the Greek comic playwright Aristophanes. In real life they seem to be "lacking" language: they talk without form or proper content, and they often search for words and help fill in each other's statements. While this is clearly a whimsical way of expressing their thoughts, it is also one that may be understood as counter-patriarchal. Following Hélène Cixous, it is through the "sweeping away syntax," that is, abandoning the linear and orderly (that is associated with traditional masculine style), that feminine speech can serve to uncover the inherent shortcomings of male speech.[38] By speaking in contradictions, she argues, women call attention to the fact that they do not, cannot, express their inner thoughts, and so, they expose the inadequacies of patriarchal language.

In a similar vein, Irigaray pushes for women to isolate themselves to develop a language of their own since they, in the current (and historical) patriarchal confinement, are locked within male language, a language that is not, cannot, and should not be theirs.[39] In *Flickorna* (The Girls), it is only in their daydreams, when reflecting over their life situation—highlighted in dramatic chiaroscuro—that they seem to "find" language: here, they speak and express their inner thoughts, their true desires. Dreams, then, the film seems to point out, are necessary for their possible liberation. The personal is political, or becomes political, when the personal is outspoken—first to oneself and then in relation to others: the "I" becomes a subject when relating to others, "The subject ... cannot remain a subject if it is voiceless."[40] Yet, in all of these films, *The Girls* included, the women characters are always represented via their (indeed, ideal) bodies, even when they express the need to be listened to and to be taken seriously. So indoctrinated is their conception of their self with the embodiment and performance of an attractive femininity, that they cannot—or will not—refuse this embodiment for actual change to happen. Trained to "perform the feminine," they are ultimately incapable of de-objectifying their physical presentation and presence for any real change to occur.

With the 1970s, women filmmakers' perception and representation of their embodiment—and their very strive for change—take on new expressions, as we will see in Chapter 5. Before that, however, we will turn to Bibi Lindström, who, in the role of "film architect," worked in what is often termed a "below-the line" position, yet whose work was indeed crucial to the many films she worked on in the mid-twentieth century.

Notes

1 Shohini Chaudhuri, *Feminist Film Theorists* (London: Routledge 2006), 61.
2 See, for example, Marjorie Rosen, *Popcorn Venus: Women, Movies, and the American Dream* (New York: Avon Books 1973); Molly Haskell, *From Reverence to Rape* (New York: Holt, Rinehart and Winston, 1974); Tytti Soila, "Kvinnors

ansikte: stereotyper och kvinnlig identitet i trettiotalets svenska filmmelodram" (Ph.D. dissertation, Stockholm University, 1991); Richard Dyer, *The Matter of Images* (London: Routledge, 1993).

3   Luce Irigaray, *This Sex which is not One* (1977; Ithaca, NY: Cornell University Press, 1985).
4   Dyer, *The Matter of Images*.
5   H. Neroni, *Feminist Film Theory and Cleo from 5 to 7* (London: Bloomington Academics, 2016).
6   It is not farfetched to compare the mother archetype with the "mothering" role on the film set—in our interviews, film producer Katinka Faragó talks about having to sit with Ingmar Bergman to comfort him before rehearsals, and about being called in to "clean up" on film productions that risked going bad. Interviews held with Faragó on several occasions in 2018 and 2019.
7   See Teresa de Lauretis, *Technologies of Gender* (Bloomington: Indiana University Press, 1987). The view of film as a technology of gender relates to film scholar Richard Dyer's long-time work on the "matter of representation." See Richard Dyer, *Gays and Film* (London: BFI, 1977), *Now You See It* (London: Routledge, 1991), *The Matter of Images*, and *WHITE* (London: Routledge, 1997). He emphasizes that representations are always *presentations*, and that "there is simply no such thing as unmediated access to reality" (Dyer, *The Matter of Images*, 3). Cultural forms always entail the use of available codes and conventions, and these forms are in turn dependent on time and space, and hence changeable. The codes: "restrict and shape what can be said by and/or about any aspect of reality in a given place in a given society at a given time, but if that seems like a limitation on saying, it is also what makes saying possible at all" (Dyer, *The Matter of Images*, 2). Accordingly, cultural forms do not have "single determinate meanings": we understand and read them differently because of our access to specific codes, which in turn depends on our social, cultural, economic, gendered, and ethnic context.
8   See, for example, Laura Mulvey, "Visual Pleasure and Narrative Cinema," *Screen*, vol. 16, no. 3 (1975), 6–18; Annette Kuhn, *Women's Pictures* (London: Verso, 1982); Teresa de Lauretis, *Alice Doesn't* (Bloomington: Indiana University Press, 1984), *Technologies of Gender*; Linda Williams, "Film Bodies: Gender, Genre, and Excess," *Film Quarterly*, vol. 44, no. 4 (1989), 2–13, *Hard Core* (Los Angeles: University of California Press, 1991); Patricia Erens, *Issues in Feminist Film Criticism* (Bloomington: Indiana University Press, 1990); and Diane Carson, Linda Dittmar, and Janice Welsch (eds.), *Multiple Voices in Feminist Film Criticism* (Minneapolis: University of Minnesota Press, 1994). Sandy Flitterman-Lewis, *To Desire Differently* (New York: Columbia University Press, 1996).
9   See, for example, Teresa de Lauretis, "Aesthetics and Feminist Theory: Rethinking Women's Cinema," in Diane Carson, Linda Dittmar, and Janice Welsch (eds.),

Multiple Voices in Feminist Film Criticism (1985; Minneapolis: University of Minnesota Press, 1994); and Liz Borden's film *Born in Flames* (USA, 1983).

10 See, for example, Chris Holmlund, "Masculinity as Multiple Masquerade," in Steven Cohan and Ina Rae Hark (eds.), *Screening the Male: Exploring Masculinities in Hollywood Cinema* (London: Routledge, 1993); Yvonne Tasker, "Dumb Movies for Dumb People: Masculinity, the Body, and the Voice in Contemporary Action Cinema," in Steven Cohan and Ina Rae Hark (eds.), *Screening the Male: Exploring Masculinities in Hollywood Cinema* (London: Routledge, 1993); Steven Cohan, *Masked Men: Masculinity and the Movies in the Fifties* (Bloomington: Indiana University Press, 1997); Louise Wallenberg, "Straight Heroes with Queer Inclinations," in Sean Griffin (ed.), *Hetero: Queering Representations of Straightness* (New York: State University of New York Press, 2009).

11 Kaja Silverman, *The Accoustic Mirror* (Bloomington: Indiana University Press, 1988).

12 Kaja Silverman, "Dis-embodying the Female Voice" (1984), quoted in Chaudhuri, *Feminist Film Theorists*, 45.

13 On women and voice in the cinema, see Mary Ann Doane, "The Voice in the Cinema: The Articulation of Body and Space," *Yale French Studies*, vol. 60, no. 60 (1980), 33–50, and *The Desire to Desire: The Woman's Film of the 1940s* (Bloomington: Indiana University Press, 1987).

14 See Marina Dahlquist, "A Queen in Her Own Right," Nordic Women in Film, February 2018, https://www.nordicwomeninfilm.com/a-queen-in-her-own-right/, accessed September 6, 2022; and Ingrid Stigsdotter, "En skandalomsusad pionjär," Nordic Women on Film, February 2016, https://www.nordicwomeninfilm.com/emelie-gor-film-om-sin-mormors-mormor-en-skandalomsusad-pionjar/, accessed September 15, 2002. For a similar negligence in the US silent film industry, see, for example, Jane Gaines, *Pink-Slipped: What Happened to Women in the Silent Film Industries?* (Champaign: University of Illinois, 2018).

15 The "Golden Age of Swedish Silent Cinema," was a cinematic period stretching approximately from 1913 to 1924, with films that were hailed internationally. For an overview of the era, see, for example, Tommy Gustafsson, *En fiende till civilisationen: manlighet, genusrelationer, sexualitet och rasstereotyper i svensk filmkultur under 1920-talet* (Lund: Sekel, 2007); Gustafsson, *Masculinity in the Golden Age of Swedish Cinema: A Cultural Analysis of 1920s Films* (Jefferson, NC: MacFarland, 2014).

16 According to several reviews published after *Den moderna suffragetten* premiered, it was Lili Ziedner who had written the film script.

17 See Louise Wallenberg, "Stilleristic Women: Gender Ambivalence in the Films of Mauritz Stiller," *Aura: Filmvetenskaplig tidskrift*, vol. 6, no. 4 (2000), 36–46, and "Moden, makar och masker. Modets funktion i två filmer av Mauritz Stiller," in

Dirk Gindt and Louise Wallenberg (eds.), *MODE: en tvärvetenskaplig introduktion* (Stockholm: Raster förlag, 2008), 250–72.

18 It should be noted that in 1923, the so-called *behörighetslagen* (Competence Law) passed in Sweden, a law that formally guaranteed women and men equal right to all public professions and positions in society, with certain specified exceptions.

19 It should also be noted that while the film script was written by Hjalmar Bergman, and the film was directed by Per Lindberg, Lindberg was married to Stina Bergman, who was Hjalmar's sister, and that she, after her husband's death, came to head the first scriptwriting department at SF. And although Stina Bergman remained a loyal warden of her husband's literary heritage throughout her life, it has been claimed that she was actually the uncredited co-author of all Hjalmar Bergman's film scripts in the early 1920s. See "Stina Bergman – i skuggan av Hjalmar" [Stina Bergman – In the Shadow of Hjalmar], Nordic Women in Film, May 2016, https://www.nordicwomeninfilm.com/stina-bergman-i-skuggan-av-hjalmar/, accessed September 4, 2022.

20 Orig. "Skall det vara absolut nödvändigt att i ett övrigt fullt acceptabelt filmskådespel ha ett banalt slut? Härigenom bringas denna konstgren i en ofta oförtjänt misskredit hos mera kräsna åskådare. I alla händelser överraskar det att Bonnierfilm, som utgår från ett fullviktigt litterärt stoff så där utan vidare gör om händelseförloppet."

21 See, for example, Esther Newton, "The Mythic Mannish Lesbian: Radclyffe Hall and the New Woman," *Signs*, vol. 9, no. 4 (Summer 1984), 557–75.

22 See, for example, Leif Furhammar, *Från skapelsen till Edvard Persson* (Stockholm: Wahlström & Widstrand, 1970), *Folklighetsfabriken* (Stockholm: PAN/Norstedt, 1979), and *Filmen i Sverige* (Stockholm: Dialogos and SFI, 2003).

23 See, for example, Furhammar, *Från skapelsen till Edvard Persson*; Furhammar, *Filmen i Sverige*.

24 Ylva Habel, "Modern Media, Modern Audiences," Ph.D. dissertation, Stockholm University, 2002.

25 For a discussion of *Valborgsmässoafton*, not least for its close connection to Alva and Gunnar Myrdal's famed book *Kris i befolkningsfrågan* (*Crisis in the Population Issue*) from 1934, see Tytti Soila, "Sweden," in Tytti Soila, Astrid Söderbergh Widding, and Gunnar Iversen (eds.), *Nordic National Cinema* (London: Routledge, 1998), and Wallenberg, "Straight Heroes with Queer Inclinations."

26 Wallenberg, "Straight Heroes with Queer Inclinations."

27 According to Fredrik Gustafsson, the 1940s are not as mediocre as described here: instead, he argues that a lot of effort was put into filmmaking, not least by screen writers, producers, and directors and that this paved the way for a "new wave" and, also, that this joint effort laid the foundation for the more prosperous 1950s. See

Fredrik Gustafsson, "Swedish Cinema of the 1940s, A New Wave," in Mette Hjort and Ursula Lindqvist (eds.), *A Companion to Nordic Cinema* (Malden, MA: John Wiley and Sons, 2016).

28 In our interviews, this was mentioned in particular by filmmakers Christina Olofson (interviewed on March 23, 2018) and Mai Wechselmann (interviewed on December 21, 2018).

29 Zetterling had made two films in the UK prior to her Swedish films, one of which was the short film *The War Game* (1962), nominated for a BAFTA award. It should also be noted that Zetterling had started out as an actress in the 1940s, and had become an international star in the UK and in Hollywood in the 1950s, filming with Danny Kay, Tyrone Power, and Dirk Bogarde.

30 See, for example, Mariah Larsson, *A Cinema of Obsession: The Life and Work of Mai Zetterling* (Madison: University of Wisconsin Press, 2019); Tytti Soila, *Att synliggöra det dolda: om fyra svenska kvinnors filmregi* (Stockholm: Brutus Östlings förlag Symposium, 2004); Lucy Fischer, *Shot/Counter Shot* (Princeton, NJ: Princeton University Press, 1989), "Feminist Forms of Address: Mai Zetterling's Loving Couples," in Kristin L. Hole, Dijana Jelača, E. Kaplan, and Patrice Petro (eds.), *The Routledge Companion to Cinema and Gender* (London: Routledge, 2017); Ingrid Ryberg, "An Elevated Feminist ahead of Her Time?" in Ingrid Stigsdotter (ed.), *Making the Invisible Visible: New Approaches to Reclaiming Women's Agency in Film History* (Stockholm: Nordic Academic Press, 2019), and "Revidera historien om auteuren Mai Zetterling!" [Revise the Story of Auteur Mai Zetterling!], Nordic Women in Film, December 2018, http://www.nordicwomeninfilm.com/revidera-historien-om-auteuren-mai-zetterling/, accessed September 6, 2022. Zetterling has also been at the center of a new generation of filmmakers, see, for example, the films *Regissören: en film om Mai Zetterling* (Lena Jordebro, 2015) and *The Woman Who Cleaned the World* (Fia-Stina Strandlund, forthcoming).

31 Bo Strömstedt, "Jag ser ...," *Expressen*, September 23, 1968.

32 Jurgen Schuldt, review in *Aftonbladet*, 1968.

33 Strömstedt, translation from "Vilka förstockade menstruationer!"

34 See Ryberg, "Revidera historien om auteuren Mai Zetterling!"

35 Cecilia Mörner, "Vissa visioner. Tendenser i svensk biografdistribuerad fiktionsfilm, 1967–1972" (Ph.D. dissertation, Stockholm University, 2000). See, for example, *Jänken* (Lars Forsberg, 1970), *Ni ljuger* (Vilgot Sjöman, 1969), *Jag heter Stelios* (Johan Bergenstråhle, 1972), *Deserter USA* (Lars Lambert and Olle Sjögren, 1970), *Misshandlingen* (Lars Lennart Forsberg, 1969), and *Made in Sweden* (Johan Bergenstråhle, 1969). It should be pointed out that these 'leftist' films were—to a certain degree—financed by the two private, and dominating, film productions companies SF and Sandrews.

36 Julia Lesage, "The Political Aesthetics of the Feminist Documentary Film," *Quarterly Review of Film Studies*, vol. 3, no. 4 (1978), 520.
37 See, for example, Bergman's *En lektion i kärlek* (*A Lesson in Love*, 1954), *Sommarnattens leende* (*Smiles of a Summer Night*, 1955), and *För att inte tala om alla dessa kvinnor* (*All These Women*, 1964).
38 Hélène Cixous, "The Laugh of the Medusa," *Signs*, vol. 1, no. 4 ([1975] 1976), 875–93, 886. Translated by Keith and Paula Cohen.
39 Irigaray, *This Sex which is not One*.
40 Tzvetan Todorov, *Mikhail Bakhtin: The Dialogical Principle* (Minneapolis: University of Minnesota Press, 1984), 18.

5

Women on Screen II

1970s–2010s

Louise Wallenberg

Introduction

This chapter picks up where Chapter 4 left off, offering a discussion of how women have been represented on screen in Swedish film from the 1970s up till the late 2010s. If the 1960s still proved difficult, with only a small handful of women filmmakers—including actor turned director Mai Zetterling—given the chance to make films for a larger audience, the following decade turned out to be more inclusive.[1] The 1970s allowed for more women to enter the industry to tell their (and others') stories, not least through their continuous enrollment and presence in the Film School and through the financial support that was offered from Sveriges Television (SVT; Swedish public television). The 1970s also saw the proliferation of the organization Svenska kvinnors filmförbund (Swedish Women Filmmakers' Association), an organization through which women film workers, including film scholars and critics, could join forces, share experiences, and exercise some pressure on a system that still was characterized by inequality and imbalance in terms of representation both in front of and behind the camera.

Following a similar chronological structure as in Chapter 4, the focus is put on a handful of films, all of which were made to "represent" a certain decade in Swedish film history. But whereas the previous chapter on women on screen only concentrated on feature films, this chapter takes into account films that belong to different genres, some of which also strive to blur the boundary between fiction and non-fiction. Further, this chapter looks solely at cinematic representations of women made by women, whereas the previous chapter looked at representations made by both women and men. Another difference between these two text-focused chapters concerns methodology: in Chapter 4, covering the years between the early 1900s and the late 1960s, the filmmakers focused upon are all no longer alive, hence I used visual analysis as my main method. For this chapter, I will use mixed methods, combining visual analysis with an ethnographic approach. The films under discussion are all made by women whom we have interviewed during the interval of our project, hence their stories and recollections from working on specific film productions constitute an important and complimentary addition to the visual analysis offered.[2] While the visual analysis accounts for women's portrayal and presence on screen, the ethnographic approach allows me to consider personal experiences of actually being present in the industry, as well as experiences of having had to struggle for authority and power. And so, while women's portrayal continues to be the focus, questions of presence and power will come into play since they figure in the interview material that will be used to support and nuance the analysis. Just like in Chapter 4, many films will be left out, and the selection made is informed both by my personal preference and by the interviews: when choosing films for analysis, I have been constricted by films made by women we have interviewed. And yet, not all of our interview participants will be represented or even referred to here. However, they do figure in other parts of this book.

The first film to be discussed is Gunnel Lindblom's award-winning drama *Paradistorg* (*Summer Paradise*, 1977), followed, in chronological order, by Suzanne Osten's semi-autobiographical drama *Mamma* (*Mother*, 1982), Christina Olofson's documentary *I rollerna tre* (*Lines from the Heart*, 1996), Maria Hedman Hvitfeldt's short children's film *Min skäggiga mamma* (*My Bearded Mum*, 2003) and Mia Engberg's semi-autobiographical and experimental *Lucky One* (2019).[3] However, before taking on the films, the chapter offers a short discussion of the relation of image and sound and of the experiences of women filmmakers when trying to deviate from existent gender stereotypes. This section will serve as a somewhat loosely constructed theoretical and empirical framework for the visual analyses that will follow.

Image, Sound, and Resisting Gender Stereotyping

While image has continued to be at the center for any discussion of women's representation on screen, whether analog or digital, so has sound—and the representation and existence of women's voices and narratives.[4] We have already touched upon how women's voices on screen historically have been tied to their bodily presentation or erotic spectacle through crying, screaming, and panting, and that when a woman's voice is made thwarted, as in mainstream film, it cannot be given any authoritative voice in the narrative.[5] Yet, in the films discussed in the first chapter on women on screen, all the films—whether made by women or men, whether mainstream or more artistic—proved to problematize women's need and desire for a voice of their own. In many ways, all of those films worked, however implicitly (as in *Norrtullsligan/The Norrtull Gang* or *Intermezzo*) or explicitly (as in *Nära livet /Brink of Life* or *Flickorna/The Girls*), to expose how women's voices and narratives are being suppressed and made insignificant in patriarchal society. Yet, all of those films still fell into the trap of tying the voice with the (erotic) body, sound and image, emphasizing—again—woman as image. Even in Zetterling's *The Girls*, this is the case: the three women are always represented via their (fashionable and ideal) bodies, and *as bodies*, even when they emphasize that they need to be listened to. So ingrained is their conception of their subjecthood with the embodiment and performance of an attractive femininity, that they cannot—will not—refuse this embodiment for any real change to happen.

Silverman argues that it is (only) in experimental feminist film practices, with a clear aim to challenge mainstream as well as malestream film, that one can find any possible liberation of the female voice from its referencing to its body. And that it is (only) by detaching the voice from the body that old stereotypes can be challenged and destructed, leaving space for new images and voices to be visualized and expressed.[6] Many experimental filmmakers have tried (see, e.g., *She Must be Seeing Things* and *Surname Nam, Given Name Vet*), with more or less successful results. Within Swedish film culture, filmmaker and producer Mia Engberg, who has been making films since the mid-1990s, stands out in her striving to counter and deconstruct stereotypical images of women by the use of disembodied sound. In her two most recent films, *Belleville Baby* (2013) and *Lucky One* (2019), both of which must be described as experimental to their form, she explores a politics and aesthetics of detachment by employing a clearly disembodied narration through her relentless taking control over the voice-over. This aesthetic and narrational grip constitute a refusal of being tied to the body (as sexed and as eroticized), and hence, it is a way to free the voice to narrate her own story, a *herstory*.

When interviewing Engberg, she was explicit about the resistance and constant questioning she has met from producers and financiers when trying to represent women characters that break with female stereotypes.[7] When making her latest feature film, *Lucky One* (2019), her choice of representing one of her characters, a young woman who is a victim of sex trafficking, was being critiqued. The French

Film Institute was approached (the film takes place in Paris to a large degree) to partly help finance the film, but she was told that they found her "portrayal of the prostitute too unnuanced since she wants to get out of prostitution" (hence insinuating that most prostitutes, even those who have been forced, want to keep on selling sex). Further, they were critical of Engberg not visually exploiting the fact that she was a prostitute, since she never "is showing the prostitute women naked."[8] Engberg also hoped to screen her film at the Cannes Film Festival and have it judged by the committee, but was told that her use of a female voice-over was too much: "These men, especially the French men of this committee, had said that they found the female voice over 'provoking and bossy' and that they felt sorry for this poor man who was to be led by this female voice. They did not only find the film to be bad, to they were provoked by it."

Through our interviews, it has become clear that Engberg's experience of having her representations questioned is shared with other women filmmakers. Breaking with conformity to gendered stereotyping calls for mistrust and critique, and women filmmakers find themselves being questioned especially when trying to create more complex and individual women characters for the screen. To try and represent women differently, that is women who deviate from the three archetypes described by Luce Irigaray (1977)—that is, the mother, the virgin, and the prostitute—is seen as controversial and, hence, these efforts are met with resistance.[9] Director Gunnel Lindblom was met with such resistance when she asked to have her film *Paradistorg* (*Summer Paradise*, 1977), a film focusing on two middle-aged women, screened at the Cannes Film Festival, and we will have reason to come back to this when discussing the film.

As for representing men, our interview participants have experienced much less resistance and questioning, which goes hand in hand with the fact that men on screen are allowed to be diverse and complex—and to act out a multitude of roles.[10] It is, however, interesting to note that when our participants were questioned regarding their portrayal of male characters, the critique regarded either the lack of male protagonists or the fact that the narrative focus was on two male protagonists. In the first scenario the director was questioned for excluding men from her story, and in the second, for thinking that she—*as a woman*—could portray men and male friendship. Director Lisa Ohlin, known for a number of critically acclaimed feature films made in the early 2000s, told us how she was involved in strenuous discussions regarding the female protagonist in her most recent film, and concluded: "Well, generally, women characters are being questioned so much more, but that is because men have a much bigger register of accepted behaviors and expressions. It is very much about the woman being *likeable*, someone [a man] has to be interested in her."[11] And she summed it all up when saying: "It is still grander with films made by men. End of story... Men are allowed to portray women, but as a woman you are being questioned when making a film about men, *and* when making a film about women. ... No matter what you do, it is wrong." This makes a very clear example of the double bind that permeates the industry when it comes to women film workers. Thus, this double bind was indeed already in place when women film workers were given the possibility to make films in the 1960s and 1970s: no matter what they did—whether in terms of portrayal, narration, and/or aesthetics—it was considered to be wrong by most critics.

1970s: A Paradise of and for Women? Gunnel Lindblom's *Paradistorg* (1977)

Societal change can happen quickly, and feminist demands and activism did come to reform Swedish society to a certain degree in the late 1960s and 1970s. While patriarchy constituted the problem in a film like *Flickorna* (*The Girls*), ten years later women's liberation and freedom were represented as possibly problematic—at least in relation to the next generation. In Gunnel Lindblom's film debut *Paradistorg* (1977), women's newly won freedom is discussed and ventilated between women themselves. *Paradistorg* was an international success when it came out, and it is indeed an interesting film to study not least because it is one that fully focuses on women and women's relations. Lindblom, known for her many roles in Ingmar Bergman's films, was offered to direct *Paradistorg*, based on the novel by Ulla Isaksson,[12] when Ingmar Bergman all of a sudden felt the urge to flee the country due to accusations of tax avoidance. Bergman had planned to film the novel, having worked closely with Isaksson before on two of his films in the 1950s, but asked Lindblom to step in as director, with him as producer.[13] It is interesting to note that after filming *The Silence* together in 1963, and following a dispute about Lindblom demanding a body double for her "nude" scenes, Bergman had left her out in the cold for a decade.[14] In 1973, when filming the TV series *Scenes from a Marriage*, he had approached her to play a small part, and she was also his assistant director for some work on screen and in the theater, and then in 1976, as he escaped to Germany, he turned to her to direct his next project. Lindblom decided to go for a next to all-woman crew—from production leader, scriptwriter, editor, and costume designer to set designer. This, she says, was a "conscious decision."[15]

Paradistorg is a story about relationships, friendship, and family. It takes place during a long summer vacation at a private family villa—called "Paradistorg" (Paradise square) by its three generations of inhabitants—situated on an island in the archipelago outside of Stockholm. The focus is Katha (Brigitta Valberg) (Figure 5.1), a middle-aged woman who runs her own medical practice and who is single, and her loving relations with her closest family members—her two daughters Sassa and Annika, her three grandchildren Eva, Kajsa, and Tomas, and her aging parents Alma and Holger. Adding to her family is her best friend of thirty-five years, Emma (Sif Ruud), a social worker (who, like Katha, is single), and an elderly married couple, Saga and Oscar, who help her parents with the household. Paradistorg is early on presented as a place of dreams and memories—many of which are tainted by a certain nostalgia. When Sassa invites her new boyfriend Puss to come with her to Paradistorg, she dreamingly describes it, in a close-up, as a place that "smells of apples and newly baked buns." Yet, by some, it is seen as suffocating and delimiting: to Emma it is a place full of bourgeois traditions and conventions, and trying to convince Katha not

Figure 5.1 On the film set of Gunnel Lindblom's *Paradistorg* (*Summer Paradise*, 1976). Lindblom at the center of the picture and Birgitta Valberg (Katha) to the right.

to go there, she reminds her that when returning to the city in late August, she is always so "tired, moody and angry after having spent two months in the comfort of the family." And Annika's husband Ture, an art critic, dreads the place so much that he makes sure to schedule his work travels abroad in the summer not to have to go there (and when he shows up on midsummer evening, unexpectedly, he sneaks into the basement and lures Annika down there to feed and bathe him—and Katha's earlier comment to Annika that she has *"three* children, not two," turns out to be accurate).

While most of the relations are depicted as intimate and loving, some are far from unproblematic: there is tension between Katha and Emma, and the source of this tension is their different take on social issues, and especially, on woman's changing role as mother, which risks ruining their friendship. There is also tension between Katha and Ingrid, Sassa's friend and neighbor and mother of King, a ten-year-old boy with aggression issues. And there is tension between Ingrid, Sassa, and Puss: it soon becomes clear that Ingrid considers Sassa to be hers, and she explicitly demonstrates her jealousy toward Puss. While all relationships turn out to be complex and far from smooth, the film puts its focus on the relationships between the women. The men are only secondary figures, they are either supportive (as in the case of Puss and Oscar) or the source of nuisance (like Ture, Annika's unfaithful and egoistic "third" child, and Holger, who still, at the mature age of eighty-five, expresses masculinity issues).

It is interesting to note that Harry Schein, CEO of the Swedish Film Institute, did not want the film to be shown at the Cannes Film Festival in 1977, and that his reluctance was tied to the film's emphasis on women, and especially elderly women. Lindblom tells us that he had asked her: "Who wants to see a film about two old women [kärringar]?" The film did screen in Cannes, at *Les yeux fertiles*, and was met with standing ovations and went on to, overnight, be sold to some fourteen countries, and hence, it was—together with some of Bergman's films— one of Sweden's largest film exports in the 1970s. This anecdote puts light on the double bind that women filmmakers find themselves in: whereas (director) Bergman (who could count Harry Schein both as his friend and his most fervent supporter) could make uncountable films about women, young and old, and have them screened at any film festival with support from the SFI, (actor) Lindblom was indirectly questioned as a director, and her film was considered uninteresting due to its focus on (middle-aged) women.

The film deals with women's "issues": it is about motherhood, daughterhood, sisterhood, and women's friendship. But it is also about the necessity for women to be both a parent and to have a career—and about the possibility to choose not to have children. The film touches on abortion, and it brings the possible disaster that comes with not being able to abort to the fore via Ingrid. We learn that in the mid-1960s, before the abortion law passed in 1975, she had tried to abort but failed, and was forced to have her child. Hence, her son King is an unwanted child, and he demonstrates his emotional and social misery through aggressive behavior. In many ways, he is *the* problematic child that Emma constantly refers to—and although she blames working mothers for not caring enough for their small children, she implicitly supports abortion as a way to avoid the upbringing of unhappy, unloved children who risk ending up in criminality. Yet, when Emma leaves Paradistorg together with Katha to go to the funeral, she too fails to notice King, and he is left there alone. No one seems to miss him.

While women's speech and dialogue (between and across generations) is central in the film, so is their visual representation—and the construction of, and invitation to, the gaze. Throughout the film, there is a resistance, if not refusal, of a gaze that invites an (erotic) objectification of women (and men). There is quite a lot of nudity (since the film takes place at a paradise in the midst of summer), yet the nakedness is used neither to objectify nor sexualize. In an early scene, Sassa is in bed with Puss, and while both are naked, the camera zooms in on both bodies, while giving her the lead as she leans over Puss, head in hand, looking at him in a manner that directs our gaze to look at him, not her. In a later scene, Annika, fully dressed, bathes a naked Ture (her "third child"), who is standing in a small zinc tub—and while this activity will eventually lead to them having sex, Lindblom for long refuses to please the straight, male gaze by forcing us all to look at (the frontally nude) Ture, not at Annika—but *with* her.

1980s: Telling a Woman's Reality, Woman at Center— Suzanne Osten's *Mamma* (1982)

In the 1980s, the political impetus that had shaped many of the films made in the 1970s was being side-tracked by a popular and mainstream turn, and the new impetus was (again) characterized by film as entertainment. And whereas the previous decade had seen an increase in women's presence in the film industry, the new decade proved even more appreciative of women filmmakers and their work, with an increasing number of films reaching critical acclaim. Among those who were most productive and popular were Marianne Ahrne (who had received a "Guldbagge" for best director in 1977, the first women ever to receive the award), Suzanne Osten, Gunnel Lindblom, Christina Olofson, Agneta Fagerström-Olsson, Marie-Louise De Geer Bergenstråhle (and Dane Susanne Bier).[16] Out of these filmmakers, Suzanne Osten's debut film *Mamma* (*Mother*) from 1982 is chosen as representative since it distinctly deals with a women's story, with her representation, and with her own desire to tell stories and to represent.

In the 1960s, while in her early twenties, Osten had established an independent theater group and since then she has been an influential force within the feminist and political theater movement. *Mamma* was her first feature film, and it was made as "a redress of the invisible, an issue that we pursued in the women's movement at that time."[17] *Mamma* is about Osten's own mother, film critic Gerd Osten, who in the 1940s and 1950s had become a film director (Figure 5.2). During our interview with her, Osten tells us that she made the film after reading her mother's diary: "[Reading it] I thought, this has never been portrayed on screen. An intellectual woman who makes film." *Mamma* depicts Gerd's strong drive and desire to tell real stories, but more so, her drive to make a film that "shows a woman's real face, a woman who loves." But traditional gender norms and expectations are clearly in her way—and while she is first encouraged by

Figure 5.2 Malin Ek as Suzanne Osten's mother Gerd, the film critic who wanted to become a filmmaker, in *Mamma/Mother* (Suzanne Osten, 1982).

men in the film industry, her ideas are later dismissed. She soon understands that the only way for her to get in, is to do it their way, not hers—and that her stories are of no interest to the men in power. The film shows how there is also another more personal obstacle in her way—her daughter Nelly. The child's presence (i.e., Suzanne Osten) is in the way of her creative work, and Osten portrays this dilemma in a manner that is simultaneously sensitive and non-judgmental. As a creative woman with artistic dreams, Gerd constantly has to fight conventions: she wants to create, she wants to be autonomous, and she wants to live a full life, yet there is little room for children in the kind of life she aspires to lead. From her point of view as both director and daughter Osten evades condemning the mother: rather, what she does is to offer a critical portrayal of how society dictates how motherhood—and never fatherhood, Nelly does after all have a father—must be altruistic, and that mothers should act self-sacrificingly. *Mamma* exposes patriarchal society as the reason why women cannot have a profession and have children at the same time—while men are expected to be able to have both. This inequality is spelled out in one scene, when Gerd is at a public indoor swimming pool with her two best friends, and exclaims: "One should be able to live with children, work, love—surely. But it doesn't work." And one of the friends answers: "The worst thing is that one wasn't told before, told that one has to make a choice." The second friend then turns to Gerd and says: "I do think your film should end with them having a child once she has liberated him. And that *he* takes care of it." The three women look at each other and fall out in wild laughter.

Encountering one setback after another, Gerd realizes that she will never get to make her film, and as a consequence she becomes depressed, and later, she will become mentally unstable. The film ends with an image of her as an old woman sitting in a mental institution, isolated from the world, and now silenced. On the soundtrack there is a voice-over that says: "Gerd continued as a film critic in the 1950s. She became mentally ill. She lost all her friends. She dies 1974. Mom never got to make her film." But whereas Gerd never got to make her film, her daughter did. In 1986, Osten made her second feature film, *Bröderna Mozart* (*The Mozart Brothers*), a film that was awarded a "Guldbagge" for Best Director (and nominated for Best Picture) in 1987. Since then, Osten has made a handful of critically acclaimed films, including *Skyddsängeln* (*The Guardian Angel*, 1990), which was awarded with a Felix, and *Bengbulan* (1996). Her last film, *Mamma, flickan och demonerna* (*The Mother, the Girl and the Demons*, 2016), was, like *Mamma*, inspired by her childhood experiences and memories, and it was indeed well received by both audiences and critics.

1990s: Doing and Undoing the "Self"—Christina Olofson's *I Rollerna Tre/Lines from the Heart* (1996)

Christina Olofson started out making films in the 1970s after having been trained as an editor at SVT between 1970 and 1971. Her first films were made within the safe and financially generous frame of SVT, and in 1974, she established her own film company, Hagafilm AB, together with her colleague Göran du Rées.[18] Olofson has made both fiction and non-fiction films, and she is still productive as a filmmaker: her most recent film, *Call Me Madame Maestro* (2021), is a follow-up to her critically acclaimed *Dirigenterna* (*A Woman is a Risky Bet*, 1987), focusing on an international group of women conductors and their struggles to survive and be recognized as professionals in a male-dominated profession.

In *I rollerna tre* (*Lines from the Heart*), Olofson brings together the three actors (and old friends) Gunnel Lindblom, Harriet Andersson, and Bibi Andersson to reflect over their joint work with Mai Zetterling for the film *Flickorna* (*The Girls*, 1968), previously discussed in Chapter 4 in this book. Zetterling, who died in 1994, had for some time planned on making a follow-up to *The Girls*, and Olofson departs from this unfinished project in her film. The three actors meet at Zetterling's villa in Provence, France, for a couple of weeks in the summer of 1995, and while the focus is on their relationships with Zetterling, they also talk about life, acting, work, love, friendship—and their relation to director Ingmar Bergman, with whom they all have made several films from the 1950s onward (apart and together).

In the film, the three actors watch *Flickorna* together, and as *In rollerna tre* evolves, sequences from *Flickorna* are interwoven with the actors' own reflections and memories of their involvement in the film and of their characters—and of their own private situation during the filming. It soon becomes apparent that they were somewhat hesitant toward their characters, but also, toward Zetterling. Later, Olofson also includes sequences filmed on other occasions, focusing on the three actors individually in various Stockholm spaces that probably have been chosen by them.

While the film is a homage to Zetterling, as stated in the opening credits, it really is a homage to the three actors. And their profession—as in *performing roles*—is very much at the center. Their very theatricality and the theatricality of their work is inscribed in the film from the start: Olofson chooses to open the film with a long take of the interior of an old and lavish theater, a take that is followed by a close-up of Lindholm rehearsing her lines in front of a mirror in her dressing room. The tone is set, and we know that what we are watching is a theatrical performance, although set within a documentary format.

I rollerna tre is indeed a documentary that is *directed*: and as the three actors engage with one another at Zetterling's villa, one becomes aware of their constant performing, even when their dialogue seems spontaneous. They are always aware of the camera and of the director, they do not look into the camera—hence they never tear down the fourth wall to beak the illusion of us and of Olofson being there as a fly on the wall. The three actors tell stories, dance, and sing, and many of their stories include memories from their professional lives, and how they have experienced being in film and theater as women professionals. The performativity with which these stories are told, however, does not risk downplaying their importance: the three women are open and honest, as they reflect upon their gendered positions in life and at work, but also on suffering from outside pressure (from the media and from audiences), feeling like they have a "split" personality, stage fear, motherhood, and the difficulty of combining professional life and having children. Olofson—from her "absent" position—gives them space and long stretches of time, individually and together. When the issues touched upon get too difficult, the three actors turn silent—and they start talking about something less burning and painful. At one point, after having discussed experiences of mental problems, first followed by silence and then a turn to discussing the melon that is being served, we hear Bibi Andersson comment: "Now, the angels walked through the room, I must say!" When the topics discussed get too painful, their performative professionality is breaking down, and the only way to get away, is to fall into silence or to change topic. Still, Olofson catches the intimacy and the pain with which the three women interact.

2000s: Unruly Mother and Wife "Becoming Horse"— Maria Hedman Hvitfeldt's *Min Skäggiga Mamma/ My Bearded Mum* (2003)

Sweden has always praised itself as a culture that makes qualitative entertainment for children—first, in terms of children's literature (with Selma Lagerlöf, Astrid Lindgren, and Maria Gripe as leading authors within this field) and, later, in terms of film. Here, the many adaptations of Lindgren's books, many of which were filmed in the late 1960s, the 1970s, and the 1980s, tend to stand out as successful adaptations. These were all set in the past, with a serious portion of nostalgia for an earlier and unmodernized Sweden affecting both form and content.

In 2003, Maria Hedman Hvitfeldt, a recent graduate from the Film School at SFI, made a short children's film based on a script by Marianne Strand, *Min skäggiga mamma* (*My Bearded Mum*). The film won a "Guldbagge" for Best Short Film in 2004, and after its success Hedman Hvitfeldt went on to direct for both film and television, before taking up a job first as instructor and then as director at Stockholm University of the Arts. In our interview with her, she describes how it was the long stretches of time that filming entailed, not seldom far away from her family and child, together with the working situation on the film set (a set that she refers to as a "playground for chaps") that made her stop filming.[19]

Min skäggiga mamma deals with two young sisters, Karin and Mirjam, who live in a small and remote house together with their depressed and withdrawn father (who not only is suffering from physical injuries after a car accident but also has been abandoned by his wife, who has left him for another man). The two sisters, much frustrated by the stagnant situation, are together trying to understand why their mother has left. Hedman Hvitfeldt and Strand tell the story from the children's perspective and they include magic components to depict how the girls try to apprehend their abandonment, and why. For example, when the older sister Karin retells the course of events leading up to their mother leaving to Mirjam, she makes up a narrative in which the mother, little by little, transforms into a horse. This narrative is paralleled with sequences showing the two sisters, isolated and lonely as they are on the remote farm, longing for a horse of their own while silently observing their estranged father and becoming-horse mother.

Making up a becoming-horse story to explain why the mother has left them, Karin indicates that their mother leaving was inevitable, since a horse "has to run free." Her narration is formulated and constructed through flashbacks showing the mother fighting the increasing growth of body hair on her legs, arms, and face. In desperation, she is shown constantly shaving and waxing her face and body, which leaves her with open and bleeding wounds (Figure 5.3).

With her bodily transformation, the mother also starts getting warmer and warmer, and at one point she flings the kitchen window open to gasp some fresh air—as in an act of trying to escape what is happening to her—that is, her becoming-horse. But her gasping for air can also be read as a sign of how she is suffocating in her role as mother and wife. Soon, all the shaving and waxing

Figure 5.3 Mother (Malena Engström) "becoming horse" in Maria Hedman Hvitfeldt's *Min skägiga mamma* (*My Bearded Mum*, 2003).

procedures are in vain, and after going through a state of pure and painful agony, she finally transforms into a big, beautiful, brown horse—and leaves.

Gaylyn Studlar's discussion on film and masochism is indeed applicable here with the (missing) mother absorbing the screen through the children's memory of her.[20] But *Min skägiga mamma* also invites us to read the mother in terms of a Deleuzian *becoming*: in becoming-horse (becoming-animal), and refuting her obligations as mother and wife, she comes close to an identity freed from gender, an identity that may be the very condition of freedom.[21]

There are similarities between Osten's *Mamma* and Hedman Hvitfeldt's *Min skägiga mamma* in that they both deal with women who are unhappy mothers and wives, women who strive for something more or else in life—and they do so without being condemned. In both cases, their daughters accept and understand, although in somewhat painful ways. Twenty years separate these two films, yet they both strongly conform to the idea that women need to run free, and that breaking the gendered rules stipulated by patriarchal society should not be doomed.

This leads me to the last film I want to discuss, and this is one that indeed serves to break well-established cinematic rules, doing so from a position that explores and expresses a feminist aesthetics.

2010s: Visual Silence and Breaking all the Rules— Mia Engberg's *Lucky One* (2019)

Mia Engberg made her first films in the mid-1990s, and while she has made mostly documentaries, including *The Stars We Are* (1998) and *Manhood* (1999), she has also made some fiction films, including *Selma och Sofie* (2002). Her two latest films, *Belleville Baby* (2013) and *Lucky One* (2019), are perhaps best described as cinematic and poetic reveries, combining elements both from fiction and non-fiction.

In a 2013 interview, Mia Engberg described how, with her latest picture, *Belleville Baby*, she "wanted to break all the rules" and that she wanted "to do something that I had never done before, and also, something that I had never seen before."[22] Her breaking of the rules is tightly connected to the employment and exploration of a feminine aesthetics—one that can be seen in *Belleville Baby* and *Lucky One*, both of which are part of what is to become a trilogy about love and loss. In the latter, she also explores the use of what she calls "visual silence," consisting of long takes of black frames. In fact, *Lucky One* opens with a black screen that is accompanied by silence for an entire minute before any sound is audible. After this long minute, there is a distant sound of children playing and a train passing by, and then, Engberg starts talking directly to us, asking us to imagine ourselves being in a dark room, counting to three, and then, letting go.

After this introduction, we are invited to listen as she calls Vincent, her former lover, late at night. Vincent lives and works in Paris, and for many years has been involved in criminality, while also providing for his child. Engberg asks what he is doing (he says that he is working, "as always") and then she starts telling him about the film she is making, and that she is struggling with its ending. Vincent says he may be able to help her, if only she tells him the story. It soon becomes clear that her film is about Vincent, but Engberg says that it may be about him, or about someone else, or *anyone*, really. It is about a man who works nights (and whose main occupation seems to be facilitating sex trafficking, transporting young girls to their clients), while caring for Adina, his fourteen-year-old daughter. It now is clear that Engberg is in charge of the story (the one we watch and the one we listen to), although Vincent at times will try to obstruct ("No, Mia, this doesn't work, you have to change your story, this is not credible") and later, at the end, ask her to add a scene to her (and now his) story. Their dialogue is accompanied by images of places shot at night (Vincent's flat, street views of Paris, most of which are taken from inside Vincent's car), of objects (Adina's things, in her room, a clock, her golden hamster Lucky), and of Adina (waiting for Vincent alone at home, watching television, searching the internet, dancing). It is unclear what is reality and what is fiction, Engberg is telling us about his life situation, but he is there to interact with her, and to try to interfere when not happy with her vision or her decisions.

Engberg is almost constantly present on the soundtrack, except when there is a dialogue between Vincent and Adina; when the girl who is a victim of trafficking speaks directly to us, the spectators; or when Vincent and she talk toward the end of the film, when she begs him to save the girl. At times, Engberg leaves her dialogue with Vincent and speaks directly to us, the spectators. In these instances, there is a slippage between us and Vincent, making us the same: Vincent, Engberg is telling us, could have been me, you, us. Engberg is never visible, never in frame, instead, she is positioning herself as the voice of God. It is *her* narrative construction that we are watching—or, rather, her construction that we are *hearing* since words are more important here. The narrative is constructed through words, and the images, together with the black frames, constitute support and instances or "spaces" where visual relaxation and calm is offered. In some scenes, such as when Vincent talks to Adina or to his boss, Engberg is silent (as if absent), yet it is her construction, her description, of these interactions that we hear. She is the master of the story and of all sounds—of voices, of the music (whether intrinsic or extrinsic), of traffic noise, etc. Yet, her voice-over is never intrusive, never total: it does not give us what Trin T. Minh-ha once referred to as "the totalizing quest of meaning."[23] Engberg does not offer one truth, one meaning: instead, she invites not only Vincent to co-construct the story with her but also her spectators, us, in sharing and constructing the story with her.

Hence, *Lucky One* constructs itself as a *relation* between director and spectator, as well as between text and spectator, indeed recalling Annette Kuhn's discussion of reading the feminine text through "passionate detachments."[24] We are becoming involved not only through her speaking to us, through her interpellation, but also through the many gaps in the narrative construction, making us fill in the missing—non-visible—pieces and images. The film experience Engberg is serving us is one that is relational, and the film, it turns out, is as dependent on us as we are of it in order to be (Figure 5.4).

When interviewing Engberg in 2018, she told us that she strives to develop a cinematic language or an aesthetics that is non-objectifying, namely, one that breaks with the malestream imagery of women.[25] Such an aesthetics clearly

Figure 5.4 Director Mia Engberg and actor Olivier Loustau during a night shoot in Paris in *Lucky One* (2019).

recalls the *de-aesthetization* that Teresa de Lauretis once proposed as an answer or solution for feminist filmmaking.[26] Already in her short erotic film *Selma and Sofie* (2002), a film that had an all-women film team, "on all posts," she wanted to explore a "feminine method" to counter and deviate from "film as a patriarchal and capitalist and violent medium that has carried the male gaze through centuries." Driving her exploration is the need to "break down this [mainstream] image, this gaze." Her own—and only—strategy is to find tools that can be used "to dismantle the master's house" following Audre Lorde.[27] The use of a black screen, of a visual silence, is one way to dismantle the dominant way films is made, and to refuse to show women in a derogatory and violently sexualized way is another. Giving voice to women, as in her last two films, in which she herself controls most of the voice-over while inquiring and pushing her male protagonist to give her answers, to remember their past *with* her, and to take responsibility, is clearly a political and conscious choice, as well as an aesthetic one.

While the passion to narrate stories is central to many of the women we have interviewed, it has become obvious that to some narrating through images is a political act. Engberg explains how to her it is both a *social ethos* ("I have a queer, feminist and clearly political agenda – in everything I do") and an *artistic creativity* that drive her to continue making films. And while conceiving of herself as a senior filmmaker, she emphasizes the importance of having role models to "hold my hand" while exploring her feminine aesthetics, pointing out Marguerite Duras, Chantal Ackerman, Agnès Varda, and Derek Jarman as important to her own work.[28] These filmmakers, indeed, were also keen on breaking the rules—exploring an aesthetics that serves both to expand and counter what is considered doable, or even possible.

Conclusion

Like many of the representations of women on film discussed in the chapter "Women on Screen I," the representations focused upon here also deviate from the conventional and mainstream. Like in the films from earlier decades, these representations consist of women who, in different ways and through somewhat different strategies, struggle to create their own place in a male-dominated society. From the four generations of women in Lindblom's feature film *Paradistorg*, via the mother who wants to make films in Osten's feature *Mamma*, the three actors in Olofson's documentary film *I rollerna tre*, and the mother who becomes horse in Hedman Hvitfeldt's short *Min skäggiga mamma*, to the narrating and disembodied voice-over in Engberg's experimental and poetic *Lucky One*, women are pluralistic as well as individualistic. They refuse any steady form, and hence they refuse the few stereotypes that mainstream cinema has stipulated for them. They are young, they are old, they have dreams and drives, they are political, they are sexually liberated, and/or they are single with no desire to (re-)enter a (hetero)sexual relationship—and they all demand their freedom and most of them demand that they be listened to.

Engberg, in *Lucky One*, strives to take the female voice further and she does so by disembodying it. She relies on her own voice-over and she refuses the image—and when she does include images of women, they are never sexualized, never objectified. Hers is an aesthetics that takes a clear step toward a liberation of the female body, since it refuses the malestream gaze. But women's liberation can also be found in and through their bodily freedom—as we have seen in the case of Sassa in *Paradistorg*, or the mother becoming-horse in *Min skäggiga mamma*.

Notes

1. Besides Mai Zetterling, who was chosen as a representative for women's filmmaking in the 1960s in Chapter 4, there were other women who started out during this period and who came into bloom in the 1970s, not seldom with financial support both from the SFI and from SVT: Mai Wechselmann, Ingela Romare, and later, Christina Olofson.
2. The interviews were carried out in 2018 and 2019 together with political scientist Maria Jansson, who was the project leader of the project Representing Women (2018–2021), of which this book is one outcome.
3. In a chapter dealing with how mothers and motherhood have been represented on the Swedish screen by women film directors, I have discussed Lindblom's *Paradistorg*, Osten's *Mamma*, and Hedman Hvitfeldt's *Min skäggiga mamma*. See Maria Jansson and Louise Wallenberg, "Negotiating Motherhood in Sweden – On and Off Screen," in Susan Liddy and Anne O'Brien (eds.), *Mothers and Motherhood: Negotiating the International Audio-Visual Industry* (London: Palgrave, 2021).
4. See, for example, Britta Sjögren, *Into the Vortex Female Voice and Paradox in Film* (Urbana: University of Illinois Press, 2006); Lisa Ehlin, "Becoming Image" (Ph.D. dissertation, IMS, Stockholm University, 2015); Ben Ogrodnik, "Listening to the 'Multi-Voiced' Feminist Film: Aspects of Voice-over, Female Stardom, and Audio-Visual Pleasure in Stephanie Beroes' *The Dream Screen* (1986)," *Journal of Art and Media Studies*, no. 15 (2018), 67–82; Kiki Tianqi Yu and Alisa Lebow (guest eds.), "Feminist Approaches in Women's First Person Documentaries from East Asia," Special Issue of *Studies in Documentary Film*, vol. 14, no. 1 (2020).
5. Kaja Silverman, "Dis-embodying the Female Voice," in Patricia Erens (ed.), *Issues in Feminist Film Criticism* (1984; Bloomington: Indiana University Press, 1990); Silverman, *The Acoustic Mirror* (Bloomington: Indiana University Press, 1988); Silverman, "A Voice to Match: The Female Voice in Classic Cinema," *Iris*, vol. 3, no. 1 (1985), 57–70; and Shohini Chaudhuri, *Feminist Film Theorists* (London: Routledge, 2006).
6. It is interesting to note that a mainstream film like *Her* (Spike Jonze, 2013), while disentangling the female voice from its physical body, not only serves to reinforce the dominant cinematic trope of the female voice being one with its (erotic) body, but also, to totally erase her agency and subjecthood, hence refusing her any narrative authority within the story.
7. Interview with film director and producer Mia Engberg on March 8, 2018.
8. Interview with Mia Engberg, March 8, 2018.
9. Luce Irigaray, *This Sex which is not One* (1977; Ithaca, NY: Cornell University Press, 1985).

10. See, for example, Hilary Neroni, *Feminist Film Theory and Cleo from 5 to 7* (London: Bloomington Academics, 2016).
11. Interview with film director Lisa Ohlin on September 12, 2018.
12. Ulla Isaksson, *Paradistorg* (Stockholm: Albert Bonnier, 1973).
13. Bergman had earlier filmed her novel *Det vänliga, värdiga* from 1954 (as *Nära livet/Brink of Life*, 1958), and she wrote the script to *Jungfrukällan* (*Virgin Spring*, 1960). In 1986, he made a television film based on her novel *De två saliga* (*The Blessed Ones*, 1962).
14. See Maaret Koskinen, *Ingmar Bergman's The Silence: Pictures in the Typewriter. Writings on the Screen* (Seattle: University of Washington Press, 2010); and Louise Wallenberg, "Making (The) Silence Speak: Remake, Retake, Rectify," in Maaret Koskinen and Louise Wallenberg (eds.), *Ingmar Bergman at the Crossroads between Theory and Practice* (New York: Bloomsbury, 2022).
15. Interview with Gunnel Lindblom on April 27, 2018.
16. The "Guldbagge" is the Swedish equivalent to the North American Academy Award and distributed at the *Guldbaggegala* in January every year. The award ceremony was installed by SFI in 1964, and it would hence take thirteen years before a woman—Marianne Ahrne—received a Bagge for best director.
17. Interview with Suzanne Osten on April 16, 2018.
18. Interview with Christina Olofson on March 23, 2018.
19. Interview with Maria Hedman Hvitfeldt on April 9, 2018.
20. Gaylyn Studlar, "Masochism and the Perverse Pleasure of the Cinema," *Quarterly Review of Film Studies*, vol. 9, no. 4 (1984), 267–82.
21. Gilles Deleuze and Felix Guattari, *A Thousand Plateaus: Capitalism and Schizophrenia*, 3rd edn (1980; London: Athlone Press, 1996); Gilles Deleuze, *Le froid et le cruel* (Paris: Les éditions de Minuit, 1967); Rosi Braidotti, "Be-coming Woman: Or Sexual Difference Revisited," *Theory, Culture & Society*, vol. 20, no. 3 (2003), 43–64.
22. DocuFest TV, "'Belleville Baby' @ DokuFest 2013," YouTube, https://www.youtube.com/watch?v=xlldfeFg6EE, accessed November 4, 2021.
23. In her chapter "The Totalizing Quest of Meaning," Trin T. Minh-ha writes that "The socially oriented filmmaker is thus the almighty voice-giver (here, in a vocalizing context that is all male), whose position of authority in the production of meaning continues to go unchallenged, skillfully masked as it is by its righteous mission." See Minh-ha in Michael Renov (ed.), *Theorizing Documentary* (London: Routledge, 1993), 96.
24. Annette Kuhn, "Passionate Detachments," in *Women's Pictures* (London: Verso, 1993), 3–18.
25. Interview with Mia Engberg on March 8, 2018.

26 Teresa de Lauretis, "Aesthetics and Feminist Theory: Rethinking Women's Cinema," in Diane Carson, Linda Dittmar, and Janice R. Welsch (eds.), *Multiple Voices in Feminist Film Criticism* (1984; Minneapolis: University of Minnesota Press, 1994). As a critique to Silvia Bovenschen's article "Is There a Feminine Aesthetic?" (*New German Critique*, no. 10 [Winter 1977], 111–37), de Lauretis argues for a feminist *de-aesthetization* in women's film, taken that many films made by women focus on a conscious de-aesthetization of the female body as well as on a de-Oedipalization of the narrative and a de-sexualization of violence.
27 Audre Lorde, "The Master's Tools Will Never Dismantle the Master's House," in *The Master's Tools Will Never Dismantle the Master's House* (London: Penguin Random House, 2018).
28 Interview March 8, 2018. See also Mia Engberg, *Den visuella tystnaden: en essä om film av Mia Engberg* (Stockholm: Pov Books, 2020).

Part Three

Routines, Practices, and Practitioners

6

Making a Living

On the Working Conditions and Salaries for Actors and Extras within Swedish Film Production 1930–1955

Tytti Soila

When the world-famous film star Ingrid Bergman (1915–1982) was a young girl and had her first roles as an extra in films, she found it wondrous and exciting not only to be allowed to perform in front of a camera but to receive a salary as well: 10 krona per day (328 krona today). She did not mind that some days were spent unpaid due to the changes in schedules as there was so much to see, so much to admire and learn.[1] From such a humble beginning, as is known, Bergman's career skyrocketed with its many working opportunities and ample monetary circumstances. Yet, it represents a giant exception: the reality for most of her fellows on stage and screen was quite different.

This chapter is about the working circumstances for film actors and extras during the first half of the twentieth century in Sweden. The study focuses on the area of the capital city—Stockholm—because it has been, and still is, the main site for production facilities for the film industry. Also, Stockholm was the home of the largest and most distinguished theater scenes, where many touring companies started their travels into the countryside and to the Swedish-speaking parts of Finland. The source material for the study consists of memoirs, articles in the press, as well as existing contracts between individuals and some of the larger film production companies in the country: AB Sandrew-Produktion, Europa Film, Wivefilm, and Svensk Filmindustri (SF). SF is the only company still active in the film production business today.[2]

Sweden, in its capacity as a small country with a homogeneous cultural sphere, provides an interesting case in the development of the theater and film production fields. The interchange between the scenic institutions and film industry has been intimate in many levels of production here: not only the staff, actors, and directors but also actual practices and customs as well as different kinds of legal and monetary agreements were taken over by film industry from theater management. Hence, it is important to begin this study with notes on the professional conditions for a stage actor at the turn of the twentieth century in Sweden.

The Profession—Actor and the Manners

When the feature film was established as the dominating and most lucrative genre of film production in the early days of the twentieth century, many producers were professional actors who nursed an interest in the new medium and its possibilities. They had the knowledge of the repertoire, audience preferences, and a large network of contacts to engage popular actors to perform in front of the camera—and a status that could grant monetary support as well. Their competence was based on their schooling and experience on the stage.

The main three routes into the acting profession during the period in question were private lessons, an apprenticeship, or a training institute, namely the Kungliga Dramatiska Teaterns Elevskola (KDTE; Royal Dramatic Training Academy). Thus, for instance, Ingrid Bergman had trained privately with a distinguished actor and pedagogue Gabriel Alw (1889–1946) before gaining admission to the KDTE at the age of eighteen in 1933. She was also engaged as an extra in a film recording thanks to the contacts her family had in the branch; her first registered appearance was in a film from 1932, *Landskamp* (*International Match*) (Gunnar Skoglund). Soon enough the leadership of the SF found her promising enough to offer her a trainee contract, which she happily accepted—whereby she became one of the first dropouts from the KDTE to develop a career as a film actor.

The KDTE was established in 1787 by the Swedish King Gustaf III who himself wrote plays and had a great interest in theater. The Royal Dramatic Theatre (hereafter Dramaten) was established the following year, in 1788. The King had invited a French theater company to perform at the court and even for the general public. To develop a cadre of domestic actors, the company members were assigned to teach at the KDTE, which was soon regarded as the most important institution of its kind in the country. The founding by royal initiative was seen as a guarantee of the eminent quality for acting—and in the future, it would set the (national) standards for the acting style for a long time.

Two of the few French performers who decided to stay in Sweden till the end of their contract period—Anne Marie Desguillons (1753–1829) and Joseph Desguillons (1750–1822)—organized and managed the curriculum at the KDTE from 1793 to 1800. The early French impact may explain the bias toward the formal, "classic" acting style with modulated declamation and formal gestures that Swedish feature films of the 1920s to mid-1940s provide eminent samples of.

From the turn of the twentieth century, *realism* became an issue in the ongoing debate about meaning and manners on the stage.[3] Yet the KDTE cadres would contribute to sustaining a stereotyped and conservative style at the major theaters and on the film screen. Due to the structural changes within the film industry toward the end of the 1930s—such as intensifying production speed with increasing numbers of premieres—the quest for new actors increased as well. Other, more low-key and more verosimile styles, practiced by new generations of professionals with their background in trainee contracts and the amateur ensembles at the vaudeville theaters, were negotiated on the silver screen.

The difficulty in the realism debate (engaged by, among others, the famous author and cultural personality August Strindberg [1849–1912]) was/is the definition of the notion itself, and a question of how to establish a plausible "set" of meaningful signs for reality, namely the meaning of signs change as time passes. There is a charming scene in a film titled *Södrans revy* (*The South Theatre Revue*) (Sven Paddock, 1950), a filmed revue containing short sketches where the celebrated operetta artist Naima Wifstrand (1890–1968) performs as a conferencier. In one of the sketches Wifstrand plays the role of an elderly actress who gives a lecture for an understudy who is apt to overtly dramatic manners. The audience laughs at the girl's conceit. Finally, the old lady pushes her to the side and shows elegantly in minuscule but marked gestures how the role should be done. The audience cheers and applauds in consent. Yet, by today's standards even the old lady's performance appears clearly exaggerated. The film, however, remains an important document for how the members of the branch themselves saw the manners and mannerisms in film and on stage.

As already indicated, the economic status of many actors was poor—and not only because of the low wages, relatively few workplaces, and short-term engagements practiced by the entire branch. Also, the routines of the profession, such as typecasting, contributed to monetary problems for many. "Typecasting"—as the expression has been in Hollywood—has deep roots in the

European acting tradition and still, at the beginning of the 1900s, the actors *in spe* became schooled in one of the standard "types." It was a system where the "type" once given becomes confirmed and cemented by the practice.

To put it roughly: a lovely young girl was schooled in the role of an *ingenue*—and would probably play that role throughout her life on stage. A more plain young girl could be schooled as an auntie or a housekeeper, such as Julia Cæsar (1885–1968) who played "the old mother" at the age of twenty and "the neighbourhood helicat" the rest of her life.[4] A big boy had a few more options: a policeman, military officer, bank director—or an emperor. A short man with a delicate build like that of Åke Söderblom (1910–1965) could play the role of an errand boy at the age of fifty—and he excelled in many plays and films with a cross-dressing theme.

Thus, first there is the physiognomy, then comes the outfit that supported the "type," and third, the arsenal of gestures and mimics. The typecasting could be an obstacle: it stalled the actor in many ways in his or her professional development while the only possibility was to refine the conventions for the character in question. Some of the conventional signs for a "type" are preserved in the earlier films: many folksy comedies from the 1930s include a character played by Fridolf Rhudin (1895–1935) or Sigurd Wallén (1884–1947), who says something amusing and stretches out his tongue. It may look odd from today's perspective but, in fact, the outstretched tongue was a gesture familiar for the audiences of the period: a theater sign meaning "funny old geezer." An *ingenue* in her turn would cast her eyes up to the skies to express youth and innocence like Astrid Holm (1893–1961) as Edith in *Körkarlen* (*The Phantom Carriage*) (Victor Sjöström, 1921).

Apart from the gestures and manner of speech, the clothes worn on stage contributed to the appearance of the "type"—and at least in the Swedish context this meant that the actors themselves were expected to obtain their stage outfits (with the exception of historical plays or professional clothing such as uniforms). This generated a considerable expense for an actor because new garments had to be bought and paid for as the program planning went on and the fashions changed. Naturally, a wardrobe could also be an asset in that it was possible to pledge. Thus, many young artists were heavily in debt at the beginning of their career: the trainee actors hardly had any salary to talk about (as we will see below) and they still needed dresses that worked well on stage. A *prima donna* of the 1920s to 1940s, Margit Manstad, writes in her memoirs: "Many male actors had to purchase both a spring costume and a tuxedo in order to get a contract, and as the salary was only one third of the cost [of an outfit] it is explicable that [many had to deal with] notes of credit." She also writes that more often than not the rehearsals had to be finished by three o'clock on payday for the staff to make it to a bank and wager the tailor's notes before closing time.[5]

The system of typecasting sustained as a mutual agreement between the scene/screen and saloon has been hard to break. It may have felt discouraging for the young Ingrid Bergman to see the verdict of a critic who—having seen her first proper film role as Elsa in *Munkbrogreven* (*The Count of Munkbron*) (Sigurd Wallén, 1935)—wrote that the film industry already had enough sweet young girls such as Birgit Rosengren (1912–2011) and Birgit Tengroth (1915–1983). So why on earth would anyone want to see yet another one like them?[6]

More well known is the devastating effect of typecasting for women, while many careers has come to an abrupt end once the young *ingenue* was not young anymore. An interesting footnote is, however, that Naima Wifstrand, after having had a splendid operetta career in the beginning of the 1900s and lost her voice and career on stage by the 1930s, was able to have a second coming within the film industry. She is especially known for her roles in Ingmar Bergman's (1918–2007) films and had a part in *Vargtimmen* (*Hour of the Wolf*) (Ingmar Bergman, 1968), which premiered only seven months before she passed away at the age of seventy-eight. Also, it has been said of another star, Karin Swanström (1873–1942), that she as the director of her touring company "played all leading female roles between 16 and 90—with panache."[7]

As time passed, there were other ways into the actor's profession outside of KDTE with its mandatory two years of practice at Dramaten. One of the earliest ways of learning was private tutoring with experienced actors, such as the above-mentioned Gabriel Alw, or Bertha Bock-Tammelin (1836–1915), the acclaimed teacher of Karin Swanström, among others. More schools and training studios were established. In Gothenburg, the first actors' school was founded by Gustaf Mallander (1840–1888) during his engagement at Nya Teatern (the New Theatre) from 1874 to 1879. One of the most valued private training studios for actors is still Calle Flygare Teaterskola (Calle Flygare Theatre School) established in 1940 with students such as Harriet Andersson (1932–) and Mai Zetterling (1925–1994). Malmö, one of the largest cities in Sweden, got its first theater in 1809 and eventually an actors' institute in 1944. Characteristic for these institutions were an interest in improvisation and realism. Worth noting is that Konstantin Stanislavsky's influential book on acting was translated into Swedish, published in 1944, and became a topic of keen discussions behind the scenes.[8]

Yet another path to the profession was offered by the touring theater companies. Young aspiring actors were promised training and engagement for low payment. Traveling was strenuous, the theater facilities in the countryside were seldom modern or first class, but if the company leadership was good, the training was rewarding: the members of the ensemble had to improvise and adjust both on stage and in real life. They had to be able to rehearse at short notice and perform more than one play per season. Consequently, they developed good skills in memorizing, contriving, and retorting; they also gained an excellent knowledge of repertoires and the feel for audience preferences in the countryside as well as in the big cities.

Some of the distinguished actors that first made their career in touring companies were Lars Hanson (1886–1965), known for instance for *The Wind* (Victor Sjöström, 1928), Gösta Ekman Sr. (1890–1938), and Karin Swanström. Swanström herself ran her touring ensemble from 1904, trained a number of known actors, and became, at the age of sixty, the artistic leader for the SF in 1930. Her profound knowledge of the field—and also her appearance on the silver screen—contributed to the company's pronounced success during the 1930s, called the Klondike period of the Swedish cinema.

A number of plays and feature films in the 1930s to 1950s described theater milieu and some were about life in touring companies. One of these films is *Karriär* (*Career*) (Schamyl Bauman, 1938), starring Signe Hasso (1915–2002)—who later emigrated to Hollywood and had a substantial career as a TV star there—and Sture Lagerwall (1908–1963). The story is a romantic comedy or comedy of errors about a young actress who makes a choice between a career and marriage, but gets both in the end. The script was written by German author Franz Winterstein and filmed during the first half of 1938 with a premiere in October the same year.[9] The director, Schamyl Bauman (1893–1966), had a team consisting of seasoned actors—among them the elderly Tollie Zellman (1887–1954)—and several younger talents in central roles: Ruth Stevens (1903–1989), Olof Widgren (1907–1999), and Sigge Fürst (1905–1984). The photographer was Hilmer Ekdahl (1889–1967), who had started his career within the film industry in 1912 in a laboratory and had stepped behind the camera when the sound film was introduced.

This was to be one of the routine productions with only some pre-PR regarding Signe Hasso, the rising star, but stands as one of the documents for a major change in acting styles in Swedish cinema. The reviews were unfavorable as far as the film's uneven narrative tempo is concerned—but completely enthusiastic otherwise. The critics praised the "natural style of acting presented by the entire ensemble," as Martin Rågberg writes in *Svenska Dagbladet*: "[It has the] feel of reality seldom seen in Swedish cinema. [This is] a comedy that really stays in touch with the ordinary human everyday life. … Most important of all: the actors speak as people do—the dialogue flows easily like in an American movie."[10]

Per Lindberg (1890–1944), himself a theater and film director, writes in *Dagens Nyheter*:

> It is a film that in its soft and tender realism is quite unique in Swedish cinema. … We, the theatre people, may feel ourselves a bit chocked while the film presents [for us] familiar people in [for us] familiar situations but in exchange, there are no formulae. … The actors seem to be just as interested in featuring real people as they are in keeping their characters within the frames of the film's basic humanism.[11]

The extraordinariness of this film lies in two things: it is an early meta-film that catches a number of issues in an actor's life, both on the conceptual and material plane. It also registers an ongoing, gradual separation between the elevated acting style of the theater with its coded mannerism and the developing style for Swedish cinema verified by the unanimous press: a low-key realism with the acting style of American films as a pronounced model.

There were many reasons for the changing style: the development of techniques during the two world wars, and the increasing understanding of cinematic possibilities for expression among critics and other professionals as promoted by imported films. Also a noteworthy fact is that actors from many different schoolings and traditions—from Dramaten to revue-theaters—were brought together during the heyday of film production, between 1935 and 1950.

The Pay—the Contracts[12]

Actors' contracts in the film industry from the 1930s are a difficult subject. This is because the forms of employment were multiple—as they, in fact, were in the whole society at this time. Some artists were employed only for one or two productions, others for a longer period of time with an agreed number roles to perform. Others worked on a weekly or daily basis, extras often per hour. Closer scrutiny may, however, reveal evidence of negotiations, working conditions, and power relationships within the film production business.

The contracts came in all forms and sizes: handwritten, typed on writing paper, with or without the logo of the company. For the majority, there existed a formal, pre-printed "standard-contract" with its prototype in those applied in theaters; the logotype of the company on the top and free space for fill-ins. Attached to the contract, most often with a maximum of four pages, were the rules of conduct—a document twice as long registering requests for constant stand-by within a reach of the film team and orders not to slander the company.

Some smaller firms could use the formal contract of a larger company with the original logotype wiped out and replaced by the other company's name handwritten on the top. This could be because the small firm actually was owned by the larger one. Thus, for instance, a subsidiary of the SF, Fribergs Filmbyrå, produced a number of profitable "light" comedies and farces that did not look *comme-il-faut* in the artistically ambitious production program of SF.

At the beginning of the 1940s all members of Förening Sveriges Filmproducenter (FSF; the Swedish Association for Film Producers) reverted to a standardized contract form, which was revised in 1944 by a mutual agreement between FSF and Teaterförbundet, the Theatre Worker's Association (from 2021 Scen och Film/Stage and Film; the Swedish Union for Performing Arts and Film). The change of name alludes to an idea of two professional fields—film and theater—but still today, the two areas are more or less inseparable in practice.

Teaterförbundet was founded in 1894—almost twenty years after the first trade union had been established in the country—recruiting nearly one hundred members during its first year. To begin with, the organization was more in line with a co-operative insurance establishment than a player in labor politics. Instead, matters considered more important than marching with the central trade unions were addressed, namely establishing reserve funds for savings, illness, and funerals for the actors.

Aging was particularly problematic for artists who in many cases lived a touring life without settling down in any place in particular. However, in 1913, Sweden—the first country in the world to do so—instigated a system of general pension insurance, easing the life situation for many, among them aging artists. Another improvement made possible by a large donation by Gustaf Fredrikson (1875–1921)—an actor, economist, and director of Dramaten—resulted in the formation of a society that would support elderly actors. In 1918, a retirement home, Pensionat Höstsol (Guest House Autumn Sun), was inaugurated at Såsta Manor, north of Stockholm.[13]

The life of a theater establishment revolved, as it still does, around two seasons, excluding summer. A reason for shooting films during the summer was not only better weather conditions with lots of light but, more importantly, because the actors were free and without an income. Many artists were looking for work in touring summer companies and, in between, acted in front of the film cameras. The expanding film production in increasingly sophisticated production facilities made recordings possible day and night, and created hectic working conditions. A film called *Fröken Julia Jubilerar* (*Miss Julia's Anniversary*) (Lau Lauridsen and Alice O'Fredericks, 1938) was a joint production between the Swedish Svea Film and Danish ASA Film A/S. According to the contract, the film recording was to take place in Denmark, at Lyngby on the outskirts of Copenhagen. However, the four leading stars—Thor Modéen (1898–1950), Annalisa Ericson (1913–2011), Katie Rolfsen (1902–1966), and Åke Söderblom—played the main characters in an evening vaudeville show in Malmö, situated on the Swedish bank of the strait between the two countries.[14]

In a system where no professional actors' agents existed (yet), the artists negotiated their salaries in a process where the producer had the upper hand. Basically, the size of remuneration was not determined by the actor's education, nor experience—nor by his or her personal contacts—but by something rather volatile as an estimated market value of each individual. This in turn was a sum of many criteria, where fame and popularity were at the center. Yet, an artist's popularity was not always based on his/her appearances on a silver screen. A well-paid actress who has not left a great mark in film history or in contemporary film magazines, the abovementioned Katie Rolfsen, provides an interesting example. Her honorary of 300 krona per recording day was quite high in 1943. However, a closer scrutiny of her career shows that the film producers aimed to exploit her fame and popularity as a vaudeville artist and agreed to pay her a higher salary.[15]

In fact, the institutional theaters and different entertainment facilities played a significant part in negotiating the actors' fees with the film producers. The leaderships at the theaters and film companies could between themselves agree not only upon salaries but also upon "loan" of a popular artist. Thus, for instance, Dagmar Ebbesen (1891–1954), who according to Leif Furhammar was the most popular female film actor during the 1930s and employed by Europa Film via prolonged contracts, worked for many different companies during her career. During five years with the beginning of March 15, 1940, her monthly salary was, without any rise, 1,000 krona. However, she received an allowance of 1,200 krona twice a year for clothes, entertainment, and travels during the filming periods. This amount rose twice to reach 5,000 krona. It is possible that such support was tax free and preferred by some artists. This particular contract agrees upon Ms. Ebbesen's request to freely accept film assignments by other producers—and in such cases, to freely negotiate her remunerations. The only condition at this point was that her extra work would not interfere with Europa Film's own planning. Yet, one year later in 1941, the company proclaimed its right to withhold 30 percent of Ms. Ebbesen's earnings from other companies.

Dramaten in its turn could demand that, as compensation, "their" actors should pay the theater 25 percent of all honoraria received by other companies. While the film *Flickornas Alfred* (*Ladies' Man Alfred*) (Edvin Adolphson, 1935) was planned in the spring of 1935, Dramaten agreed to "lend" a number of their employed actors to Wivefilm (among them Sture Lagerwall and Hilda Borgström [1871–1953]) for a few days, unless they were not needed at Dramaten. Olof Molander (1892–1966), the director of the theater, signed the "transfer document" requesting the "agreed compensation" in advance.

It is hard not to associate this to a slave trade here. A popular star from the 1930s onward, Sickan Carlsson (1915–2011) cannot hide her bitterness in her memoirs as she states that, in fact, the system exploited the actors twice: "first, the company that held the first-hand contract paying the low salary, and then the other company that hired the actor for a few days—and the first company laid hands on parts of the agreed extra payment."[16]

As previously noted, it was not customary for the artists to rely on agents, but there were exceptions among the most famous and most wanted. Thus, for instance, an agreement between the Danish film star Marguerite Wiby (1909–2001) and Wvivefilm in 1940 is written in Danish on writing paper with the logotype of a Danish lawyer, V. Falbe-Hansen. Clearly, Ms. Wiby had the leverage here; she was one of Denmark's most celebrated stars and had made a number of films in Sweden since 1927. This particular contract is regarding *Fröken Kyrkråtta* (*Miss Church-Mouse*) (Schamyl Bauman, 1941). Ms. Wiby accepts the role of the main character Eva Holm and the engagement for three months beginning in January 2, 1941. Her honorarium will be 20,000 krona plus taxes that are to be paid in Sweden. Ms. Wiby wants to have Sundays off, and she also wants the company to consult her regarding the choice of director for the film. The contract is signed on December 9, 1940, and a clause stipulates that if Stockholm or its surroundings be subject to bombardment during the film's recording, she would immediately be allowed to leave the country. In her turn, she agrees to return and complete the recordings after the political situation has stabilized. Sweden was not attacked by any enemy, the film had its premiere in April 1941, and Ms. Wiby got excellent reviews.

Needless to say that the remuneration mentioned in the contract was for a star; another star was Signe Hasso. She had received an honorary of 600 krona for her first film in 1933, but six years later with SF she was paid 45,000 krona for two films. In addition, she would travel in first class and have a daily allowance when traveling. Another rising star, Alice "Babs" Nilson (later Sjöblom, 1924–2014), aged sixteen, played the role of young Inga in *Swing it, Magistern!* (*Swing It, Teacher!*) (Schamyl Bauman, 1940)—the story of a schoolgirl who surprises the new music teacher with her swing melody. The teacher and Inga perform in a restaurant and Inga risks being expelled from the school. However, it all ends well while the vicious headmaster and Inga sing a duet.

The film was a success and Alice Babs Nilson—now on a first name basis with her audiences—became the first teenage idol in the country. Wivefilm, the production company decided for a sequel in haste. The new film had a planned budget of 213,200 krona, of which 45,000 krona was reserved for cast actors and 3,000 krona for extras. Alice Babs's honorarium was 10,000 krona, circa 20 percent of the entire salary budget. But already at this point Ms. Nilson had her economic advisors with her, and she was even granted a share of 5 percent of the film's rental income in Sweden and part of the license income in case the film was sold abroad.

Whether such agreements—at that time—were customary or not is not easy to say because the contracts of the real leading stars were confidential. Also, the fact is that even if the examples above concern women, it is clear that their salaries were small when compared to those of men. Edvard Persson, who was the most celebrated film star in all categories during the 1930s, had a contract with Europa Film already in 1932 that guaranteed him an annual income of 24,000 krona. The films related to the contract were premiered in 1933 and they, without exception, became blockbusters.[17] In comparison, Erik "Bullen" Berglund, number four in the popularity race during the 1930s, did not reach that kind of annual honorarium until 1944, with 27,000 krona from SF.[18]

The discrepancy in salaries—not only between men and women but also between women and women—was of course a reason for much bitterness among the disadvantaged: Annalisa Ericson—a versatile actress, singer, and dancer who worked in numerous revues and stage plays, starring in almost seventy films during her career—writes in her memoirs that in 1932 she accepted a one-year contract by SF that offered a guaranteed basic salary of 10,000 krona plus an additional 1,500 krona for her leading role as Anna in *Värmlänningarna* (*The People of Värmland*) (Gustaf Edgren, 1932).[19]

The system of trainee contracts was a common trait that exploited young actors. As seen above, there existed different means for learning the ropes of the profession and none of them were lucrative in monetary terms, especially considering the amount of work that was asked for the minuscule pay. Ingrid Bergman, who was a dropout of KDTE, was offered 75 krona per day with a guaranteed annual salary of 5,000 krona during 1933. In addition, she also collected 2,000 krona for private lessons in acting. The following year, she was paid 6,000 krona and thereafter she had another rise of 1,000 krona. Bergman wrote in her diary that she thought the company was exploiting her: from the fall of 1933 she worked in four films with premieres in 1935; she earned a sum of 18,000 krona over three years.[20] Sickan Carlsson, who also thought she worked hard, did not think she was paid as she deserved: she was employed as a trainee at the same time as Ingrid Bergman, but three years later she earned 1,000 krona less—and had played in seven films.[21]

When holding a discussion of matters referred to above, it is not possible to avoid bringing forth the issue of favoritism. Annalisa Ericson, Sickan Carlsson, and Birgit Tengroth write that Karin Swanström—the artistic leader of SF— favored Ingrid Bergman and paved the way for her at SF.[22] Swanström held, together with her husband—the Stage Master of the company, Stellan Claësson (1886–1970)—a unique position of power and clearly ensured that Bergman was given opportunities to demonstrate her talents, which Bergman confirms in her diary, speaking well of Ms. Swanström.[23]

Yet another document that bears witness to the unfairness within the film industry is a confidential report set up by FSF, a document with the association's logotype and titled "Advisory tariff," regarding actors' remunerations. It is dated September 1943, listing 323 names of actors and the recommended payment per day for each of them. However, the actors with annual contracts, namely the best paid ones, are not included. The highest honorarium listed is 400 krona per day and is advised for four individuals: Carl Barklind (1873–1945), Holger Löwenadler (1904–1977), Marianne Löfgren (1910–1957), and Tollie Zellman. The reason why just these four are considered worth the best pay is hard to know—all were well-known professionals; Barklind and Zellman were trusty old troupers whereas Löwenadler and Löfgren were younger, versatile professionals.

Those actors that had annual contracts were surely considered elite and privileged in many ways. Thus, for instance, the companies took out collective accident insurance, even if it only covered each film recording (from 12:00 p.m. the first day of filming to 12:00 p.m. on the last day). Wivefilm, for instance, took out accident insurance for the film *Anderssonskans Kalle* (*Andersson's Kalle*) (Sigurd Wallén, 1934) for a period of one month, covering thirteen individuals altogether. The five main characters were insured for 10,000 krona in case of death, 20,000 krona in case of permanent disability, and 10 krona per day in case of sick leave. The insurance amount for the other eight individuals was half of each sum. In regard to this specific case, the insurance did not cover the star of the film, Thor Modéen, probably because he was "lent" to Wivefilm and was covered by his regular employer SF.

As seen in the case of Dagmar Ebbesen's contract, the actual compensation for work done could take many forms, not just the actual salary. The clothes were one quite important issue. As previously stated, in the early days clothes—as well as make-up, wigs, and other attributes that created a character on the stage and later in film—were the responsibility of the actor. Within the modern film industry, this was not a sustainable system. The clothing was a considerable expense—but it also was an asset, and one manner of benefiting this asset was to make it part of the compensation for the actor's work. Another aspect was that the large majority of films were set in a contemporary frame, and the clothing of the actors soon became an important part of the system with tie-ins.

To use clothes as a part of the salaries was stipulated in the contracts, and the many cross-outs, add-ons, and other handwritten alterations show that this was a spot for hard negotiations, and probably the one where especially a female actor was able to exercise influence. After all, the clothes were custom-made for the specific actor, and a film star on the streets of the city could be seen as a walking advertisement for both the film and the tailor. Both Ingrid Bergman and Sickan Carlsson describe their enthusiasm when they realized that it was possible to keep the outfits fashioned for them personally.[24] The contracts show that there were many different options for the terms: for instance, (1) the actor brings his/her own clothing (to the recording site), (2) the company provides the clothing but it remains as the property of the company after recording, (3) the clothing may be purchased by the actor, (4) the clothing may be purchased by the actor at a discount, or (5) the clothing will remain as the actor's property.

An example of the praxis comes from the production of a film called *Hem från Babylon* (*Home from Babylon*) (Alf Sjöberg, 1941). The female lead was Gerd

Hagman (1919–2011). In the case, the wardrobe would remain as the producer's property—probably because this was Hagman's second film and she was new to the business. The clothes were made at Firma Modeträdgårdh, one of the most fashionable ateliers in the city. The producer writes to the atelier that the price of the wardrobe should not exceed 2,100 krona. Included is an order list counting "an elegant evening gown—all in white and rhinestone," "an evening dress—dark, distinguished" as well as three mourning dresses of which one should be elegant. A nightgown is included in the list, as well as a number of hats and other accessories: "elegant" seems to be one of the favorite definitions of the day.

Conclusion

The Swedish film critic and producer of TV show *Filmkrönikan* (*Film Chronicle*), Torsten Jungstedt, presented a number of episodes in the fall of 1980 where he brought up issues regarding the Swedish company Europa Film and others. In one of them he focused on the discrepancies in the salary system and stated that there was no doubt that "the entire production system laid on the delicate shoulders of young women."[25] This chapter accounts for a number of circumstances regarding the working conditions of the actors within the Swedish entertainment industry during the first half of the 1900s. It might explain why the existing production companies are still, after nearly a hundred years, so protective of their documents, contracts and minutes from meetings on different levels of decision-making. The system of "loans" of actors between different production companies and institutions, the use of trainee contracts and "clothing-as-salaries" recalls the medieval guild system where an apprentice more or less belonged to the master's house before gaining a mastership him/herself. In that regard, the founding of Teaterförbundet and especially its membership organization, the Swedish Confederation of Professional Employees (TCO), in 1944, has made a difference in the lives of professional actors, artists, and musicians.

Notes

1   Ingrid Bergman and Alan Burgess, *Mitt liv* (Stockholm: Norstedts, 1981), 37. The filming site probably was that of *Landskamp* (Gunnar Skoglund, 1932).

2   This chapter shares some of the material used in Tytti Soila, "Thalias magra bröd," in Tytti Soila (ed.), *Dialoger. Feministisk filmteori i praktik* (Stockholm: Aura Förlag Stiftelsen Filmvetenskaplig tidskrift, 1997).
3   Among others, August Strindberg (1849–1912) partook in the debate both in newspaper articles and by developing his dramas, moving from a naturalistic style towards symbolic plays.
4   Tytti Soila, "Kvinnors ansikte, stereotyper och kvinnlig identitet i trettiotalets svenska filmmelodram" (Ph.D. dissertation, Stockholm University, 1991), 52–77.
5   Margit Manstad, *Och vinden viskade så förtroligt* (Stockholm: Läsarförlaget, 1987), 54.
6   Filmson, *Arbetarbladet*, January 22, 1935, 12.
7   *Veckojournalen*, no. 31 (1959).
8   Konstantin Stanislavskij, *My Life in Art* (Boston: Little, Brown & Co, 1924).
9   Not much information of this writer exists: he probably was a German refugee who left Sweden for Spain round 1940.
10 Martin Rågberg, aka "Esq," *Svenska Dagbladet*, October 12, 1938, 13.
11 Per Lindberg, *Dagens Nyheter*, October 12, 1938, 10–11. Lindberg seems to refer to the character played by Tollie Zellman, who even in real life "took help of Bacchus to be able to serve Thalia."
12 The material in this chapter is partly from the archives of the author. The original documents are kept in the Centre for Business History in Stockholm. Among these documents there exists a confidential agreement by the association stating the recommend remunerations for over 300 actors and entertainers.
13 The Guest House in Såsta was sold in 1981 due to the outmoded facilities and diminishing demand. Instead, the foundation Höstsol still manages a property with thirty-two senior apartments in the center of Stockholm City.
14 Ulf Kjellström, *Åke, boken om författaren, artisten, revy- och filmskådespelaren Åke Söderblom* (Arvika: Norlén & Slottner 2002), 143.
15 See note 12.
16 Sickan Carlsson, *Sickan, minnen berättade för Anna Nyman* (Stockholm: Bonniers 1977), 76–7.
17 Kjell Jerselius, *Hotade reservat, Spelfilmerna med Edvard Persson* (Uppsala: Filmförlaget 1987), 41.
18 Leif Furhammar, *Filmen i Sverige En historia i tio kapitel* (Wiken: Höganäs Förlags AB, 1991), 159.
19 Annalisa Ericson, *Mina sju liv* (Stockholm: Norstedts, 1982), 70.
20 Bergman and Burgess, *Mitt liv*, 18.
21 Carlsson, *Sickan*, 156.

22 Ericson, *Mina sju liv*, 70; Birgit Tengroth, *Jag vill ha tillbaka mitt liv: Minnen* (Stockholm: Bonniers, 1972), 59–61.
23 Bergman and Burgess, *Mitt liv*, 44.
24 Carlsson, *Sickan*, 156.
25 Torsten Jungstedt, *Filmkrönikan. 50 år med Europafilm 1–4* (Stockholm: Sveriges Television TV2, 1980).

7

Bibi Lindström

"Easy to Work With"

Tytti Soila

In May 1954 the major newspapers in Sweden published reportages about Bibi (Birgit) Lindström (1904–1984), a film architect who during her career had worked on ninety film productions. Before her retirement in the 1970s, the number of films and TV programs with her contribution would amount to over 150. The reason for the attention was the prestigious award she had received from Svenska Filmsamfundet (then the equivalent of the Academy Award), which had an interest in promoting cinema culture in Sweden.

The rationale for the award was her work on *Fröken Julie* (*Miss Julie*) (Alf Sjöberg, 1951)—the Golden Palm winner in Cannes in the same year—*Gycklarnas afton* (*Sawdust and Tinsel*) (Ingmar Bergman, 1953), and *Barabbas* (Alf Sjöberg, 1953). The two other artists awarded on the same occasion were the film director Arne Mattsson (1919–1995) and the actor Ulf Palme. Palme was praised for his title role in *Barabbas* and as the male lead in *Fröken Julie*. Arne Mattsson was awarded for his films *Hon dansade en sommar* (*One Summer of Happiness*, 1951) and *Kärlekens bröd* (*The Bread of Love*, 1953). In fact, of these five films, Bibi Lindström had worked on four—she was at the peak of her career.

This chapter aims to explore the oeuvre of Lindström, a woman film architect within the Swedish film industry. In addition, the goal is to understand the probable prerequisites that contributed to the fact that she managed to make her way in an all-male profession and to stay in her position for almost half a century. My stimulus derives from ideas developed by Pierre Bourdieu regarding "cultural fields"—in this specific case pertaining to the film industry, media, and cultural institutions concentrated in the area of the capital city of Sweden. However, the purpose has not been to use Bourdieu's thoughts as a kind of explanatory model, but to let them inspire the questions arising in the working process.

The basic sources for the investigation come from archival studies; studies of film scripts; film reviews in magazines and major newspapers; and, to some extent, interviews with individuals who knew Lindström. Regrettably, the source material is scarce and scattered: the material found in the printed media is random, and the archival material seldom includes records on the process of planning and building the scenery. Immaculate copies of scripts have been saved instead of the scrapped ones with doodles and reminders that might have revealed something about the work process. However, by carefully putting together the puzzle out of bits and pieces of information—with the generous help of knowledgeable archive personnel—it has been possible to create a plausible image of a professional and resourceful person: Bibi Lindström.[1]

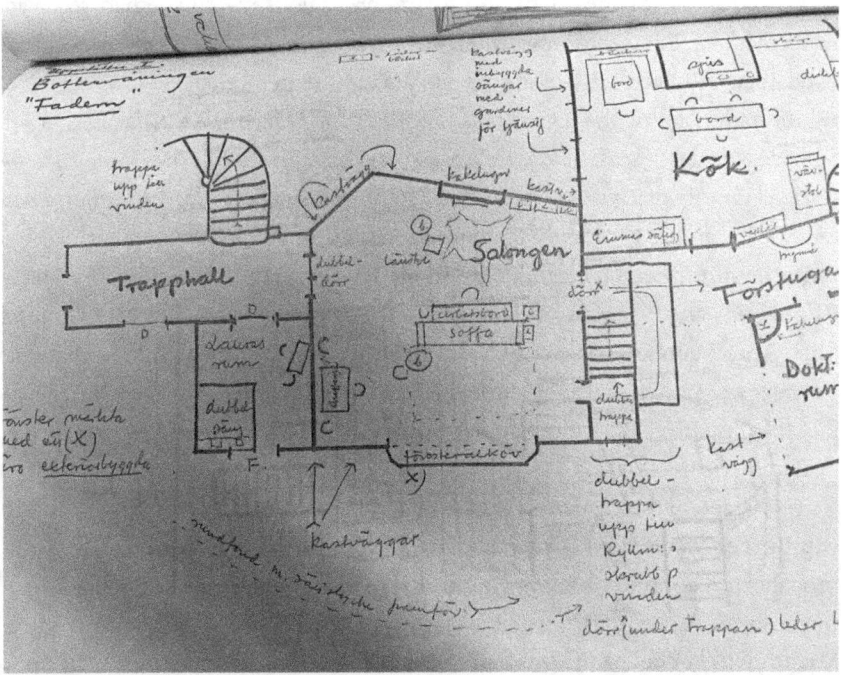

Figure 7.1 A sketch for studio floor plan of *Fadern* (Alf Sjöberg 1969). SFI Archival material.

The Milieus

Bibi Lindström was born in a well-to-do middle-class family. Her father Arthur (1882–1936) was a chief accountant at one of the engineering industries in a small community of Arbrå, north Sweden. However, Bibi's parents separated when she and her brother, Jan-Gunnar (1911–1969), were quite young, and their mother Sigrid (1881–1942) moved to Stockholm with them. Leaving her marriage—in that day and age—shows the independence of Sigrid Lindström's personality, and of her economic status that made the separation possible. In Stockholm, the small family lived an unassuming life, but due to her ambition and cultural interest, Sigrid ensured that her children received a good education.

The beginning of the twentieth century was a period of economic, political, and social upheaval manifesting itself in many levels of society, a turmoil that would develop into a world war. In Sweden, three powerful popular movements—the *godtemplar*, socialist, and religious revivalist movements, all nursing ideas about reforming the society as well as its individual members—had a palpable effect on public societal thought.

The overarching issue debated at the turn of the century was about general suffrage. A law passed in 1909 still excluded women, whose right to vote was not confirmed until 1921. Other public disputes in Sweden that may serve as examples of the intertwined cultural and political ideas and their effects in practice are the so-called Strindberg feud that raged throughout the press from 1910 to 1920, initiated by the famous author August Strindberg, who—with the wholehearted support of the leftist press—attacked the (national romantic) personal cult of great (Swedish) men; and also the debate caused by feature film *Ingeborg Holm* (*Margaret Day*) (Viktor Sjöström, 1913).[2] The film was based on a book about a widowed woman who, because of her poverty, lost the custody of her children and was sent to the almshouse. The fierce debate launched by the film would eventually lead to progressive changes in the Poverty Law in 1918.

The modern world was under formation, and Bibi Lindström, a young woman with artistic talent, wanted to experience the sources of the new. She chose Munich, with its architecture, museums, and art institutions. Munich had an unblemished reputation built up during the second half of the nineteenth century as the center of art education, ranking alongside Paris, and being the number one "Kunststadt" (art city) in Central Europe.[3] Also, as the architecture scholar Douglas Klahr has stated, the identity of Munich as an art city was firmly associated with the artist's role as an integrated part of the society (and not as an outcast, for instance). Another important ingredient in this "city identity" was the general emphasis on the notion of *Gesamtkunstwerk* as an ideal.[4] New art institutes were designed and built at the turn of the century. Events such as the three avant-garde exhibitions with works by Picasso, Rouault, Kogan, and others were arranged in 1909 to 1912 by Die Neue Kunstlervereinigung Munchen (the Munich New Association of Artists), established by Wassily Kandinsky, among others.

Ten years later, in 1922, Bibi Lindström, now eighteen years old, was admitted to Münchener Lehrwerkstätten (Munich Educational Workshops) to study decorative painting. It should be safe to say that the ideas on art embraced in Munich—namely, co-working, reciprocal societal relationships, and shared, modern visions—made an impact on the young woman, and were eventually carried on in her work on the theater stages and studio floors. Thus, for instance, in the future she would stress the importance of teamwork during the film production and tactfully point out the significance of those with supporting functions—for example, carpenters and electricians—for her work.[5] In an interview regarding the award touched on above, she explained: "Characteristic for film ateliers is the collective work: everybody is helping out. It is extremely important that the craftsmen use their fantasy when handling their tools, because the result is very much dependent on their inventiveness."[6]

Stage and Screen

After returning to Stockholm in 1923, Bibi Lindström was admitted to Filip Månsson's Painter School situated at the Institute of Technology in Stockholm for four years. She then continued her education at the Royal College of Fine Arts' department of decorative painting and graduated in 1932. In 1930, toward the end of her student years, Lindström had the opportunity to work at the Stockholmsutställningen (Stockholm exhibition) as an aide to Isaac Grünewald (1889–1946), considered the leading character of early Swedish Modernism. The years spent in Munich were most certainly a good recommendation for such an employment. Being a major event with four million visitors during the opening months, the exhibition signified the introduction of modern design and functionalism to Sweden. The most visited department was the one bestowing architecture and the building of practical and functional new homes.

Lindström worked, among others, with the architect Sven Markelius (1889–1972), famous for his functionalist construction design. This experience would later open up a position for her to design the Swedish pavilion at the World Exhibition in New York in 1939. Also, while still a student, Lindström worked as a trainee stage decorator in small private theaters such as Oscarsteatern, which was led by Gösta Ekman, one of the most celebrated actors in the country. It was not difficult to get an extra job as a staff member in theaters in Stockholm; the city boasted—apart from the two national stages—almost twenty theaters with regular repertoire. In addition, the revue was an extremely popular genre of entertainment, and makeshift stages were built in larger restaurants, assembly halls, and summer theater facilities.

However, come 1931, Bibi Lindström's career path changed. Another field of the modern world, namely cinema, was well established in Sweden with its internationally celebrated productions during the silent era. The new sound technology was cautiously introduced in 1929 in the country, in the midst of an economic crisis. Yet, it proved itself a success already at the launch of the first two films with some dialogue and musical themes in 1931. All film thereafter was produced with sound and contributed to a significant expansion of domestic film production.[7]

Bibi Lindström's education was in decorative painting with a focus on murals, namely ornamenting large surfaces in sizeable spaces. The techniques to create such pieces of art—planned to be regarded at a distance—were especially apt for work on stage and the film screen. In addition, Lindström had also developed a skilled hand in architecture and building construction. She was credited as a film architect (a title that today may translate as production designer or even scenographer) throughout her career, and this was also the title that appeared in the press, stressing her position as a woman in a male-coded profession, at the time something with considerable news value.

The expanding market in the field of cinema and at times the hectic production tempo naturally led to a quest for more staff for the newly built studios and—given that the productions became more complicated and technology more sophisticated—also more qualified professionals. During the early 1900s the way into the profession of film architect had many different openings, mainly by a sort of an apprentice system. But during the studio era, when entire houses and vast landscapes were built inside large atelier facilities, it was not a surprise that the newcomers had the backgrounds of a civil engineer such as Vilhelm Bryde (1888–1974), who contributed to seventy-two films, or of an architect such as Arne Åkermark (1902–1962). Åkermark was the only one of Lindström's colleagues that passed her record with more than fifty productions at Svensk Filmindustri, the country's oldest and largest production company.

In the early 1930s, the job descriptions between different occupations were vague, and a sound technician, for instance, might also be the one to edit the entire film. Likewise, the profession of a prop master became only gradually defined. A newspaper article about a day in Bibi Lindström's life in 1940 reports her driving around the city in a pickup or her bicycle in search of objects to furnish a scene with. She tells the reporter that it feels like constantly moving from one home to another, trying to find furniture with the right style and "atmosphere" for a certain setting.[8] Later she would note:

> My task is to draw sketches and arrange the interiors and even exteriors if they are to be built in a studio. We are always in a hurry when a film is in the making. Sometimes it is a bit difficult to get hold of things—we need to rent from furniture store, borrow, look into the cellars and attics. Actually, it is easier to furnish an ancient castle than a modern apartment.[9]

Later on, she would be able to entrust this work to a professional props master.

A title in Swedish such as "Inspicient" may today translate to Unit Director or Studio Manager. For Lindström, it corresponded to one of the most important functions on the site. She has explained that the first thing for her to do after receiving a film script was to get in touch with the "Inspicient," and intense planning would start. She even said playfully that: "The Inspicient is a magic man, he can get hold of everything from a locomotive to speaking parrots!"[10] During her stay at Europa Film, Lindström worked most often with Olle Brunaeus (1896–1962) as well as Emil A. Pehrsson (1898–1984), who, besides his other responsibilities, often was responsible for the sound editing of films. "Most often" in this case means no more than five productions of the fourteen she participated in at Europa Film, which suggests she needed to adjust to new faces in a constant flow.

Start of a Long Career

Bibi Lindström's younger brother Jan-Gunnar was a film buff—he wrote articles on film and was one of the founding members of the Stockholm "ciné studio" in the 1930s.[11] He was aware of the expansion plans within the film business and encouraged his sister to apply for work at a studio. An opportunity turned up while she was working at Ekman's Oscarsteatern; a frantic man from a film team asked for help with their décor and no one except for Bibi Lindström had time to rush over—and the rest is, as they say, history.[12] Soon enough, in the spring of 1932, she was engaged by the newly (1930) established production company Europa Film. Her first film was a comedy called *Muntra musikanter* (*Jolly Musicians*) (Weyler Hilebrand, 1932). The film had its premiere at the end of November the same year, and a few months later she was already working on two new productions in the modern studios the company had rented in Sundbyberg at the northwestern fringes of the city.

One of Bibi Lindström's favorite productions from her first years in the business was *Flickorna från Gamla Sta'n* (*The Girls from the Old Town*) (Schamyl Bauman, 1934).[13] The story is a romantic comedy about two young women and an aspiring artist living in the picturesque Old Town of Stockholm. Most of the buildings there are from the sixteenth and seventeenth centuries, and must have been a challenge for Lindström and the photographers Harald Berglund (1904–1980) and Hilding Bladh (1906–1982). The exteriors for the film were shot on location while the interiors were filmed in Sundbyberg. When designing the sets for the studio, the film architect had to make estimates of the interiors in relation to the proportions of the exteriors of the house and to plan for the movements for the camera as well as space for all the equipment.

Another, perhaps more pleasing, part in designing the interiors for *Flickorna* was to create the artist of the story's paintings and sketches, which would hang on the walls of his house (Figure 7.2). Even *Muntra musikanter* had contained a scene where two of the characters appear on the stage in front of an "amateurishly" painted prop, most certainly created by Lindström.

Europa Film produced folksy comedies and romantic, rural melodramas. Within ten years it would develop into one of the three largest fully integrated film companies in Sweden. In spite of the increasing film production, the owners of the studio facilities could not let them stay vacant; instead they let other producers rent them as well. Most of the workers on the studio floor were full-time employees. An external producer would be charged not just for the facilities but also on an hourly basis for the work. Yet, this did not benefit the staff, who only received their rather modest monthly salary. Consequently, it was not unusual for employees to take on freelance assignments. Such a practice contributed to a developing network of studio professionals across the companies, familiar with each other's ways of working.

Figure 7.2 The style of the paintings on the wall in the film *Flickorna från Gamla Sta'n* (1934) correspond to the style common for the artists in 1930s Stockholm, but were likely to have been created by Bibi Lindström. © AB Svensk Filmindustri (1934) Foto: Filminstitutets bildarkiv.

On the other hand, many of those professionals Bibi Lindström made an acquaintance with in the 1930s would meet her in different teams during different periods. Thus, for instance, Hilding Bladh—the photographer who was first engaged as a B-photographer in *Kvinnorna kring Larsson (The Women around Larsson)* (Schamyl Bauman, 1934) at Europa Film—would later shoot many praised films with Lindström as the architect, such as the Ingmar Bergman (1918–2007) film *Persona* and the Mattsson thrillers produced by Sandrews.

Lindström would also work with many new film workers from the younger generations such as Sven Nykvist (1922–2006), who was first a B-photographer on *En kvinna ombord* (*Woman On-Board*) (Gunnar Skoglund 1941) and would later reach world fame as the photographer of a number of films directed by Bergman. Nykvist also shot the only film Lindström ever directed: *En Stockholmssilhouett* (*Stockholm Silhouette*) (1943), a short film journal about a workday in Berns salonger (Bern's salons), the legendary house of entertainment in Sweden.

Moving On

During the years of the Second World War, film production in Sweden topped its annual production rates, doubling the results made ten years earlier. This was partly due to the unceasing popularity of the domestic film, but also due to the fact that importing from abroad was difficult during the war.[14] In 1939, Bibi Lindström had several freelance assignments, among others the design of the exhibition "Sweden Speaks: Of Present Achievements and Future Aspirations" for the World Fair in New York.[15]

The Swedish pavilion was created by Sven Markelius, whom Lindström had worked with during the Stockholm exhibition. At the planning stage of the exhibition in 1938 she had, together with an advertising designer Anders Beckman (1907–1967), presented a proposal for the interior design of the Swedish pavilion.[16] They won the contest and a newspaper article reports of her success, simultaneously pointing out the fact that she had handed over the eighteen large sketches for the competition only two days before she gave birth to her son Jonas.[17]

Bibi Lindström had married a colleague, architect Viking Göransson (1900–1985), in 1929, and the couple belonged—due to their academic education and the modern style they favored professionally—to those devoted to the idea of the welfare state and modernization of society. Thus, for instance, the family lived in an experimental lodging—a "Collective House"—created by Sven Markelius, built in 1935 and designed "to relieve the burden of professional, married women in their work with children and household."[18]

The apartments were small, but there were common areas and service facilities such as a restaurant, laundry, and a children's daycare center managed by employed staff. Markelius himself lived on the top floor of this house that carried unmistakable features of functionalist architecture. Among the tenants were many radical personalities of the period, including members of the anti-Nazi group Kulturfront. The architecture scholar Eva Rudberg quotes a "contemporary assessor" as follows: "A considerable number of the radical intellectuals in Sweden would probably be killed if someone placed a bomb in the Collective House."[19]

AB Sandrew-Produktion a.k.a. Sandrews

Bibi Lindström had worked at Europa Film with the film director Schamyl Bauman (1893–1966), who also was one of the two founders of the company. In 1938, Bauman decided to move on and established first an enterprise named after himself, before making a cooperation agreement in 1939 with the expanding distribution company of Anders Sandrew. The new corporation called AB Sandrew-Produktion—shortened to Sandrews—had the ambition to focus on "quality film production" by employing younger film critics with academic backgrounds such as Rune Waldekranz (1911–2003) and Lorens Marmstedt (1908–1966). With their shared ideas on film as art rather than entertainment, they would in the future contribute to Sandrews' reputation as a company for "prestigious" film.

Perhaps due to the production tempo, and the fact that practically every film returned their investments, a lesser (artistic) quality of the film supply was observed in many instances. The "yardstick" used was the world fame of the Swedish film in the 1920s with its artistic and innovative solutions, which was, perhaps, an unfair comparison. The criticism was harsh, led by the Swedish Authors' Association (Svensk Författarförening) and the chair of the Swedish Pen Club, Carl Björkman (1901–1961). The campaign orchestrated by the association was implemented by indignant open meetings and articles in the media. The establishment of Sandrew-Produktion came as a promise of better days ahead, even if the actual prime motivation was to guarantee the supply of films for their own distribution net.[20]

The debates may have contributed to the fact that Bibi Lindström accepted Schamyl Bauman's offer and left Europa Film for the newly established company. She was part of the cultural elite that was for the "better," namely more artistic, films. Her husband Viking Göransson, for instance, lectured at a Society for Fiber Arts meeting in 1937, criticizing Swedish films for their "harmful influence on the public taste" regarding interior design: "[However,] the inept interior design seen in contemporary films [still] generates a feel of reality that may appear acceptable for [someone with] an untrained eye and invite to imitation."[21] In addition, an interview indicates that Bibi Lindström's own preferences regarding film as a medium were with the experimental, short, and children's film rather than with the mainstream feature film.[22]

Also, after ten years in the business Lindström was quite competent and perhaps looking for more challenging opportunities: during the heyday of the 1930s production boom, the same décor was sometimes used in several films (a fact that even Viking Göransson referred to), and she may have wanted freer hands. Indeed, during the twenty-odd years to follow, Lindström was to work at Sandrews with some of the most distinguished Swedish film directors, including Olof Molander (1892–1966), Arne Mattsson, Ingmar Bergman, Alf Sjöberg (1903–1980), and Mai Zetterling (1925–1994)—to name but a few.

Lindström's first task for Sandrews, however, was *En sjöman i frack* (*A Sailor in Tailcoat*) (Ragnar Arvedson, 1942), which did not differ much from the genres of Europa Film; it was a comedy starring the popular Adolf Jahr that gave the two architects, Lindström and Arthur Spjuth (1904–1989), an opportunity to stage many different milieus: from a bourgeois residence to a shady bar in a harbor. This film was recorded in the studios of Centrumateljéerna at Gärdet, next to the center of the city. The Sandrews' studios were first situated in Djurgården on the outskirts of Stockholm, but as the facilities grew insufficient, the company moved the production corps to Gärdet, which was closer to the city. In 1948, the company bought the entire plant and changed its name to Sandrewateljéerna. Bibi Lindström worked in these facilities until the mid-1960s. However, she had many interesting freelance employments on the side, such as creating décor for Swedish Television and participating in feminist theater productions in 1960s Stockholm.

Art and Crafts

Kan doktorn komma? (*Can You Come, Doctor?*) (Rolf Husberg, 1942), Bibi Lindström's second film for Sandrews, was more of a challenge, based on a novel of a doctor's work in the milieu among the Sámi people. The work required a number of trips to Lapland, and the film was shot in different places in Arjeplog, close to the Norwegian mountains. The filming of exteriors took place from the end of June to the beginning of the fall—the completing takes were shot in October.

The production manager for *Kan doktorn* was Rune Waldekranz, who also participated in writing the script. It is interesting to note that this project enrolled more women than usual: in addition to Bibi Lindström, there was Britta Bergquist as the script supervisor, Birgitta Pramm (1924–1991), responsible for stills and C-photo, and Inga Lindeström (1915–1994) for masks. Also, yet another woman should be mentioned, namely Alva Lundin (1889–1972), a personal friend of Lindström. Lundin was a painter and advertising designer who created hundreds of credit tableaus—*Kan doktorn* was her twenty-fourth film that year alone.

Bibi Lindström has admitted that before showing her sketches to the director and producer she visited archives and museums for inspiration and accuracy. While planning for *Kan doktorn* she studied the specific building style in the north of Sweden to find out, for instance, how people used to furnish their homes.[23] If necessary, she took advice from experts, and while *Gycklarnas afton* (*Sawdust and Tinsel*) (Ingmar Bergman, 1953) was prepared for filming, she interviewed workers at a circus to find out how to erect a circus tent.

Kan doktorn was met with quite positive reactions for its "no-nonsense" approach: "This film owns a deeper value that emanates from love to all it describes [without communicating] any wild life romanticism."[24] In fact in every review it became praised for its "authenticity and low key atmosphere"—which in this context signified realism.

Realism was a central notion, and Bibi Lindström stressed quite often that she felt she had succeeded in her work if the spectator did not particularly pay attention to the constructions or décor but accepted them without further reflection: "It may sound like a paradox, but if the milieu is correctly done, you do not react, but if it is wrong, it may ruin the whole impression."[25]

The quest for realism—or verisimilitude—as a sign of qualified crafting had its consequences for the life of the film workers: among other things, it has meant many and long travels. It was a common praxis that Lindström traveled to different places with the director at the early stages of a production. Even if it was economically sensible to find locations for the story as close to Stockholm as possible—where all the facilities stood within reach—it was not worth one's while to film in the Stockholm archipelago if the action was meant to take place on the Swedish west coast. It was not *real*, it would look unprofessional, and would upset, if not audiences, then at least the critics.

Thus, for instance, the critic of Italian newspaper *Il Messagero* reacted forcefully having seen the Swedish film *Barabbas* (Alf Sjöberg) at Cannes Film

Festival in April 1953. It is a story by the 1951 Nobel Prize winner Pär Lagerkvist about a villain whom the people wanted pardoned to crucify Jesus instead. Among other things, the critic pointed out that it was quite wrong to let the modern Viktor Emanuel monument in Rome function as a background for the emperor Nero's persecution of the Christians 1,800 years before the building was erected.[26]

Yet, when preparing for this ambitious work the members of the film team made trips to Italy and Israel with the director Alf Sjöberg. Much of the story takes place outdoors, describing Barabbas' wanderings from Jerusalem to Rome in his search for the answer to the mystery of early Christianity. Notwithstanding the *faux pas* with Viktor Emanuel, it was important for the team to create an authentic feel, and they agreed, for instance, that certain scenes would be more effective if filmed "real," such as those in the Roman catacombs.

Barabbas had its Swedish premiere in May 5, 1953, and had been under production for more than a year at the cost of 1.5 million krona, twice as much as the estimated budget the year before (and in its turn half of the entire production budget of Sandrews for the year in question).[27] During two months from the beginning of March 1952, and again in October for extra takes, the team worked in Rome and Israel. Meanwhile, the interior scenes such as the whorehouse, the potter's workshop, and the mill with its huge millstones handled by Barabbas and the other slaves, were built at the Sandrewateljéerna to be ready for filming in the summer.

The applause at the Cannes Film Festival had been merely polite, reports Ellen Liliedahl of *Svenska Dagbladet*, who also wrote a very positive review of the film.[28] In all, *Barabbas* met with understanding reactions at home. The influential Bengt Idestam-Almquist, for instance, was very positive: "As for me, I like this film very, very much."[29] Even Carl Björkman—the merciless critic of 1930s Swedish film production—was positive in spite of the weak points he found in the film, such as its solemn slow pace and confusing flashbacks.[30] The work of the photographer Göran Strindberg was also greeted with praise.

Despite the fact that so many of the films Bibi Lindström worked with were extremely successful, she was sometimes sad, feeling that the results of her work were ephemeral and rarely recognized by critics[31]—which, as stated above, in a sense was a consequence of work well done.[32] There are, however, exceptions and they were always positive. One review of her contribution for the film *Hemsöborna* (*The People of Hemsö*) (Arne Mattsson, 1955)—based on the novel with the same name by August Strindberg—was written by Ellen Liliedahl:

> The architect Bibi Lindström's coloured elements and décor, designed in discreet and convincing manner, adapt themselves in the wholeness of the exterior takes, conserving the interior takes within an exemplary tasteful frame. When juxtaposing Hemsöborna with the whole lot of dreadfully coloured Hollywood-spectacles, the former stands out as a blameless piece of art in colour.[33]

Bengt Idestam-Almquist in his turn writes of *Vägen till Klockrike* (*The Road to Klockrike*) (Arne Mattsson, 1953):

> I even think about the architect Bibi Lindström [,] her work is superb. *Klockrike* is a costume film, the story takes place in 1902. Bibi Lindström has understood to provide the scenes with correct colour of the period, but in a quite discrete manner without constituting an eyesore, it does not smell Nordic Museum—and yet, the tune of the film does not conflict with [its topic,] a timeless dream.[34]

Yet another film based on a novel of a (then future) Nobel Prize winner, Halldor Kiljan Laxness (1902–1998), named *Salka Valka* (Arne Mattsson, 1954) demanded extensive travels in search of sufficient sites. This tragic story takes place among the extremely poor fishermen on the stormy shores of Iceland. The young Salka (Gunnel Broström/Birgitta Petersson) is torn between two men: Arnaldur, her young lover, and Steinthor, the partner of her mother. The mother (Margareta Krook) drowns herself when she finds out about the man's desire for her daughter.

Salka Valka was a challenging endeavor merely because of the capricious Icelandic weather conditions, and the press reported on the process on several occasions. Laxness—who was to win the Nobel Prize in literature in 1955—was a celebrity and visited the filming sites in person. The main location for the story was a small town named Grindavik in the southwestern corner of Iceland. However, some of the exterior takes were filmed at Hovs hallar in Båstad, in the south of Sweden. A newspaper article reports under the header "Icelandic tragedy in Skåne" that the death of Salka's mother, for example, was shot in Hovs hallar.[35] Two years later Ingmar Bergman decided to film the famous chess scene in *Sjunde inseglet* (*The Seventh Seal*) (1957) in the same location.[36]

A reporter of *Svenska Dagbladet* was in awe when visiting the studios in March 1954, where Bibi Lindström with her craftsmen had built an Icelandic Salvation Army prayer house; a lowly hall with citations from the Bible on the walls, an organ next to the preacher's pulpit, and a reeking iron stove in the corner. After the takes were finished in the house, the walls were torn down and the workers erected a farmer's cottage of peat and stone, next to a barn that sheltered real cows borrowed from Skansen (the open air museum nearby). The studio halls were also to host a rudimentary general store and a number of other interiors.[37]

Salka Valka was produced by Nordisk Tonefilm, which owned studios in Jungfrugatan in the center of the city. Bibi Lindström had already worked there on three other Mattsson films before *Salka*. At the same time, she had handled her projects at the Sandrewateljéerna as well: *Fröken Julie* and two films directed by Hasse Ekman (1915–2004), one of them *Flicka och hyacinter* (*The Girl with Hyacinths*, 1950). She even worked on two projects for a company called Film AB Imago that had its studios in Stocksund, slightly north of the city.

This means that during a period of circa five years, Lindström was working on two, sometimes three films simultaneously—normally preparing for recordings that would take place during the spring and summer. Further, the films were produced by different companies that used three studio facilities: Sandrewateljéerna in Gärdet, Nordisk Tonefilm's atelier at Jungfrugatan, and Film AB Imago's facilities in Stocksund. All the studios were situated in the northeastern part of the city. Yet the distance from Gärdet to Stocksund with Jungfrugatan in between was about 10 kilometers, and Lindström had to commute almost daily. It was, of course, not necessary for an architect to be present on location while the filming went on, but she needed to supervise the building and rebuilding of the sceneries, and to be at hand if something went wrong. Toward the mid-1950s, however, Bibi Lindström worked mostly for Nordisk Tonefilm, which financed films directed by Arne Mattsson and the rising "star" Kenne Fant (1923–2016), who both preferred working with her.

Changing Techniques

Having a career that lasts almost half a century means adjusting to many changes in techniques. As shown by the reviews cited above, Bibi Lindström was happy to work with color film productions: "With black and white it is only possible to work with shades and nuances—to juxtapose dark against light and shiny against lacklustre."[38] Among others, she worked on three thrillers directed by Arne Mattsson: *Damen i svart* (*The Lady in Black*) (1958) was—not surprisingly— black and white, but the other two, *Mannekäng i rött* (*Mannequin in Red*) (1958) and *Ryttare i blått* (*Rider in Blue*) (1959), were shot in Eastman Colour, the first in ratio 1.66:1 whereas the latter was shot in Agascope—the Swedish equivalent of Cinemascope—in ratio 2:35:1.

Not only colors but also the widescreen format asked for a new kind of thinking. Bibi Lindström found it a bit challenging to work with Mattsson, albeit in a positive way: he often wanted to do takes from extreme angles and at times it was challenging to build scenery that would make his wishes possible and still guarantee four prerequisites—enough light to accomplish decent photography, the concealment of the equipment, the avoidance of reflections into the camera, and finally, to keep the buildings from falling in.[39]

In *Mannekäng i rött* and *Ryttare i blått* the interiors are spacious and furnished with good taste according to the latest in Swedish design, as if on display. In a much distributed picture from the former, an interior take at the home of the main characters, the Hillmans, depicts older Gustavian furniture, signaling classy bourgeois taste—present in the life of the couple but still in the rear, as if being a bit passé. Instead, the modern design is displayed in the foreground with a coffee table and bookshelf in teak, the woodwork in vogue. The easy chair at the front is in curved veneer, probably "Mingo" by Yngve Ekström (1913–1988).

The costumes were created by the celebrated German-born designer Magó (Max Goldstein, 1925–2008) to match the surrounding colors. The cooperation between the architect, costume designer, photographer—Hilding Bladh—and the director resulted in a color palette that in extension brings to mind the Italian directors Mario Brava's and Dario Argento's films created later in the 1960s and 1970s.

An Alf Sjöberg film, *Karin Månsdotter* (1954), had its premiere in Stockholm the same day as *Salka Valka*. *Karin Månsdotter* was based on August Strindberg's play *Erik XIV* and was, due to uncleared property rights, delayed several times. Sjöberg had successfully staged this popular historical play for the Royal Dramatic Theatre, with the premiere on November 15, 1950. After *Barabbas*, he decided to return to *Erik XIV*, this time with the unhappy queen Karin Månsdotter in focus. Due to the aforementioned legal problems, the film formed a triptych, where the first part is an animated parody of a silent film in color—a short "chap book" about Karin, the poor man's daughter whom the King wanted to marry (the animation work was by Ulrika Friberger, an artist and scenographer). The second part followed the Strindberg play, and the last part is a free fantasy about the life of Karin after the King's death.

The data available on the film production identifies a number of sites in the vicinity of Stockholm, but the film consists mostly of interior takes—not surprising perhaps because of its focus on dialogue, and perhaps because Sjöberg's mind was still preoccupied by the play staged for a theater. Bibi Lindström's efforts to give life to the milieu were concentrated on two things: to reproduce the historical characters' dwellings mentioned in the play, and to adapt the scenery for Sjöberg's *faiblesse* for deep focus. By cooperating with Sven Nykvist, the result turned out commendably in spite of the fact that the film otherwise was considered a fiasco.[40] The kind-hearted critic of *Svenska Dagbladet* Ellen Liliedahl stated that "Bibi Lindström's 'skilled hand' has created magnificent sceneries, and Sven Nykvist's camerawork, using deep focus, is excellent."[41] Undoubtedly, the takes in deep focus on the long, arched corridors did reflect the situation of the main characters: distance, on the one hand, and incarceration, on the other.

Lindström revealed in an interview that, after receiving the script, she first tried to form an idea of how the characters were and to imagine what kind of things they might want to have around them.[42] Indeed, it seems that this was a method she practiced throughout her professional days—trying to understand the mindset of the people in a story and to create milieus that corresponded to their likings in a plausible manner.

Figure 7.3 A sketch on the throne hall in *Karin Månsdotter* made on a graph sheet. SFI Archival material.

Television: A New Medium

Bibi Lindström's son Jonas Göransson remembers her reflecting upon her last major work, *Godnatt jord* (*Goodnight Earth*) (1979), a TV series based on the novel by Ivar Lo-Johansson (1901–1990) and directed by Keve Hjelm (1922–2004) for Swedish Television. The novel was published in 1933; an autobiographical story about the life of the oppressed and extremely poor farm workers in the Swedish countryside in the beginning of the twentieth century.

Lindström took pains to provide the actors with the kind of properties the characters of the story might have had. For décor, she was looking for two kinds of things: first, plain everyday articles and, second, those of a "special sort" that carried meaning within the scenic discourse and were specified by the instructions in the script. Under the direction of Keve Hjelm, every "family" in the story chose certain furniture and interior details, such as curtains, carpets, and perhaps paintings or pictures for the walls. Then Lindström saw it as her job to make everything fit in the whole, namely, in the exclusively overarching visual style of the actual film: "It is difficult to catch but not impossible to create," she had said. "The point was to make the details play with a number of larger, supporting constructions and to reflect the dramatic action and its consequences."[43]

Godnatt jord was produced for the Swedish broadcasting company in 1979, shot in color and with wide-angle framing, which created problems when viewed on TV sets that still had the ratio 4:3. Keve Hjelm followed Andrew Bazin's idea of a long take with a wide angle allowing the spectator's gaze to roam freely over the screen, as in reality. The idea, in itself quite interesting, asked for wide, in-depth staging arrangements but turned into a nuisance when the widescreen photography was squeezed into the ratio of a TV set in the spectators' living rooms—but sixty years later, the series has become pronounced an often-streamed masterpiece.

Regular TV broadcasting in Sweden had started in 1957, twenty-odd years earlier, and even at this time Bibi Lindström had participated in the development of the new technology from early on. The first TV years in Sweden were characterized by experimentation and innovation but also imitating both British and American TV programs. Series were imported, but surprising co-operative enterprises took place as well. One of them was the horror series *13 Demon Street* (Curt Siodmak, 1959–1960), produced by the US company Herts Lion Productions, filmed in the studios of Nordisk Tonefilm in Stockholm, where Lindström worked. The language of the dialogue was English and many actors were Americans. Lindström is credited as the Art Director. The series included a dozen 25-minute long episodes directed by Curt Siodmak (1902–2000), a Hollywood scriptwriter and brother of the famous film director Robert Siodmak (1900–1973).

How the project got started remains still to be clarified. But in 1947 the Swedish twin brothers and dancers Gustaf (1920–1995) and Bertil (1920–1990) Unger had emigrated to the United States and established themselves in Hollywood. Gustaf Unger still had contacts in the Swedish entertainment business and he was to produce all the episodes with suggestive titles such as "The Vine of Death," "The Book of Ghouls," and "Black Nemesis" during 1960. The series imitates *Alfred Hitchcock Presents* (1955–1965), where the famous director introduces the story of the day. Number 13 Demon Street is the address and purgatory of sorts where a doomed criminal dwells, played by Lon Chaney Jr. (1906–1973), trying to invent more hideous crimes than he himself has committed, to be set free.[44]

Every episode follows the same pattern: it begins with a thunderstorm; it is dark, the shadows are long, and among them the street sign is shown from extreme and disturbing angles. The camera approaches a heavy door surrounded by branches of ivy, with the number thirteen in the middle. The door opens and a voice-over by the doomed man explains the conditions of his imprisonment. There is a cut to his face as he looks in the camera and opens another door or a window, inviting the spectator to come and see. There is no doubt about the artificiality of the décor that reminds of the sceneries used in the early 1920s and 1930s horror films, a subtle reminder of the fact that this is but another make-believe. An interesting fact is that now, after decades of striving for realism, a meta-aspect of narration is introduced in a new medium.

As with so many other works for early television, *13 Demon Street* was a low-budget production. The television aesthetics adapted for the ratio of 4:3 allowed a limited range of action that made it necessary for the actors to stay close to each other and perform *en face* in front of the cameras. Consequently, the settings do not show much—yet, it is possible to see that the furnishing does adhere to the predicaments of the characters, such as in "The Black Hand," where a dark and heavy semicircular window frames the unlucky couple in the scene where they are informed that they have been in contact with a psychopathic killer.

Swedish Television had, as a part of the public service function, a division called TV theater assigned to stage (classic) theater plays. Over time, the division initiated cooperation with independent film producers as part of the outsourcing of their production. Bibi Lindström participated in staging some of the series, such as *Den vita stenen* (*The White Stone*) (Göran Graffman, 1973) and the Strindberg play *Fadern* (*The Father*) (Alf Sjöberg, 1969). The assistant director for the latter was Pelle Berglund (1939–). He recalls in an interview that at this time and age, Bibi Lindström was just as laid back as she was experienced. Sjöberg insisted on having a certain type of iron fence in a take, maintaining that he had seen a fence like that round one or two manors outside Stockholm. It would take at least half a day to drive and find the places, but Sjöberg was quite adamant in spite of the actual hurry. However, when the film director turned his back, Lindström quietly said to the assistant: "Down in Östermalm, at the Artillery Depot, there is a similar kind of fence—why don't you go there instead!"[45]

Later, when Berglund would direct films of his own, he would engage Lindström first of all. She worked with him on *Den magiska cirkeln* (*The Magic Circle*) (Pelle Berglund, 1969) and *Ture Sventon—privatdetektiv* (*Ture Sventon— The Private Detective*) (Pelle Berglund, 1972): "it was so easy to work with her!"[46] Bengt Forslund, film historian and former artistic leader of the Swedish Film Institute, writes: "The fact that she was so well liked and often requested was due to her solid routine for working swiftly and effectively; she also was knowledgeable in art history, cost conscious and kept her budget without bargaining on the quality of her work."[47]

Conclusion

When the aspiring young actress Lena Nyman (1944–2011) started rehearsing her role in a play directed and written by Vilgot Sjöman called *Hattasken* (1964), she writes in her diary *en passant* that Bibi Lindström has designed the décor for the play, and that she even will help with the costumes. The way she notes it signals that this young theater student knew who Lindström was, and thinks it is worth her while to mention her and her contribution—yet, they are not closer acquainted because Nyman writes down her whole name.[48]

Who, then, was Bibi Lindström as a person, aside from her professional self? She was described in terms such as discrete, shy, friendly, hard-working, intuitive, artistic—in short, a picture of a person with great integrity appears. A family "legend" tells that when Ingmar Bergman arrived in Gotland to inspect the constructions for *Persona*, he was so enthusiastic over the work done that he spread his arms wide to give Lindström a big hug—and she froze stiff: the spontaneous closeness did not appeal to her.[49]

Bibi Lindström loved to dance, and in her youth she took classes at the Musikaliska Akademien in "plastic dance," which according to an interview, would later be of help, not only with keeping her balance when she had to climb up high on the studio constructions but also to understand the rhythm in movements of the figures she wanted to paint.[50] Her friendliness and politeness was witnessed by many, but she could get angry and, allegedly, she never got along with the successor of Josef Andersson, the chief of Sandrewateljéerna, after Andersson's retirement in 1964.[51]

Issues regarding women's work, leisure activities, and housing were important for Lindström, and she was engaged in women's associations in several ways. She figured in the press, sometimes just in small notes such as the one where she and her son Jonas are said to have contributed to a Christmas tree exhibition arranged by the Housing Advisor of the city.[52] Another small notice contradicts allegations of her shyness while reporting that she was asked to give a lecture on her work as a film architect at Zonta Club Stockholm in 1945.[53] She also gave lectures at Film Week in Stockholm when she received the honorary plaque: "Bibi Lindström presented her work unassumingly, in short notes, and guided round the small special exhibition with sketches, floor plans and small models arranged at the Technical Museum."[54]

What about the question of her position in the "cultural field" of the Swedish film culture? How could she break into a branch and a profession with an all-male representation? Pierre Bourdieu says that in conditions where there emerges a lack—of labor or positions—or unease of some kind, new individuals for the otherwise closed cultural field may find their way in. This was quite true of the first decades of the Swedish society at large, and the film branch in particular. To manage, a person needed to have guidance, support that fostered a sense of what is valued within the society or field, or to put it in the words of Bourdieu, a sense of "a system of internalized structures, schemes of perception and action common to all members of the same group or class."[55] Bibi Lindström had plenty: she had a supporting family that gave her social status, and her husband and brother encouraged her and were interested in her work. She had an exclusive education granted to few. Through her journalist friends, she became not a celebrity but a "name" in the cultural field where she had contact with many powerful people.

Last, but not least, she was there to mold the new field. While acknowledging a structural sociological pattern that may highlight a life course and work—a when, where, and how of an individual—it does not make manifest the *primus motor*, the power that makes use of the agency that certain familiarity with the valid rules and structures in a field allow. Bibi Lindström was a talented person who in her own right made her contacts through hard and innovative work. Her oeuvre also shows that she was able to adapt to new working conditions and changing techniques. From early on, she was interested in functionalism and modernist design as well as ideas on social engineering promoted by the social democratic rationale in the country. At first glance, it seems like a contradiction that in her work she was involved in the production of popular mass entertainment—a form of culture that most often supported conformist, traditional, and conservative values—while her own life did not quite coincide with them: she lived in a modernist milieu with radical intellectual friends, far from underprivileged working-class problems. While working in the film production business, her preferences, as far as it comes to film as a means of expression, perhaps were on the side of international cooperation and experimental film than on folksy, rural comedy.[56] In a sense, the work and art of Bibi Lindström was about furnishing; furnishing the stage, the scene, and the silver screen. Her work was a novelty, it was academic, and her being a woman had news value. Undoubtedly, she allowed different values and cultural spheres to enlighten the others.

Acknowledgments

The author wishes to extend her warmest thanks to the helpful and most supportive staff at the Library and Archives of the Swedish Film Institute, and to Pelle Berglund, Jonas Göransson, and Mikael Lindström for generously sharing their memories of Bibi Lindström.

Notes

1 Particularly important was the input of the members of her family.
2 Ironically, this feud would lead to another cult, namely the Strindbergian one.
3 Douglas Klahr, "Munich as Kunststadt," *Oxford Art Journal*, vol. 34, no. 2 (2011), 179–201, 172.
4 Ibid., 184.

5   "C-a," *Svenska Dagbladet*, June 15, 1940, 8; [Anna Greta Ståhle], "Age," *Dagens Nyheter*, May 9, 1954, 13.
6   [Anna Greta Ståhle], "Age," *Dagens Nyheter*, May 9, 1954, 20.
7   Leif Furhammar, *Filmen i Sverige En historia i tio kapitel* (Wiken: Höganäs Förlags AB, 1991), 133.
8   *Svenska Dagbladet*, July 15, 1940, 8.
9   Anonymous, "På lördagen 90 filmer," *Svenska Dagbladet*, May 9, 1954, 18. As for the profession of "film architect," different countries announced different terms: in English handouts Lindström was titled as the Art Director or Set Designer; in Germany, the actual handicraft was stressed with the expression "Bauten"— namely "Construction[s made by]." In Sweden the term film architect remained in use as long as the first generation of professionals were active (i.e., to the mid-1970s) and then became gradually replaced by the term scenographer. Also, following the development of new technology and educational career paths, the title scenographer may appear in TV productions she worked on in the 1960s and 1970s.
10 "C-a," 8.
11 Bengt Bengtsson, "Filmstudion och drömmen om den stora uppsalafilmen: Uppsala Studenters Filmstudio som filmproducent och skola," in Erik Hedling and Mats Jönsson (eds.), *Välfärdsbilder—svensk film utanför biografen*, Mediehistoriska arkiv, vol. 5 (Stockholm: Statens Ljud- och bildarkiv. Stockholm, 2008), 205–27, 209. Jan-Gunnar Lindström went on to study film in the United States and become a director at Statens Biografbyrå, the Swedish film censorship organ. During the 1950s he held a position as the Acting Director of the United Nations' Films and Visual Information Division in New York.
12 [Ståhle], "Age," 20.
13 "Col," *Dagens Nyheter*, June 18, 1938, 13.
14 Furhammar, *Filmen i Sverige En historia i tio kapitel*, 174.
15 Probably due to the threatening political situation in Europe, the exhibition in New York that presented news on design, technology, and innovations did not get the attention it deserved. The Second World War prevented further series of exhibitions until the tradition was re-established in 1958 by World Expo "Atomium" in Belgium.
16 Jeff Werner, *Medelvägens estetik. Sverigebilder i USA*, part 1 (Hedemora: Gidlunds förlag, 2008), 320.
17 *Svenska Dagbladet*, December 4, 1949, 18.
18 Eva Rudberg, "Sven Markelius 1889–1972," *Arkitekturmuseet*, October 28, 1989– February 4, 1990, 7.
19 Ibid., 7–8.

20 Tytti Soila, "Sweden," in Tytti Soila, Astrid Söderbergh Widding, and Gunnar Iversen (eds.), *Nordic National Cinemas* (New York: Routledge, 1998), 175–76.
21 *Svenska Dagbladet*, April 28, 1937, 16.
22 *Svenska Dagbladet*, December 31, 1949, 11.
23 [Ståhle], "Age," 20.
24 [Sven Hanson], "Filmson," *Arbetarbladet*, December 22, 1942.
25 Anonymous, *Svenska Dagbladet*, June 15, 1940, 8.
26 *Dagens Nyheter*, May 5, 1953, 7.
27 "-gram," *Svenska Dagbladet*, April 28, 1952, 20; Anonymous, *Dagens Nyheter*, May 17, 1952, 14.
28 [Ellen Liliedahl], "Lil," *Svenska Dagbladet*, April 25, 1953, 11.
29 [Bengt Idestam-Almquist], "Robin Hood," *Stockholms-Tidningen*, May 5, 1953.
30 Carl Björkman, *Dagens Nyheter*, May 6, 1953, 7.
31 This was still long before any significant archival methods.
32 Jonas Göransson, letter to Tytti Soila, October 20, 2020.
33 [Ellen Liliedahl], "Lil," *Svenska Dagbladet*, December 18, 1955, 21.
34 [Bengt Idestam-Almquist], "Robin Hood," *Stockholms-Tidningen*, July 21, 1953, 11.
35 Anonymous, *Dagens Nyheter*, March 28, 1954, 19.
36 Bibi Lindström worked with Ingmar Bergman three times: *Gycklarnas afton* (1953), *Nära livet* (1958), and *Persona* (1966).
37 "Age," *Dagens Nyheter*, March 3, 1954, 11; "Age," *Dagens Nyheter*, May 9, 1954, 20.
38 Anonymous, "På lördagen 90 filmer," 18.
39 Jonas Göransson, on-site interview with Tytti Soila in Gothenburg, March 7, 2019.
40 [Carl Björkman], "C. B-n," *Dagens Nyheter*, November 2, 1954, 12.
41 [Ellen Liliedahl], "Lil," *Svenska Dagbladet*, November 2, 1954, 13.
42 Anonymous, "På lördagen 90 filmer," 18.
43 Jonas Göransson, letter to Tytti Soila, October 20, 2020.
44 Don G. Smith, *Lon Chaney Jr Horror Film star 1906-1973* (Jefferson, NC: McFarland & Company, 1996), 146. Chaney's father Lon Sr. was a celebrated horror movie actor during the silent era.
45 Pelle Berglund, on-site interview with Tytti Soila in Stockholm, October 19, 2021.
46 Ibid.
47 Bengt Forslund, *Svensk Filmdatabas,* https://www.svenskfilmdataba.se/sv/, accessed September 6, 2022.
48 Lena Nyman, *Dagböcker och brev 1962-1974* (Stockholm: Ellerströms, 2011), 111.
49 Mikael Lindström, on-site interview with Tytti Soila in Stockholm, October 18, 2021.
50 Brodjaga, "En duktig dekorationsmålarinna," *Stockholms-Tidningen*, October 3, 1931.

51 Jonas Göransson, on-site interview with Tytti Soila in Gothenburg, March 7, 2019.
52 *Svenska Dagbladet*, December 4, 1949, 18.
53 *Svenska Dagbladet*, February 6, 1945, 14.
54 [Ellen Liliedahl], "Lil," *Svenska Dagbladet*, May 26, 1954, 15.
55 Pierre Bourdieu, *Outline of a Theory of Practice* (Cambridge: Cambridge University Press 1977), 86.
56 Casper, "Filmiska nyårsönskningar," *Svenska Dagbladet*, December 31, 1949, 11.

8

Lisa Langseth

"Make Sure That What's in Your Heart is Done, So it Doesn't Drown and Stay in the Heart"

Maaret Koskinen

Introduction

Lisa Langseth (b.1975) is considered one of the most significant film auteurs (male or female) to have emerged from Sweden during the last decade. In her case, the term auteur is doubly apt, as she is always also her own scriptwriter—something she will delve into in the interview below.[1] Significantly, her very first feature, *Till det som är vackert* (*Pure*, 2010), was not only nominated for Best Film Direction at the Golden Beetle Awards (the Swedish Oscars) in 2011 but also awarded the prize for Best Screenplay. In addition, the female lead, Alicia Vikander, won the Golden Beetle for Best Actress. (Later Vikander became internationally noted for films such as *A Royal Affair* [Nicolaj Arcel, 2012], *The Danish Girl* [Tom Hooper, 2015], *Jason Bourne* [Paul Greengrass, 2016], *Tomb Raider* [Roar Uthaug, 2018], and *The Glorias* [Julie Taymor, 2020]). Langseth reunited with Vikander in her next feature film, *Hotell* (2013; Figure 8.1), which was very well received by both critics and audiences, and again rendered Langseth a Golden Beetle nomination for Best Screenplay. Her next feature, *Euphoria* (2018), was an international co-production, with noted actors such as Charlotte Rampling and Eva Green. Here too Langseth continued her collaboration with Alicia Vikander as lead actress, but also as co-producer, through Vikander's newly founded production company Vikarious Productions, the ambition of which is to promote women in the film industry. Since then, Lisa Langseth has secured her presence on the international scene even further through her

Figure 8.1 Lisa Langseth instructing Alicia Vikander in *Hotell* (2013). Photo: Dan Lepp.

successful Netflix series *Love & Anarchy* (2020). The second season of the series was being edited as the interview below took place and was scheduled to premiere in May 2022.

This chapter can (and perhaps should) be read as a complement to the chapter on Anna Serner and the Swedish Film Institute, giving a perspective from a film practitioner's point of view not only on Swedish film policy but also on other aspects of Swedish film culture, for instance, film schools.

***

Maaret Koskinen (MK): Let's start from the beginning, so to speak. What's your background, education-wise? What led up to you becoming a film director?

Lisa Langseth (LL): It started at the Kulturama school in the mid-1990s, where I took courses on so-called physical theater. I guess that I wanted to test what it meant to be on stage. But I only did that for a year until coming to the conclusion that I wanted to be in charge—so the role of actress was not an option! So, then I applied to the so-called folk college Biskops Arnö's scriptwriting course. There I later noticed that many wanted to apply for something called DI. What was DI? Daily Industry? Anyway, I too ended up applying to DI, Dramatiska Institutet (now SK, Stockholms Konstnärliga Högskola/Stockholm University College of the Arts), to which I was accepted in 1999. I was very young at the time, had a problem with structures of all sorts, and did all kinds of other things, for instance leading my own electronic band. I was probably not easy to deal with!

Anyway, I had applied to their program on writing for the theater, and had thought that it would be a bit like the curriculum at the Academy of Fine Arts, where you're expected to find your own path. But DI was very structured. For example, when I was about to graduate in 2002, I was not allowed to direct my own final production myself. But I did it anyway! I found actors who were willing to work for free, and even managed to get an actor who was completely unknown then—Noomi Rapace [later internationally well known for her portrayal of the Lisbeth Salander character in Niels Arden Oplev's *The Girl with the Dragon Tattoo* in 2009, and Ridley Scott's *Promotheus* in 2012]. The script that I had written was quite provocative. It dealt with four men who talked about pornography and buying women's bodies, so it became quite talked about. And so when it ended up at the City Theatre (Stadsteatern) in 2003, I had suddenly become a director anyway!

MK: So you really started as a playwright?[2]

LL: Yes. But I always strove to direct my own plays. I basically became a director because I wasn't happy with the stage productions of my texts that were directed by others. Even so I have written for others, for instance, several plays at Uppsala

City Theatre. But after some time I got bored doing this, so I got the idea of making a short film based on my graduation production at DI called *Godkänd* (Approved), which ended up receiving an honorable mention for Best Screenplay in the Short Film Competition in Gothenburg in 2006.

But still, I really didn't know how to make film. So it was very good advice when cinematographer Simon Pramsten, simply said "but you know what you want to say—and that solves it." Then I learned more at the editing how to go forward. But still, when it was time just a few years later to shoot my first feature *Till det som är vackert* (*Pure*, 2010), with Simon as cinematographer, it was a huge step. It was based on a monologue that I had done with Noomi Rapace for Dramaten (the Royal Dramatic Theatre in Stockholm). First of all, it was *truly* disgusting to make a screenplay out of this monologue. At that time I went through hell in my private life as well—and on top of it there was the shoot, which was tough, as I had very little previous experience or even education in film. But it turned out all right.

MK: Well—you can say *that* again!

LL: But the funny thing is that people kept telling me that "it's not really a love story." Exactly—it's *not* a love story! Perhaps that's why that now, several years later, the film has gained momentum. Because it's about cultural capital and about class structures, in a way that relates to the #MeToo scandal surrounding the Swedish Nobel Academy and Jean-Claude Arnault—although it came ten years too early.[3] Because the film is about how the male lead uses his superior education and the cultural world that this young woman longs for. I've noticed that many young people now have it as a favorite film.

MK: In fact, I used your next film, *Hotel*, in my teaching at the university, because I noticed how much the students became engaged by it.

LL: *Hotel* is very close to my heart. As for *Pure*, I've received many requests to make similar films. But I'm so done with that film, I've so put it behind me. On the other hand, in my mind I like to return to *Hotel*, because it's both sad and playful. This particular combination seems to suit my temperament—which I think is also evident in *Love & Anarchy*.

MK: *Hotel* is also very much an actor's film, and it's really quite amazing that after only two features you got to work with actors such as Charlotte Rampling in *Euphoria*. And talking about actors, I'm reminded of a stage talk you had the other year with another grand old lady, Gunnel Lindblom (1931–2021), this iconic actor in films by, for instance, Mai Zetterling and Ingmar Bergman, and who (just like you) was also both stage and film director.[4] In your conversation you said something to the effect that "writing and acting belong together. The author in me hangs out with actors."

LL: I still think so. Because the actor's most common question is: Why do I say this? How does it become credible? These questions are also the author's questions: Why do I say and write this? I need to know who's talking! In that sense acting comes close to writing. It's a shared psychology. Directing, on the other hand, is stressful. Schedule, images, takes—everything has to work. So the director in me is dogmatic, colder, looking from the outside rather than inside: I need a dramaturgical breakthrough here, and another there—the interesting "why" questions aren't there. It makes me think of when I tested acting as a youngster. Sometimes you got lines that were just so bad—which made me realize that the only thing good actors need are good lines and a good script. Then it's almost enough just to film it straight up, as is.

MK: So that the context itself substitutes for the direction, in a way?

LL: Yeah right! I have a good friend who's a film director, but who very much has entered the profession from the image side, so to speak. She has another take on film—almost wordless. Take the film *Titane* [Julia Ducournau, 2021] that won the Golden Palm at Cannes this year. It's completely bananas, and here the lead character doesn't say much, hardly anything at all—but goddamn, does she *do* things! However, I come from the side of words, the text, and that was and still is the way I approach directing.

MK: It strikes me that often the best directors in Sweden in the younger generation—like you—come from other places and practices than film. Think, for example, of Anna Odell [who directed *Återträffen* (*The Reunion*, 2013)] and Jens Jonsson [*Ping-pongkingen* (The King of Ping Pong, 2008) and *Snabba Cash 3* (*Easy Money 3*, 2013)] who both went to art school, which I think has enriched their films, both ideologically and aesthetically. And by the way—you've studied history of ideas, haven't you?

LL: Yes, I did so at the university before I took that course in physical theater. It really meant a lot to me. I mean, take a closer look at physical theater—it's so completely unintellectual and corny. What I learned from the history of ideas is that you can think about and approach life in so many and completely different ways, and that people in all times have thought of and tried other things. Take for example when I and cinematographer Rob Hardy [who shot *Mission: Impossible—Fallout*, 2018] were walking around in a forest checking out locations for *Euphoria*, and all the while I was harping on about the shooting schedule being too tight, or worrying about the placements of the lights—and he interrupted me and said: "This is my job. The important thing is: What do you see in front of you? What is your *vision*? I'll solve it!" And although he was completely limitless and crushed our budget 1,000 times over, this was important for me—that what he was interested in was the vision, the underlying idea of the film. This is what the history of ideas help you realize—that if you don't have it, it will be boring. This is what happens too often in Swedish film. It's all just about: how does it "function"?

MK: You mean it's too pragmatic and not driven by ideas?

LL: Yeah! My stuff is idea-driven. Although often my films have been interpreted only psychologically. But take *Hotel*. It's a drama comedy about a therapy group that checks in to a hotel, in order to take a vacation from themselves, as it were. But the underlying question is: what *is* a thing like "the self"? It's the same with *Love & Anarchy*: should everything be measurable, or are there other, non-measurable values? While *Euphoria* is about euthanasia, as idea and practice, and my first film is about accountability. To refer again to the #McToo scandal surrounding the Swedish Academy, and Arnault, the question that could be asked in hindsight is: but what, then, is my own responsibility? Think of the young woman in the lead role in *Pure*, and the way she uses the older man of culture to rise socially, and be close to everything "beautiful," while being really disgusting towards her boyfriend. Also it's actually she who kills the older man, that is, she's the only one in the film who actually commits a crime, legally speaking. And yet people reacted: "Oh, how good that he died …"! But—hello? That's actually a question for modern feminism, because earlier when things were actually devilish [for women], well then it was all right just smash the shit out of it! But now everything is much more complicated, and we are more involved in the morally dubious.

MK: But aside from ideas and themes, what about your narrative style? For instance, you usually emphasize your delight in genre mixing. Do you think you have enough space to experiment and push the boundaries? Or is it on the contrary good to have certain boundaries that you then can stretch from within?

LL: Good question. But if you want to cross borders like, for example, Lars von Trier, you have to be so terribly strong. And you have to have a whole staff around you, fighting for you, and Lars has precisely that in [the production company] Zentropa. It seems that women have had a harder time finding or creating those kinds of platforms. Just take Mai Zetterling, who in the end just fluttered about, without finding any contexts for her projects. Of course there are several reasons for this. First of all, a woman is generally not considered a genius, that is, someone worth investing in. In my case, for example, they said that "now that you have made a short story film, maybe it's time that you make a youth film? For example about horses—after all you are a girl!"

Here you can only put your hope in the younger, tougher girls who are coming along now, like Ninja Thyberg [director of *Pleasure*, 2021]. Then, when I started, you just got a pat on the head. There are so many ways to grind you down in the film industry, because, let's say, unlike in the sphere of literature, in film you must first learn to manage the entire film funding system, then tackle the actors, then editing, then … There are so many conquests that you have to make—while at the same time trying to stick to your original idea and not compromise it.

MK: What you say about platforms, and the importance of collaborators, is generally underestimated in film, I think. Because as an outsider one imagines that all the while a person is artistically active, that person also builds a context over time, a staff or a support system, as you put it—but that there is a risk that women have, so to speak, been left or left themselves out, on that score. There I have to say that I envy guys, if I may generalize. They seem to have a greater talent for backing each other up.

LL: Yeah! Because the moment they see a "genius," then at least ten guys turn up and want to hang on. While, as I read in an interview, even a Jane fucking Campion has had a hard time gaining confidence from the powers that be. In addition, it's often the case that when you finally get the chance, you're often over thirty years old, when life has happened, so to speak. After all, we have our bodies and pregnancies. So when young girls ask me for advice, I usually say: if you want a family—get a man who takes care of your children! I've seen so many women whose careers just stop, especially if they've paired up with another filmmaker. So do *not* team up with a genius!

MK: Yes—become like Ruth Bader Ginsburg and find yourself the right kind of man! But let me return to another kind of support system or infrastructure, rather—the Swedish Film Institute (SFI). I'm curious about what or if you learned something when you were in that "think tank" that SFI organized around 2013. How was that? Were there any interesting ideas or suggestions discussed, and did you reach any useful conclusions?

LL: If I'm a bit hard about it, we were probably there so that Anna [Serner], who was still fairly new at her post as CEO, would get a better grip on what was going on in the film industry at the time. Because, as I remember it, nothing became of anything important that we discussed. What happened was that someone wrote on a white board: What does Swedish film need? And then the answer: We need to make films that end up in Cannes, and that many want to see, and finally more equality and diversity. Okay, everyone knows that, and you can figure that out with your behind. But then—how? The think tank never came to this how question, that is, how to fix a structure in order to get there. This must come from a film culture, and the artists themselves—and a *trust* in those artists, instead of in some administrative machine.

Let's take *Titane* again. It's made by a strong writer-director, with a voice all her own, who no one has managed to stop. Here, in Sweden, there is more often a belief that a smart *film commissioner* will fix it—but this person must first have a film idea that (s)he won't destroy … ! As I've experienced it, that kind of idea-driven film far too often comes in second place. And as for SFI now, there is a big conflict presently, namely how much of the commercial film should be supported by SFI? I am thinking here for instance of the so-called automatic support that is given to films that are deemed as having box office potential, and that goes straight to the big production companies. Or should SFI primarily be there as support for the individual artists and creators?

MK: You are referring here to what you and all the other film directors wrote in that open letter to SFI in *Dagens Nyheter* earlier this year? [See Chapter 7.]

LL: Precisely. That's something that I think Anna dodged. Yes—I've been mad at Anna, but not anymore. Because she has put SFI on the map, and many female voices in film emerged thanks to her. But that's not the main issue today. Now we have to ask ourselves: Why should SFI exist at all? Should there be tax-financed film at all? Because no one has managed to explain to me why SFI should finance broad films, which receive automatic support, but are not seen by anyone (as promised). While so-called narrow films, such as *Återträffen* or *Gräns* [*Border*, Ali Abbasi, 2018, which received two Academy Award nominations] have attracted large audiences for very little production money. But this just goes to show that it's not possible to identify what's "narrow" or "wide." So I'm not *for* "narrow" art house film, as seemingly narrow film apparently can get wide! Take the Danish film *Druk* [*Another Round*, Thomas Vinterberg, 2020]. I'm sure that someone [at SFI] would have classified it as "narrow." We seem to have some strange templates of what's a narrow and wide film—and who makes those decisions?

What I'm basically worried about is that SFI cannot justify its existence in the future. Especially now that Netflix, Amazon, C-more, and Viaplay are just thundering onto the market. I myself get several suggestions a week from them, and now there's even a shortage of film staff, in Sweden and above all in Stockholm. So the question becomes—should SFI compete with Netflix? I think that France is a role model here, because they are better at regulating. There, cinema owners must show a certain percentage of French films in the cinemas. Here, on the other hand, a small Swedish film doesn't have a chance when a blockbuster comes along. So if we do want to keep the system we have, we must regulate. It's also thanks to France that we can now make films in Swedish for Netflix—otherwise we would have made films in the English language directly. These are questions that SFI has not taken hold of, and if it doesn't soon, it will just be reduced to a strange and irrelevant hole that only costs tax money. And I say this not just because I now work in and for Netflix. Because they also produce a lot of shit. But it's all a question of SFI's identity.

MK: That's precisely why the recruitment of a new CEO will be very important, someone who has the ability to see the big picture and understand the new media landscape. Perhaps a contemporary Harry Schein? Otherwise, the risk is that it will only be a person who becomes steward of what has already been achieved. And the same thing I think goes for the recruitment of consultants (despite what you say about them). After all, they are key when it comes to identifying, for example, the so-called broad quality film.

LL: Yes, but when was the last time we saw one of those? Lukas Moodysson's *Tillsammans* [Together, 2000] perhaps? Don't forget that the people who make these films are usually auteurs, and the system must help give birth to more such artists. That's what drove me crazy when I sat in that think tank, because "broad quality films" are not something that can come from calculations on a whiteboard. They are made by people with a ton on their minds and in their hearts.

MK: It's often said that Denmark has succeeded on that score—but how did they achieve it? Is there something in their support system or infrastructure around film? For example, do they provide more long-term support that promotes continuity, which perhaps even in the long run creates work teams, or those important platforms that we talked about before?

LL: Well, there you have it—they have cultivated a film *culture*! First of all, all their great creators—Thomas Vinterberg, Lars von Trier, Susanne Bier—come from their film school, which works closely with the film industry. So when you go to film school there, you are automatically also a trainee. For instance, if you know that Susanne Bier is going to be there for four weeks—then certainly you sit there in your bench and listen! This also provides a direct link between the younger generation and the older, established one. Then of course you can and probably will revolt at some point against what you've learned. But first you must understand how the industry works, so that your criticism is relevant in the first place.

When I was at DI twenty years ago, we had no contact with the industry at all, and all teachers had done their thing in the 1960s and 1970s. While I give credit to their work in and of itself, there was no link to the contemporary situation in the film industry, and it's a big problem when so many who leave school just don't find their way—they just disappear. I even think that traditionally the school in a way has tried to protect itself against the commercial film industry. But the young people must know what it looks like, in order to enter it and take it over! I remember when DI wanted Lukas Moodysson to teach, and he said fine, I want to set up my teaching like this—well that didn't fit the ready-made course modules of the school. As far as I know it's not much better today. For instance, the students don't have a clue about how Netflix works, with regard to technology and tempo. Bottom line—you must know the alphabet and be able to spell in order to grasp the language. If you don't, you can't revolt either!

MK: Add to this that in Sweden, for incomprehensible historical reasons, there's an almost schizophrenic division between theory and practice with regard to teaching film. I myself teach film and media—history, theory, aesthetics, etcetera—at the university, with hundreds of screenings, while SK is almost only practically oriented—right?

LL: Yes. I have a friend who was a teacher at the school who told me that the students hardly see any movies! When she wondered about this, the management said: no we are a practical training institution. But in that case, there's the risk that you as a student reinvent the wheel thirty-eight times, without even knowing it. Take me: I have no film education but on the other hand I watch *everything* instead! You learn by looking. It makes me remember that when I went to DI, they *hated* Bergman. But—hello? Here we were, students at a film school—and we never saw any movies by Bergman … When I told Charlotte Rampling, she didn't believe me: Huh? Hate Bergman?

MK: Isn't it all about getting some food for thought, that is, something either to resist or be inspired by. If you don't bring it to the table and show the palette, it doesn't exist.

LL: I myself am very inspired by both Ingmar Bergman and Mai Zetterling. Such energy! They just did stuff, just floored it! It's important to get past the contempt for artists that I think exists in Sweden, and also the ideology that "you should not think you amount to anything"—which is an even worse provocation if you happen to be a woman.[5] Fortunately I didn't understand how difficult it was to make a feature film when I made my first film … Anyway, as SK is about to move (to the so-called Slaughterhouse area south of Stockholm), I'm actually involved in creating a kind of film village there—that is, a home or a room where you can meet across generational boundaries, with the aim of creating a more vital industry.

But the bottom line is this: you have to have something on your mind, and see that the industry is just a tool that you have to use. The important thing is to make sure that what's on your mind and in your heart is done, so it doesn't drown and stay in the heart.

Notes

1. The interview took place on December 15, 2021.
2. For a more detailed overview of Langseth's career, particularly as playwright, see Freya Kilander's text on the Swedish Film Institute site, "Lisa Langseth," Nordic Women in Film, https://www.nordicwomeninfilm.com/person/lisa-langseth/, accessed September 6, 2022.
3. Arnault is the husband of a (now former) member of the Swedish Academy, who was publically accused by nearly twenty women at the height of the #MeToo movement for sexual predatory behavior, including toward women who worked for him in professional capacities. He was eventually convicted for rape in two cases.
4. Lindblom acted in, for instance, Ingmar Bergman's *The Seventh Seal* (*Det sjunde inseglet*, 1957), *The Virgin Spring* (*Jungfrukällan*, 1960), *The Communicants* (also known as *Winter Light, Nattvardsgästerna*, 1962), and *The Silence* (*Tystnaden*, 1963); and in Mai Zetterling's *Loving Couples* (*Älskande par*, 1964) and *The Girls* (*Flickorna*, 1968). Later she directed features such as *Summer Paradise* (*Paradistorg*, 1977) and *Sally and Freedom* (*Sally och friheten*, 1981).
5. Here, Langseth refers to the "Jante-law," a notion used by Nobel Prize-winning Norwegian-Danish author Aksel Sandemose in one of his novels, the meaning of which is that "no one is better than anyone else," and should success befall you, then be absolutely sure not to brag about it. Thus, in the public sphere and in vernacular parlance, it is thought of as part of a particularly Scandinavian psychological mindset, and therefore sometimes also the basis of (egalitarian) ideology.

Afterthoughts

Louise Wallenberg

Anna Serner decided to step down from her post as CEO of the Swedish Film Institute in late 2021. After ten years of relentless equality work, she had by then become a key player in transforming the film industry to become more gender inclusive. Her work and her active engagement in public events, advocating gender and diversity policies, influenced a number of other film nations—and her quest for "50/50 by 2020," pronounced at the Cannes Film Festival in 2016, has left a huge mark not only on other film cultures internationally but also on film history.

But that was then, this is now. As of December 2021, the SFI no longer is obliged to push for diversity: the Swedish government decided to take out the demand to always try and "integrate equality, diversity and children's perspectives" in their stipulated guidelines to the SFI.[1] Instead, "artistic freedom" is now being emphasized. And while SFI still advocates gender equality, the erasure of the previous demand or request surely means that the previous work for gender equality and diversity will lose some of its impetus and effectiveness.[2] This backlash, because it is a backlash, must be seen either as a short-sighted contentment with Swedish film now having reached its equality goals as the first nation worldwide (with women *almost* reaching the 50/50, we should all be happy and no longer need to think about gender), or as a giving in by the government to the many critical voices that over the years have argued that artistic quality and freedom should always come before forced quotas— and that political power must be kept at least at an arm's length from art. Either way, gender is a problem that we should no longer see as a problem: if we are all convincing ourselves (clearly in tune with postfeminist discourse and beliefs) that there are no inequalities and that everyone entering the industry has a fair chance of making it if they only work hard enough, and that success in this industry all has to do with artistic quality, individuality, and skill, then all is well. If women do not make it, it must because they do not work hard enough, or that they lack all of these qualities, and not because of male homosocialism (or homophilia) still pervading the industry. The risk of going back to the film set, and film production, as "a playground for chaps" (only)—as our interview participant Maria Hedman Hvitfeldt expressed it—is overwhelmingly large.³ 50/50 is never going to be made a reality if we stop working for and demanding it—and to achieve gender equality, in this specific industry as in all other areas of society, private as well as public, constant work is indeed needed.

Maybe we should have seen it coming. Someone who actually did warn us about this backlash was actor and director Gunnel Lindblom. In an interview made for public Swedish radio in 1974 (that is, some twenty-five years before gender equality policies in the film industry were introduced), she was asked about her experience of "stepping into a traditionally male sphere—the director's," and she responded:

> Of course, as a woman you think that you need to be more sharp and not show any flaws [to be accepted as director] … On the surface level, the world of theater is more democratic than other areas of society, but when you start scratching that surface you can see the many prejudices that exist … I cannot help but wonder how long it will take before men start realizing that women directors and producers are their rivals … and I think that they will never allow us to continue once they feel threatened … and that there is no doubt that they will strike back … for women can only do this as long as they let us.

And while the erasure of the request for equality and diversity perspectives to pervade the work carried out by the SFI cannot be said to be a "strike back" on men's behalf, it surely says something about the last decade of women's accomplishments as successful directors, producers, and scriptwriters as indeed threatening. While this turn (or giving in) is depressing, there is some light at the end of the tunnel—and it comes from outside of both the industry and governmental policies. Turning to all the research on gender and diversity in the screening industries that is being published and made available, there is reason to be filled with some hope. In the last two decades, the scholarly interest for gender, diversity, and (in-)equalities in these industries have increased steadily, in film and production studies, as well as in management and work life studies. Humanities scholars and social scientists join forces in analyzing the gendered politics and the gendered experiences that pervade these industries, pointing out how much gender equality policies are needed to change these industries and to help make them more inclusive. Edited volumes and special issues, next to individual books, book chapters, and journal articles, dealing either with gendered experiences or statistics (and sometimes with both), or with women's agency and representation in film history, or with gender equality policies and their effects, come in abundance, and they tell of both global and more local and regional situations, and in all parts of the world.[4]

Now About All These Women in the Swedish Film Industry, focusing on one single (and rather small and specific) film industry and culture, is one contribution to this growing field, and we hope that our readers find it inspirational and useful. It is also our hope that this research field, taken together, and much of which also aims at having an impact on stakeholders and policymakers, will help contribute to the strive for a real 50/50 split, if not by 2020, then in the very near future. It is not too late.

Notes

1 Elisabeth Andersson, "Regeringen stryker krav på mångfald," *Svenska Dagbladet*, December 28, 2021, https://www.svd.se/a/WjeK7k/ny-riktlinjer-for-filminstitutet-mangfaldskrav-stryks, accessed September 6, 2022.

2 See the SFI report *406 Days: It's About Time. Gender Equality Report for 2022/2022*, https://www.filminstitutet.se/globalassets/2.-fa-kunskap-om-film/analys-och-statistik/publications/other-publications/406-days--its-about-time.-gender-equality-report-2021-2022.pdf, accessed September 6, 2022.

3 Interview with Maria Hedman Hvitfeldt on April 9, 2018.

4 See, for example, Deborah Jones and Judith K. Pringle, "Unmanageable Inequalities: Sexism in the Film industry," *The Sociological Review*, vol. 63, S1 (2015), 37–49; Emma Bell and A. Sinclair, "Re-envisaging Leadership through the Feminine Imaginary in Film and Television," in Chris Steyaert, Timon Beyes and Martin Parker (eds.), *The Routledge Companion to Reinventing Management Education* (London: Routledge, 2016); Erin Hill, *Never Done: A History of Women's Work in Media Production* (New Brunswick, NJ: Rutgers University Press, 2016); Jane Gaines, *Pink-Slipped: What happened to Women in the Silent Film Industries?* (Champaign: University of Illinois, 2018); Anne O'Brien, *Women, Inequality and Media Work* (London: Routledge, 2019); Ingrid Stigsdotter (ed.), *Making the Invisible Visible: Reclaiming Women's Agency in Swedish Film History and beyond* (Lund: Nordic Academic Press, 2019); Susan Liddy (ed.), *Women in the International Film Industry* (London: Palgrave, 2020); Orianna Calderón-Sandoval, "Implementing Gender Equality Policies in the Spanish Film Industry: Persistent Prejudices and the Potential of Feminist Awareness," *International*

Journal of Cultural Policy (2021), https://doi.org/10.1080/10286632.2021.197843 9; Susan Liddy and Anne O'Brien (eds.), *Media Work, Mothers and Motherhood: Negotiating the International Audio-Visual Industry* (London: Routledge, 2021); Louise Wallenberg and Maria Jansson (eds.), "On and Off Screen: Women's Work in the Screen Industries," Special Issue of *Gender, Work and Organization*, vol. 28, no. 6 (2021); Louise Wallenberg and Maaret Koskinen (eds.), "The Politics of Gendered Work and Representation in the Nordic Screen Industries," Special Issue of *Journal of Scandinavian Cinema* (2022); Ingrid Ryberg, *Swedish Film Feminism: Between Grassroots Movements and Cultural Policies* (London: Bloomsbury, forthcoming). Also see the Women Film Pioneer Project, https://wfpp.columbia.edu/pioneers/?sort=occupation, accessed September 6, 2022, and the research project "Calling the Shots," led by PI Shelley Cobb in the UK, https://womencallingtheshots.com, accessed September 6, 2022.

Bibliography

Adams, R., and Funck, P. (2012). "Beyond the Glass Ceiling: Does Gender Matter?" *Management Science*, vol. 58, 219–35.

Adeniji, A., and Habel, Y. (2020). *Which Women? Gender Equality Report 2019/2020*. Stockholm: Swedish Film Institute. Available online: https://issuu.com/svenskafilminstitutet/docs/gender-equality-report_19_20_english (accessed September 16, 2022).

Ahlborg, H., and Nightengale, A.J. (2018). "Theorizing Power in Political Ecology." *Journal of Political Ecology*, vol. 25, no. 1, 381–401.

Allen, A. (1999). *The Power of Feminist Theory*. London: Routledge.

Allen, A. (2014). "Feminist Perspectives on Power." In E.N. Zalta (ed.), *The Stanford Encyclopedia of Philosophy*. Stanford: Stanford University Press.

"Almedalen Week." (2022). Wikipedia, August 1. Available online: http://en.wikipedia.org/wiki/Almedalen_Week (accessed September 6, 2022).

"Almedalen Week: At Sweden's One- of- a-Kind Festival, All Political Parties Gather in One Place." (2014). Democracy Now! July 2. Available online: https://www.democracynow.org/2014/7/2/dn_at_almedalen_week_at_swedens (accessed September 6, 2022).

Andersson, E. (2021). "Regeringen stryker krav på mångfald." *Svenska Dagbladet*, December 28. Available online: https://www.svd.se/regeringen-stryker-krav-pa-mangfald (accessed September 6, 2022).

Asp, J. (2018). "Enväldiga beslut om vem som får göra film" [Autocratic Decisions on Who Is Allowed to Make Films]. *Aftonbladet*, July 17. Available online: https://www.aftonbladet.se/kultur/a/WLAn2K/envaldiga-beslut-om-vem-som-far-gora-film (accessed September 2, 2022).

Asp, J. (2020). "Publiktapp, politisering och locket på" [Loss of Audiences, Pollicization, and a Cover Up]. *Point of View*, no. 72, October 29. Available online: https://www.povfilm.se/72/publiktapp-politisering-och-locket-pa-banar-vag-for-existentiell-kris-i-svensk/ (accessed September 2, 2022).

Astruc, A. ([1948] 1992). *Du Stylo à la caméra et de la caméra au stylo. Écrits (1942–1984)*. Paris: l'Archipel.

Austin-Smith, B., and Melnyk, G. (eds.). (2010). *The Gendered Screen: Canadian Women Filmmakers*. Waterloo, ON: Wilfrid Laurier University Press.

Baixauli-Soler, J.S., Belda-Ruiz, M., and Sanchez-Marin, G. (2017). "An Executive Hierarchy Analysis of Stock Options: Does Gender Matter?" *Review Management Science*, vol. 11, 737–66.

Banks, M. (2009). "Gender Below-the-Line: Defining Feminist Production Studies." In V. Mayer, M. Banks, and J.T. Caldwell (eds.), *Production Studies: Cultural Studies of Media Industries*. New York: Routledge.

Banks, M. (2018). "Production Studies." *Feminist Media Histories*, vol. 4, no. 2, 157–61.

Banks, M., Conor, B., and Mayer, V. (eds.). (2016). *Production Studies, The Sequel!* London: Routledge.

Barthes, R. ([1968] 1977). *The Death of the Author, Image, Music, Text*. London: Fontana.

Bartky, S.L. (1990). *Femininity and Domination*. London: Routledge.

Bartow, A. (2006). "Fair Use and the Fairer Sex: Gender, Feminism and Copyright Law." *Journal of Gender, Social Policy and the Law*, vol. 14, no. 3, 551–58.

Belcher, A. (2000). "Feminist Perspective on Contract Theories from Law and Economics." *Feminist Legal Studies*, 8, 29–46.

Bell, E., and Sinclair, A. (2016). "Re-envisaging Leadership through the Feminine Imaginary in Film and Television." In Chris Steyaert, Timon Beyes and Martin Parker (eds.), *The Routledge Companion to Reinventing Management Education*. London: Routledge.

Bengtsson, B. (2008). "Filmstudion och drömmen om den stora uppsalafilmen: Uppsala Studenters Filmstudio som filmproducent och skola." In E. Hedling and M. Jönsson (eds.), *Välfärdsbilder – svensk film utanför biografen*, Mediehistoriska arkiv, vol. 5. Stockholm: Statens Ljud- och bildarkiv.

Bergfelder, T. (2015). "Popular European Cinema in the 2000s: Cinephilia, Genre and Heritage." In M. Harrod, M. Liz, and A. Timoshkina (eds.), *The Europeanness of European Cinema*. London: I.B. Tauris.

Bergman, H. (1925). *Flickan i frack*. Stockholm: Albert Bonnier.

Bergman, I., and Burgess, A. (1981). *Mitt liv*. Stockholm: Norstedts.

Betz, M. (2013). "High and Low and in Between." *Screen*, vol. 54, no. 4, 495–513. https://doi.org/10.1093/screen/hjt044.

"Bibi Lindström – pionjär och influencer". Nordic Women in Film. Available online: https://www.nordicwomeninfilm.com/bibi-lindstrom-pionjar-och-influencer/ (Published August 2018)

Blair, H. (2001). "'You're Only as Good as Your Last Job': The Labour Process in the British Film Industry." *Work, Employment and Society*, vol. 15, no. 1, 149–69.

Bourdieu, P. ([1972] 1993). *The Field of Cultural Production*. Cambridge: Polity Press.

Bourdieu, P. (1977). *Outline of a Theory of Practice*. Cambridge: Cambridge University Press.

Bourdieu, P. (1986). "The Forms of Capital." In J.G. Richardson (ed.), *Handbook of Theory and Research for the Sociology of Education*. New York: Greenwood Press.

Bourdieu, P. (1994). *The Field of Cultural Production*. New York: Columbia University Press.

Bourdieu, P. (1998). *The State Nobility: Élite Schools in the Field of Power*. Palo Alto, CA: Stanford University Press.

Bovenschen, S. (1977). "Is there a Feminine Aesthetic?" *New German Critique*, no. 10 (Winter), 111–37.

Bowrey, K. (1996). "Who's Writing Copyright History?" *European Intellectual Property Review*, vol. 18, no. 6, 322–29.

Braak, M. ter (1931). *De absolute film*. Rotterdam: W. L. en J. Brusse's Uitgeversmaatschappij N.V.

Braidotti, R. (2003). "Be-coming Woman: Or Sexual Difference Revisited." *Theory, Culture & Society*, vol. 20, no. 3, 43–64.

Brammer, S., Millington, A., and Rayton, B. (2007). "The Contribution of Corporate Social Responsibility to Organizational Commitment." *International Journal of Human Resource Management*, vol. 18, no. 10, 1701–719.

Brooks, D.A. (2000). *From Playhouse to Printing House: Drama and Authorship in Early Modern England*. Cambridge: Cambridge University Press.

Bruno, G. (1992). *Streetwalking on a Ruined Map: Cultural Theory and the City Films of Elvira Notari*. Princeton, NJ: Princeton University Press.

Buccafusco, C. (2016). "A Theory of Copyright Authorship." *Virginia Law Review*, vol. 102, no. 5, 1229–295.

Burke, S. (1992). *The Death and Return of the Author: Criticism and Subjectivity in Barthes, Foucault and Derrida*. Edinburgh: Edinburgh University Press.

Burke, S. (1995). "Feminism and the Authorial Subject." In S. Burke (ed.), *Authorship: From Plato to the Postmodern*. Edinburgh: Edinburgh University Press.

Bygren, M., and Gähler, M. (2012). "Family Formation and Men's and Women's Attainment of Workplace Authority." *Social Forces*, vol. 90, no. 3, 795–816.

Byrnes, P. (2015). "How Sweden Hit Its 50:50 Gender Target for Film Production in Record Time." *The Sydney Morning Herald*, May 24. Available online: www.smh.com.au/entertainment/movies/how-sweden-hit-its-5050-gender-target-for-film-production-in-record-time-20150519-gh489a.html#ixzz41CyTwsjc (accessed September 6, 2022).

Calderón-Sandoval, O. (2021). "Implementing Gender Equality Policies in the Spanish Film Industry: Persistent Prejudices and the Potential of Feminist Awareness." *International Journal of Cultural Policy* (2021). https://doi.org/10.1080/10286632.2021.1978439.

Callahan, V. (2010). *Reclaiming the Archive: Feminism and Film Theory*. Detroit: Wayne State University Press.

Calling the Shots. (2020). Available online: https://womencallingtheshots.com (accessed September 6, 2022).

Canudo, R. ([1911] 1988). "Naissance d'un Sixième Art - Essai sur le Cinématographe." Translated as "The Birth of the Sixth Art." In R. Abel (ed.), *French Film Theory and Criticism: A History/Anthology, 1907–1930*, vol. 1. Princeton, NJ: Princeton University Press.

Carlsson, S. (1977). *Sickan, minnen berättade för Anna Nyman*. Stockholm: Bonniers.

Carson, D., L. Dittmar, L., and Welsch, J. (eds.) (1994). *Multiple Voices in Feminist Film Criticism*. Minneapolis: Minnesota University Press.

Chaloner, E. (2010). "A Feminist Critique of Copyright Law." *I/S: A Journal of Law and Policy for the Information Society*, vol. 6, no. 2, 221–55.

Cham Wing-Fai, L., Gill, R., and Randle, K. (2015). "Getting in, Getting on, Getting out? Women as Career Scramblers in the UK Film and Television Industries." *The Sociological Review*, vol. 63, no. S1, 50–65.

Chaudhuri, S. (2006). *Feminist Film Theorists*. London: Routledge.

Cixous, H. ([1975] 1976). "The Laugh of the Medusa." Trans. Keith and Paula Cohen. *Signs*, vol. 1, no. 4, 875–93.

Clare, J. (2012). "Shakespeare and Paradigms of Early Modern Authorship." *Journal of Early Modern Studies*, vol. 1, no. 1, 137–53.

Cobb, S. (2020). "What about the Men: Gender Inequality Data and the Rhetoric of Inclusion in the US and UK Film Industries." *Journal of British Cinema and Television*, vol. 17, no. 1, 112–35.

Cobb, S., and Williams, L.R. (2020). "Gender Equality in British Film-making: Research, Targets, Change." In S. Liddy (ed.), *Women in the International Film Industry*. Cham: Palgrave Macmillan.

Cohan, S. (1997). *Masked Men: Masculinity and the Movies in the Fifties*. Bloomington: Indiana University Press.

Cohan, S., and Hark, I.R. (1993). *Screening the Male: Exploring Masculinities in Hollywood Cinema*. London: Routledge.

Coombes, R.J. (1998). *The Cultural Life of Intellectual Properties: Authorship, Appropriation, and the Law*. Durham, NC: Duke University Press.

Council of Europe. (n.d.). Available online: https://www.coe.int/en/web/eurimages/gender-equality-documents (accessed September 15, 2022).

Craig, C.J. (2007). "Reconstructing the Author-Self: Some Feminist Lessons for Copyright Law." *Journal of Gender, Social Policy and the Law*, vol. 15, no. 2, 207–68.

Craig, C.J. (2015). "Feminist Aesthetics and Copyright Law: Genius, Value and Gendered Visions of the Creative Self." In I. Calboli and S. Ragavan (eds.), *Diversity in Intellectual Property Law*. Cambridge: Cambridge University Press.

Creed, B. (1993). *The Monstrous Feminine: Film, Feminism, Psychoanalysis*. London: Routledge.

Crisp, V. (2015). *Film Distribution in the Digital Age: Pirates and Professionals*. Basingstoke: Palgrave Macmillan.

d'Acci, J. (1994). *Defining Women: Television and the Case of Cagney and Lacey*. Chapel Hill: University of North Carolina Press.

Dahlberg, L. (2003). "Rätt och litteratur." *Tidskrift för litteraturvetenskap*, vol. 32, no. 3, 3–15.

Dahlquist, M. (2018). "A Queen in Her Own Right." Nordic Women in Film, February. Available online: https://www.nordicwomeninfilm.com/a-queen-in-her-own-right/ (accessed September 6, 2022).

de Lauretis, T. (1984). *Alice Doesn't*. Bloomington: Indiana University Press.

de Lauretis, T. ([1985] 1994). "Aesthetics and Feminist Theory: Rethinking Women's Cinema." In D. Carson, L. Dittmar, and J.R. Welsch (eds.), *Multiple Voices in Feminist Film Criticism*. Minneapolis: University of Minnesota Press.

de Lauretis, T. (1987). *Technologies of Gender: Essays on Theory, Film, and Fiction*. Bloomington: Indiana University Press.

Deleuze, G. (1967). *Le froid et le cruel*. Paris: Les Éditions de Minuit.

Deleuze, G., and Guattari, F. ([1980] 1996). *A Thousand Plateaus: Capitalism and Schizophrenia*. 3rd edn. London: Athlone Press.

Delmestri, G., Montanari, F., and Usai, A. (2005). "Reputation and Strength of Ties in Predicting Commercial Success and Artistic Merit of Independents in the Italian Feature Film Industry." *Journal of Management Studies* vol. 45, no. 5, 975–1002.

Doane, M.A. (1980). "The Voice in the Cinema: The Articulation of Body and Space." *Yale French Studies*, vol. 60, no. 60, 33–50.

Doane, M.A. (1987). *The Desire to Desire: The Woman's Film of the 1940s*. Bloomington: Indiana University Press.

Doane, M.A. (1989). Untitled contribution to the "Spectatrix," Special Issue of *Camera Obscura*, vol. 21, no. 20, 142–43.

Dobranski, S.B. (2008). "The Birth of the Author: The Origins of Early Modern Printed Authority." *DQR Studies in Literature*, vol. 43, 23–45.

DocuFest TV (2013). "'Belleville Baby' @ DokuFest 2013." YouTube. Available online: https://www.youtube.com/watch?v=xlldfeFg6EE (accessed November 4, 2021).

Drassinower, A. (2018). "Copyright, Authorship and the Public Domain: A Reply to Mark Rose and Niva Elkin-Koren." *Jurisprudence*, vol. 9, no. 1, 179–85.

Durie, J., Pham, A., and Watson, N. (2000). *Marketing and Selling Your Film around the World*. Los Angeles: Silman-James Press.

Dyer, R. (1977). *Gays and Film*. London: BFI.

Dyer, R. (1991). *Now You See It*. London: Routledge.

Dyer, R. (1993). *The Matter of Images*. London: Routledge.

Dyer, R. (1997). *WHITE*. London: Routledge.

Eagly, A. (2005). "Achieving Relational Authenticity in Leadership: Does Gender Matter?" *The Leadership Quarterly*, vol. 16, no. 3, 459–74.

Ebbers, J.J., and Wijnberg, N.M. (2009). "Latent Organizations in the Film Industry." *Human Relations*, vol. 62, no. 7, 987–1009.

Eberstein, G. (1923). *Den svenska författarrätten*. Stockholm: Norstedts.

Eddleston, K., Ladge, J., Mitteness, C., and Balachandra, L. (2016). "Do You See What I See? Signaling Effects of Gender and Firm Characteristics on Financing Entrepreneurial Ventures." *Entrepreneurship: Theory and Practice*, vol. 40, no. 3, 489–584.

Ehlin, L. (2015). "Becoming Image." Ph.D. dissertation, IMS, Stockholm University.

Engberg, M. (2020). *Den visuella tystnaden: en essä om film av Mia Engberg*. Stockholm: Pov Books.

Erens, P. (1990). *Issues in Feminist Film Criticism*. Bloomington: Indiana University Press.
Ericson, A.L. (1982). *Mina sju liv*. Stockholm: Norstedts.
European Women's Audiovisual Network (EWA) (2015). "Where Are the Women Directors?" Available online: https://www.ewawomen.com/wp-content/uploads/2018/09/Complete-report_compressed.pdf (accessed September 6, 2022).
Feather, J. (1994). *Publishing, Piracy and Politics: An Historical Study of Copyright in Britain*. London: Mansell.
Fischer, L. (1989). *Shot/Counter Shot*. Princeton, NJ: Princeton University Press.
Fischer, L. (2017). "Feminist Forms of Address: Mai Zetterling's Loving Couples." In K.L. Hole, D. Jelača, E.A. Kaplan, and P. Petro (eds.), *The Routledge Companion to Cinema and Gender*. London: Routledge.
Flitterman-Lewis, S. (1996). *To Desire Differently*. New York: Columbia University Press.
Fornstam, P. (2021). "Staten hade inte räknat med den globala konkurrensen" [The State Did Not Count on the Global Competition]. *FLM*, June 3. Available online: https://flm.nu/2021/06/peter-fornstam-staten-hade-inte-raknat-med-den-globala-konkurrensen/ (accessed September 2, 2022).
Foucault, M. ([1969] 2008). "Vad är en författare?" In *Diskursernas kamp*. Stockholm: Symposion.
Foucault, M. ([1975] 1991). *Discipline and Punish: The Birth of a Prison*. London: Penguin.
Foucault, M. ([1976] 1998). *The History of Sexuality: The Will to Knowledge*. London: Penguin.
Fredman, S. (2013). "The Legal Construction of Personal Work Relations and Gender." *Jerusalem Review of Legal Studies*, vol. 7, no. 1, 112–22.
Fredriksson, M. (2010). *Skapandets rätt*. Gothenburg: Daidalos.
French, L. (2020). "Gender Still Matters: Towards Sustainable Progress for Women in Australian Film and Television Industries." In S. Liddy (ed.), *Women in the International Film Industry*. London: Palgrave Macmillan.
Furhammar, L. (1970). *Från skapelsen till Edvard Persson*. Stockholm: Wahlström & Widstrand.
Furhammar, L. (1979). *Folklighetsfabriken*. Stockholm: PAN/Norstedt.
Furhammar, L. (1991). *Filmen i Sverige En historia i tio kapitel*. Wiken: Höganäs Förlags AB.
Furhammar, L. (2003). *Filmen i Sverige*. Stockholm: Dialogos and SFI.
Gabaldon, P., de Anca, C., Mateos de Cabo, R., and Gimeno, R. (2016). "Searching for Women on Boards: An Analysis from the Supply and Demand Perspective." *Corporate Governance: An International Review*, vol. 24, no. 3, 371–85.
Gaines, J. (2018). *Pink-Slipped: What Happened to Women in the Silent Film Industries?* Champaign: University of Illinois.
Gaines, J. (1984). "Women and Representation." *Jump Cut*, no. 29 (February), 25–7.

Galbreath, J. (2011). "Are There Gender-Related Influences on Corporate Sustainability? A Study of Women on Boards of Directors." *Journal of Management & Organization*, vol. 17, no. 1, 17–38.

Galloway, K. (2019). "The Role of Pateman's Sexual Contract in Beneficial Interests in Property." *Feminist Legal Studies*, 27, 263–85.

Garba, T., and Abubakar, B.A. (2014). "Corporate Board Diversity and Financial Performance of Insurance Companies in Nigeria: An Application of Panel Data Approach." *Asian Economic and Financial Review*, vol. 4, no. 2, 257–77.

Gardiner, M., and Tiggemann, M. (1999). "Gender Differences in Leadership Style, Job Stress and Mental Health in Male- and Female-Dominated Industries." *Journal of Occupational and Organizational Psychology*, vol. 72, 301–15.

Gedin, P.I. (1997). *Litteraturen i verkligheten: Om bokmarknadens historia och framtid.* Stockholm: Rabén Prisma.

Goodrich, P. (1996). "Gender and Contracts." In A. Bottomley (ed.), *Feminist Perspectives on the Foundational Subjects of Law*. London: Cavendish.

Government Bill 2015/16:132. (2016). *Mer film till fler—en sammanhållen filmpolitik 2015/16: 132.* Available online: https://www.riksdagen.se/sv/dokument-lagar/dokument/proposition/mer-film-till-fler—en-sammanhallen-filmpolitik_H303132 (accessed January 6, 2022).

Gregory-Smith, I., Main, B., and O'Reilly III, C. (2014). "Appointments, Pay and Performance in UK Boardrooms by Gender." *Economic Journal*, vol. 124, no. 574, F109–F128.

Gustafsson, F. (2016). "Swedish Cinema of the 1940s, A New Wave." In M. Hjort and U. Lindqvist (eds.), *A Companion to Nordic Cinema*. Malden, MA: John Wiley and Sons.

Gustafsson, T. (2007). *En fiende till civilisationen: manlighet, genusrelationer, sexualitet och rasstereotyper i svensk filmkultur under 1920-talet.* Lund: Sekel.

Gustafsson, T. (2014). *Masculinity in the Golden Age of Swedish Cinema: A Cultural Analysis of 1920s Films*. Jefferson, NC: MacFarland.

Habel, Y. (2002). "Modern Media, Modern Audiences." Ph.D. dissertation, Stockholm University.

Halbert, D. (2006). "Feminist Interpretations of Intellectual Property." *Journal of Gender, Social Policy & the Law*, vol. 14, no. 3, 431–60.

Haskell, M. (1974). *From Reverence to Rape*. New York: Holt, Rinehart and Winston.

Hedling, E., Hedling, O., and Jönsson, M. (eds.). (2010). *Regional Aesthetics: Locating Swedish Media*. Stockholm: KB/Mediehistoriskt arkiv 15.

Hedling, O. (2016). "Cinema in the Welfare State: Notes on Public Support. Regional Film Funds and Film Policy in Swedish Film." In M. Hjort and U. Lindqvist (eds.), *The Blackwell Companion to Nordic Cinema*. London: Blackwell.

Hedrén, K. (2021). "Ingen kan sudda ut visionen om jämställdhet" [No One Can Erase the Vision of Equality]. *FLM*, June 11. Available online: https://flm.nu/2021/06/katarina-hedren-ingen-kan-sudda-ut-visionen-om-jamstalldhet/ (accessed September 2, 2022).

Heggestad, E. (1991). *Fången och fri:1880-talets svenska kvinnliga författare och hemmet, yrkeslivet och konstnärskapet*. Uppsala: Uppsala universitet.

Heilman, M. (2001). "Description and Prescription: How Gender Stereotypes Prevent Women's Ascent up the Organizational Ladder." *Journal of Social Issues*, vol. 57, no. 4, 657–74.

Helmersson, E. (2018). "Ledare: Normkritiken tar över kulturen och ingen vågar klaga" [Editorial: Norm-Critics Take Over Culture, and No One Dares to Complain]. *Dagens Nyheter*, January 3.

Hemmungs Wirtén, E. (2004). *No Trespassing: Authorship, Intellectual Property Rights, and the Boundaries of Globalization*. Toronto: University of Toronto Press.

Hermele, V. (2002). *Män, män, män och en och annan kvinna*. Stockholm: Swedish Film Institute.

Hermele, V. (2004). *Hur svårt kan det vara?: Filmbranschen, jämställdheten och demokratin*. Stockholm: Swedish Film Institute.

Hill, E. (2016). *Never Done: A History of Women's Work in Media Production*. New Brunswick, NJ: Rutgers University Press.

Holmlund, C. (1993). "Masculinity as Multiple Masquerade." In S. Cohan and I.R. Hark (eds.), *Screening the Male: Exploring Masculinities in Hollywood Cinema*. London: Routledge.

Homestead, M. (2005). *American Women Authors and Literary Property*. New York: Cambridge University Press.

Huang, X. (2014). "In the Shadow of Suku (Speaking-bitterness): Master Scripts and Women's Life Stories." *Frontiers of the History in China*, vol. 9, no. 4, 584–610.

Huyssen, A. (1988). "Mass Culture as Woman: Modernism's Other." In *After the Great Divide: Modernism, Mass Culture, Postmodernism*. Basingstoke: Macmillan.

Hviid, M. (1996). "Relational Contracts and Repeated Games." In D. Campbell and P. Vincent Jones (eds.), *Contract and Economic Organisation*. Aldershot: Dartmouth.

Hyvönen, M., Snickars, P., and Vesterlund, P. (2015). *Massmedieproblem*. Lund: Lunds universitet.

Ihrfors, C.G. (1926). *Om författarerätt och äganderätt: med särskild hänsyn till svenska lagen den 30 maj 1919 om rätt till litterära och musikaliska verk*. Stockholm: Norstedts.

Ilshammar, L., Snickars, P., and Vesterlund, P. (2010). *Citizen Schein*. Stockholm: Kungliga biblioteket.

Irigaray, L. ([1977] 1985). *This Sex Which Is Not One*. Ithaca, NY: Cornell University Press.

Isaksson, U. (1973). *Paradistorg*. Stockholm: Albert Bonnier.

Jansson, M. (2017). "Gender Equality in Swedish Film Policy: Radical Interpretations and 'Unruly' Women." *European Journal of Women's Studies*, vol. 24, no. 4, 336–50. https://www.doi.org/10.1177/1350506817692387.

Jansson, M., and Wallenberg, L. (2020). "Experiencing Male Dominance in Swedish Film Production." In S. Liddy (ed.), *Women in the International Film Industry: Policy, Practice and Power*. London: Palgrave Macmillan.

Jansson, M., and Wallenberg, L. (2021). "Negotiating Motherhood in Sweden – On and Off Screen." In S. Liddy and A. O'Brien (eds.), *Mothers and Motherhood: Negotiating the International Audio-Visual Industry*. London: Palgrave.

Jansson, M., Papadopoulou, F., Stigsdotter, I., and Wallenberg, L. (2020). "Studying Women in Swedish Film Production: Methodological Considerations." *Journal of Scandinavian Cinema*, vol. 10, no. 2, 207–14.

Jansson, M., Papadopoulou, F., Stigsdotter, I., and Wallenberg, L. (2021)."'The Final Cut': Directors, Producers and the Gender Regime of the Swedish Film Industry." In L. Wallenberg and M. Jansson (eds.), "On and Off Screen: Women's Work in the Screen Industries," Special Issue of *Gender, Work and Organization*, vol. 28, no. 6, 2010–025.

Jaszi, P. (1991). "Toward a Theory of Copyright: The Metamorphoses of 'Authorship'." *Duke Law Journal*, no. 2, 455–502.

Jerselius, K. (1987). *Hotade reservat, Spelfilmerna med Edvard Persson*. Uppsala: Filmförlaget.

Johnston, C. (1973). "Women's Cinema as Counter-Cinema." In C. Johnston (ed.), *Notes on Women*. London: SEFT.

Johnston, C. (ed.). (1975). *The Work of Dorothy Arzner: Towards a Feminist Cinema*. London: BFI.

Jones, D., and Pringle, J.K. (2015). "Unmanageable Inequalities: Sexism in the Film industry." *The Sociological Review*, vol. 63, S1, 37–49.

Jungstedt, T. (1980). *Filmkrönikan. 50 år med Europafilm 1–4*. Stockholm: Sveriges Television TV2.

Kael, P. (1963). "Circles and Squares." *Film Quarterly*, vol. 16, no. 3, 12–26.

Kamina, P. (2016). *Film Copyright in the European Union*. 2nd edn. Cambridge: Cambridge University Press.

Kaplan, A.E. (1983). *Women and Film: Both Sides of the Camera*. London: Routledge.

Kaplan, B. (1967). *An Unhurried View on Copyright*. New York: Columbia University Press.

Kernell, A. et al. (2018). "Svenska toppregissörer i upprop: Låt skattepengarna utveckla svensk films särart!" [Appeal by Swedish Top Directors: Let Tax Money Develop the Specificity of Swedish Film!]. *Dagens Nyheter*, February 11. Available online: https://www.dn.se/kultur/svenska-toppregissorer-i-upprop-lat-skattepengarna-utveckla-svensk-films-sarart/ (accessed January 6, 2022).

Kerrigan, F. (2009). *Film marketing*. Oxford: Butterworth-Heinemann.

King, A. (2004). "The Prisoner of Gender: Foucault and the Disciplining of the Female Body." *Journal of International Women's Studies*, vol. 5, no. 2, 29–39.

Kjellström, U. (2002). *Åke, boken om författaren, artisten, revy- och filmskådespelaren Åke Söderblom*. Arvika: Norlén & Slottner.

Klahr, D. (2011). "Munich as Kunststadt." *Oxford Art Journal*, vol. 34, no. 2, 179–201.
Knapp, J. (2005). "What is a Co-Author?" *Representations*, vol. 89, 1–29
Knoph, R. (1931). "Om ophavsmannens 'moralske' rett til sitt verk efter den nye lov om åndsverker." *Festskrift tillägnad Presidenten Juris doktor Herr Friherre Erik Marks von Würtemberg den 11 maj 1931*, 316.
Knutson, M. (2018). "Anna Serners utbrott: Det du säger är vulgärt!" [Anna Serner's Outburst: What You Say Is Vulgar]. *Expressen,* July 4. Available online: https://www.expressen.se/kultur/film--tv/anna-serners-utbrott-det-du-sager-ar-vulgart/ (accessed September 2, 2022).
Koskinen, M. (2010). *Ingmar Bergman's The Silence: Pictures in the Typewriter. Writings on the Screen*. Seattle: University of Washington Press.
Koskinen, M., and Wallenberg, L. (eds.). (2017). *Harry bit för bit*. Stockholm: Carlsson förlag.
Kuhn, A. (1993). *Women's Pictures*. London: Verso.
Kuhn, A. (1995). *Queen of the B's: Ida Lupino behind the Camera*. Westport, CT: Greenwood Press.
Larsson, M. (2019). *A Cinema of Obsession: The Life and Work of Mai Zetterling*. Madison: University of Wisconsin Press.
Lauzen, M.M. (2019). "Where Are the Film Directors (Who Happen to Be Women)?" *Quarterly Review of Film and Video*, vol. 29, 310–19. https://doi.org/10.1080/10509201003601167.
Lenken, S. (2021). "Jag hoppas mer pengar hamnar hos de modiga, inte hos jättarna" [I hope that More Money Is Awarded the Brave, Not the Giants]. *FLM*, June 11. Available online: https://flm.nu/2021/06/sanna-lenken-jag-hoppas-mer-pengar-hamnar-hos-de-modiga-inte-hos-jattarna/ (accessed September 6, 2022).
Lesage, J. (1978). "The Political Aesthetics of the Feminist Documentary Film." *Quarterly Review of Film Studies*, vol. 3, no. 4, 507–23.
Levine, E. (1998). "Toward a Paradigm for Media Production Research." *Critical Studies in Media Communication,* vol. 18, no. 1, 66–82.
Liddy, S. (2017). "In Her Own Voice: Reflections on the Irish Film Industry and beyond." In "Networking Knowledge," Special Issue of *Gender and the Screenplay: Processes, Practices, Perspectives*, vol. 10, no. 2, 19–31.
Liddy, S. (ed.) (2020). *Women in the International Film Industry: Policy, Practice and Power*. London: Palgrave Macmillan.
Liddy, S., and O'Brien, A. (eds.). (2021). *Media Work, Mothers and Motherhood: Negotiating the International Audio-Visual Industry*. London: Routledge.
Liljedahl, E. (1975). *Stumfilmen i Sverige: Kritik och debatt – hur samtiden värderade den nya konstarten*. Stockholm: Svenska filminstitutet.
Lindblad, H. (2020). "Filminstitutets Anna Serner bör bredda sin repertoar eller lämna vd-stolen" [Anna Serner Should Broaden Her Repertoire or Leave Her CEO Chair]. *Dagens Nyheter*, September 17.

Lindblad, H. (2021). "Nu behövs en efterträdare som kan återupprätta det brustna förtroendet med publiken" [What Is Needed Now Is a Successor Who Can Restore the Broken Trust with the Audience]. *Dagens Nyheter*, April 27.

"Lisa Langseth." (n.d.). Nordic Women in Film. Available online: https://www.nordicwomeninfilm.com/person/lisa-langseth/ (accessed September 6, 2022).

Liyanto, C. (2008). "The Discrete, the Relational, the Selfish, and the Societal: Elements Present in all Transactions." *Hastings Business Law Journal*, vol. 4, 315–32.

Lodderhouse, D. (2021). "International Disruptors: Outgoing Swedish Film Institute CEO Anna Serner on Her Commitment to Gender Parity and Why 'the Old Industry needs to Change.'" *Deadline*, September 15. Available online: https://deadline.com/2021/09/international-disruptors-anna-serner-gender-parity-swedish-film-institute-1234833086/ (accessed October 7, 2021).

Lorde, A. (2018). "The Master's Tools Will Never Dismantle the Master's House." In *The Master's Tools Will Never Dismantle the Master's House*. London: Penguin Random House.

Lundkvist, T. (2016). *Svenska Filminstitutets konsulentsystem: En reflekterande studie* [The SFI's Commisssioner System: A Reflexive Study]. Stockholm: The Media Mentors.

Luthersson, P. (1986). *Modernism och individualitet: en studie i den litterära modernismens kvalitativa egenart*. Stockholm: Symposium.

Lögdberg, Å. (1957). *Auktorrätt och film*. Lund: Gleerup.

Mackay, F. (2014). "Nested Newness, Institutional Innovation, and the Gendered Limits of Change." *Politics and Gender*, vol. 10, no. 4, 549–71. https://doi.org/10.1017/S1743923X14000415.

Mackenzie, C., and Stoljar, N. (2000). "Autonomy Refigured." In C. Mackenzie and N. Stoljar (eds.), *Relational Autonomy: Feminist Perspectives on Autonomy, Agency and the Social Self*. New York: Oxford University Press.

Macneil, I. (1978). "Contracts: Adjustment of Long-Term Economic Relations under Classical, Neoclassical and Relational Contract Law." *Northwestern University Law Review*, vol. 72, no. 6, 854–902.

Manstad, M. (1987). *Och vinden viskade så förtroligt*. Stockholm: Läsarförlaget.

Marghitu, S. (2018). "'It's just art': Auteur Apologism in the post-Weinstein Era." *Feminist Media Studies*, vol. 18, no. 3, 491–94. https://doi.org/10.1080/14680777.2018.1456158.

Martin, B. (1982). "Feminism, Criticism and Foucault." *New German Critique*, no. 27, 3–30.

Mayer, V. (2009). "Bringing the Social Back In: Studies of Production Cultures and Social Theory." In V. Mayer, M.J. Banks, and J.T. Caldwell (eds.), *Production Studies*, New York and London: Routledge.

Mayer, V. (2011). *Below the Line: Producers and Production Studies in the New Television Economy*. Durham, NC: Duke University Press.

Mayer, V., Banks, M., and Caldwell, J.T. (eds.). (2009). *Production Studies: Cultural Studies of Media Industries*. New York: Routledge.

McMahan, A. (2002). *Alice Guy Blaché: Lost Visionary of the Cinema*. New York: Continuum.

Meyers, D. (2000). "Intersectional Identity and the Authentic Self? Opposites Attract!" In C. Mackenzie and N. Stoljar (eds.), *Relational Autonomy: Feminist Perspectives on Autonomy, Agency and the Social Self*. Oxford: Oxford University Press.

Meziani, N., and Cabantous, L. (2020). "Acting Intuition into Sense: How Film Crews Make Sense with Embodied Ways of Knowing." *Journal of Management Studies*, vol. 57, no. 7, 1384–419.

Miklo. (2015). "Svensk films representation av Sverige" [The Representation of Sweden in Swedish Film]. Swedish Film Institute, February. Available online: https://www.filminstitutet.se/globalassets/2.-fa-kunskap-om-film/analys-och-statistik/publikationer/utredningar/2015/svensk-films-representation-av-sverige.pdf (accessed September 6, 2022).

Miller, N. (1986). "Changing the Subject: Authorship, Writing, and the Reader." In T. de Lauretis (ed.), *Feminist Studies/Critical Studies. Language, Discourse, Society*. London: Palgrave Macmillan.

Miller, T., and Del Carmen Triana, M. (2009). "Demographic Diversity in the Boardroom: Mediators of the Board Diversity–Firm Performance Relationship." *Journal of Management Studies*, vol. 46, 755–86.

Milliken, F., and Marins L. (1996). "Searching for Common Threads: Understanding the Multiple Effects of Diversity in Organizational Groups." *The Academy of Management Review*, vol. 21, no. 2, 402–33.

Modleski, T. (1988). *Women Who Knew too Much: Hitchcock and Feminist Theory*. New York: Methuen.

Mukherjee, A. (2018). "Representational Politics in Bollywood Sports Movies of the 21st Century: Empowering Women through Counter Cinema." *PostScriptum: An Interdisciplinary Journal of Literary Studies*, vol. 3, 65–80.

Mulvey, L. (1975). "Visual Pleasure and Narrative Cinema." *Screen*, vol. 16, no. 3, 6–18.

Mörner, C. (2000). "Vissa visioner. Tendenser i svensk biografdistribuerad fiktionsfilm, 1967–1972." Ph.D. dissertation, Stockholm University.

Narayan, U. (2002). "Minds of Their Own: Choices, Autonomy, Cultural Practices, and Other Women." In L. Antony and C. Witt (eds.), *A Mind of One's Own: Feminist Essays on Reason and Objectivity*. New York: Routledge.

Neroni, H. (2016). *Feminist Film Theory and Cleo from 5 to 7*. London: Bloomington Academics.

Newton, E. (1984). "The Mythic Mannish Lesbian: Radclyffe Hall and the New Woman." *Signs*, vol. 9, no. 4, 557–75.

Nordic Women in Film. (2018). Available online: https://www.svenskfilmdatabas.se/sv/nordic-women-in-film/ (accessed September 6, 2022).

Nordlund, A. (2014). "Selma Lagerlöf in the Golden Age of Swedish Silent Cinema." In Helena Försås-Scott, Lisbeth Stenberg, and Bjarne Thorup Thomsen (eds.), *Remapping Lagerlöf*. Lund: Nordic Academic Press.

Nyman, L. (2011). *Dagböcker och brev 1962–1974*. Stockholm, Elleströms.

O'Brien, A. (2015). "Producing Television and Reproducing Gender." *Television & New Media*, vol. 16, no. 3, 259–74.

O'Brien, A. (2019). *Women, Inequality and Media Work*. London: Routledge.

Ogrodnik, B. (2018). "Listening to the 'Multi-Voiced' Feminist Film: Aspects of Voice-over, Female Stardom, and Audio-Visual Pleasure in Stephanie Beroes' *The Dream Screen* (1986)." *Journal of Art and Media Studies*, no.15, 67–82.

Ohlin, L. (2018). *Ravinen; Så du vill bli regissör?* Stockholm: Type & Tell.

Okin, S.M. (1990). "Feminism, the Individual, and Contract Theory." *Ethics*, vol. 100, no. 3, 658–69.

Olsson, G.H. (2021). "Ingen VD på SFI har gjort någon större skillnad" [No CEO at the SFI Has Made Much Difference]. *FLM*, May 31. Available online: https://flm.nu/2021/05/goran-hugo-olsson-ingen-vd-pa-sfi-har-gjort-nagon-storre-skillnad (accessed September 6, 2022).

Olsson, J. (1990). *I offentlighetens ljus. Stumfilmens affischer, kritiker, stjärnor och musik*. Stockholm: Symposium.

Pallas, H. (2011). "Vithet i svensk spelfilm 1989–2010" [Whiteness in Swedish Feature Film 1989–2010]. Ph.D. dissertation, Stockholm University.

Pallas, H. (2015). "Reducera inte filmkonsten till politik" [Don't Reduce the Art of Film to Politics]. *Expressen*, June 18.

Pallas, H. (2018). "Svensk film politiseras—men var är debatten?" [Swedish Film Is Being Politicized—But Where's the Debate?]. *Expressen*, August 14. Available online: https://www.expressen.se/kultur/ide/svensk-film-politiseras-men-var-ar-debatten/ (accessed September 6, 2022).

Parment, A. (2006). *Distributionsstrategier: kritiska val på konkurrensintensiva marknader*. Malmö: Liber.

Paydar, S. (2017). "Boys Club behind the Scenes: Using Title VII to Remedy Gender Discrimination in Hollywood." *Law School Student Scholarship*, 870.

Peterson, B. (2003). *Välja och sälja: Om bokförläggarens nya roll under 1800-talet, då landet industrialiserades, tågen började rulla, elektriciteten förändrade läsvanorna, skolan byggdes och bokläsarna blev allt fler*. Stockholm: Norstedts.

Petri, G. (2008). *Författarrättens genombrott*. Stockholm: Atlantis.

Pletzer, J.L., Nikolova, R., Kedzior, K.K., and Voelpel, S.C. (2015). "Does Gender Matter? Female Representation on Corporate Boards and Firm Financial Performance – A Meta-Analysis." *PLoS ONE*, vol. 10, no. 6. https://doi.org/10.1371/journal.pone.0130005.

Powell, G., and Butterfield, A.D. (2003). "Gender, Gender Identity and Aspirations to Top Management." *Women in Management Review*, vol. 18, nos 1–2, 88–96.

Powell, G., and Greenhaus, J.H. (2010). "Sex, Gender, and Decisions at the Family → Work Interface." *Journal of Management*, vol. 36, no. 4, 1011–039.

ProductionStudies Research. (n.d.). Available online: https://productionstudies.net (accessed September 7, 2022).

Ramazanoglu, C. (ed.). (1993). *Up Against Foucault: Explorations of some Tensions between Foucault and Feminism*. London: Routledge

Regev, R. (2016). "Hollywood Works: How Creativity Became Labour in the Studio System." *Enterprise and Society*, vol. 17, no. 3, 591–617.

Ricketson, S., and Ginsburg, J. (2006). *International Copyright and Neighbouring Rights: The Berne Convention and Beyond*, vol. 1. Oxford: Oxford University Press.

Rose, C. (1992). "Women and Property: Gaining and Losing Ground." *Virginia Law Review*, vol. 78, no. 2, 421–59.

Rose, C. (1995). "Bargaining and Gender." *Harvard Law Journal & Public Policy*, vol. 18, 547–63.

Rose, M. (1996). "Mothers and Authors: Johnson v. Calvert and the New Children of Our Imaginations." *Critical Inquiry*, vol. 22, no. 4, 613–33.

Rosen, M. (1973). *Popcorn Venus: Women, Movies, and the American Dream*. New York: Avon Books.

Rudberg, E. (1989). "Sven Markelius 1889–1972." *Arkitekturmuseet*, October 28, 1989–February 4, 1990. Stockholm: Arkitektur förlag.

Ryberg, I. (2018). "Revidera historien om auteuren Mai Zetterling!" *Nordic Women in Film*, December. Available online: http://www.nordicwomeninfilm.com/revidera-historien-om-auteuren-mai-zetterling/ (accessed September 6, 2022).

Ryberg, I. (2019). "An Elevated Feminist ahead of Her Time?" In I. Stigsdotter (ed.), *Making the Invisible Visible: New Approaches to Reclaiming Women's Agency in Film History*. Stockholm: Nordic Academic Press.

Ryberg, I. (forthcoming). *Swedish Film Feminism: Between Grassroots Movements and Cultural Policies*. London: Bloomsbury.

Sawicki, J. (1991). *Disciplining Foucault: Feminism, Power, and the Body*. London: Routledge.

Schatz, T. (1988). *The Genius of the System: Hollywood Filmmaking in the Studio Era*. New York: Pantheon Book.

Schottenius, M. (2021). "Vem ska hålla vakt vid luftslottet där konstnärlig frihet bor?" [Who Is to Guard at Castles in the Air Where Artistic Freedom Resides?]. *Dagens Nyheter*, June 16.

Schultz, M.M. (1991). "The Gendered Curriculum: Of Contracts and Careers." *Iowa Law Review*, vol. 70, 55–71.

Serner, A. (2011–2021). [Blog]. Available online: https://annasernersfi.wordpress.com (accessed September 6, 2022).

Serner, A. (2018). "Så ser vi bortom hudfärg och gör svensk film bättre" [This Is How We Look beyond Skin Color and Make Swedish Film Better]. *Expressen*, August 16.

Silverman, K. ([1984] 1990). "Dis-embodying the Female Voice." In P. Erens (ed.), *Issues in Feminist Film Criticism*. Bloomington: Indiana University Press.

Silverman, K. (1985). "A Voice to Match: The Female Voice in Classic Cinema." *Iris*, vol. 3, no. 1, 57–70.

Silverman, K. (1988). *The Acoustic Mirror*. Bloomington: Indiana University Press.

Simon, J. (ed.). (2009). *Alice Guy Blaché: Cinema Pioneer*. New Haven, CT: Yale University Press.

Sjögren, B. (2006). *Into the Vortex Female Voice and Paradox in Film*. Urbana: University of Illinois Press.

Sjöström, V. (1941). "Selma Lagerlöf och filmen." In S. Thulin (ed.), *Mårbacka och Övralid; minnen av Selma Lagerlöf och Verner von Heidenstam/av 40 författare*. Uppsala: J.A. Lindblad.

Smith, D.G. (1996). *Lon Chaney Jr Horror Film star 1906–1973*. Jefferson, NC: McFarland & Company.

Smith, S.L., Choueiti, M., Scofield, E., and Pieper, K. (2013). *Gender Inequality in 500 Popular Films: Examining on-screen Portrayals and behind the Scenes Employment Patterns in Motion Pictures Released between 2007–2012*. Los Angeles: Annenberg School for Communication & Journalism, University of Southern California.

Soila, T. (1991). "Kvinnors ansikte: stereotyper och kvinnlig identitet i trettiotalets svenska filmmelodram." Ph.D. dissertation, Stockholm University.

Soila, T. (1997). "Thalias magra bröd." In T. Soila (ed.), *Dialoger. Feministisk filmteori i praktik*. Stockholm: Aura Förlag Stiftelsen filmvetenskaplig tidskrift.

Soila, T. (1998). "Sweden." In T. Soila, A. Söderbergh Widding, and G. Iversen (eds.), *Nordic National Cinemas*. London: Routledge.

Soila, T. (2004). *Att synliggöra det dolda: om fyra svenska kvinnors filmregi*. Stockholm: Brutus Östlings förlag Symposium.

Soila, T. (2014). "The Phantom Carriage and the Concept of Melodrama." In H. Forsås-Scott, L. Stenberg, and B.T. Thomsen (eds.), *Re-mapping Lagerlöf*. Lund: Nordic Academic Press.

Soila-Wadman, M. (2003). "Kapitulationens estetik: Organisering och ledarskap i filmprojekt." Ph.D. dissertation, Stockholm University.

Stacey, J. (1994). *Star Gazing: Hollywood Cinema and Female Spectatorship*. London: Routledge.

Staiger, J. (2003). "Authorship Approaches." In D.A. Gerstner and J. Staiger (eds.), *Authorship and Film*. London: Routledge.

Stamp, S. (2015). "Feminist Media Historiography and the Work Ahead." *Screening the Past*, vol. 40. Available online: http://www.screeningthepast.com/2015/08/feminist-media-historiography-and-the-work-ahead/ (accessed September 6, 2022).

Stanislavskij, K. (1924). *My Life in Art*. Boston: Little, Brown & Co.

Stigsdotter, I. (2016). "En skandalomsusad pionjär." *Nordic Women in Film*, February. Available online: https://www.nordicwomeninfilm.com/emelie-

gor-film-om-sin-mormors-mormor-en-skandalomsusad-pionjar/ (accessed September 15, 2002).
Stigsdotter, I. (ed.). (2019). *Making the Invisible Visible: Reclaiming Women's Agency in Swedish Film History and beyond*. Lund: Nordic Academic Press.
Stigsdotter, I. (2020). "Women Film Exhibition Pioneers in Sweden: Agency, Invisibility and First Wave Feminism." *Nordic Women in Film*, April. Available online: https://www.nordicwomeninfilm.com/women-film-exhibition-pioneers-in-sweden-agency-invisibility-and-first-wave-feminism/ (accessed September 6, 2022).
"Stina Bergman—i skuggan av Hjalmar" [Stina Bergman—In the Shadow of Hjalmar] (2016). *Nordic Women in Film*, May. Available online: https://www.nordicwomeninfilm.com/stina-bergman-i-skuggan-av-hjalmar/ (accessed September 4, 2022).
Straub, C. (2007). "A Comparative Analysis of the Use of Work-Life Balance Practices in Europe." *Women in Management Review*, vol. 22, 289–304.
Strömholm, S. (1964). *Europeisk upphovsrätt: En översikt över lagstiftningen i Frankrike, Tyskland och England*. Stockholm: Norstedts.
Strömholm, S. (1970). *Upphovsrättens verksbegrepp*. Stockholm: Norstedts.
Strömholm, S. (1975). "Upphovsmans ideella rätt—Några huvudlinjer." *Tidsskrift for rettsvitenskap*, vol. 88, 289–338.
Strömholm, S. (2005). "Upphovsrätten som nationell disciplin – exemplet droit moral." *NIR: Nordiskt immateriellt rättsskydd*, vol. 74, 650–63.
Studlar, G. (1984). "Masochism and the Perverse Pleasures of the Cinema." *Quarterly Review of Film Studies*, vol. 9, no. 4, 267–82.
"Superdirektrisen Karin Swanström". (2016). *Nordic Women in Film*, August. Available online: https://www.nordicwomeninfilm.com/superdirektrisen/.
SVT. (2018). "65 metoo-grupper lämnar kravlista till regeringen." March 6. Available online: https://www.svt.se/nyheter/inrikes/65-metoo-grupper-lamnar-kravlista-till-regeringen (accessed September 6, 2022).
Swedish Film Institute (SFI). (2007). "Harry Scheins kvalitetsbegrepp" [Harry Schein's Concept of Quality]. Available online: https://www.filminstitutet.se/sv/nyheter/2007/harry-scheins-kvalitetsbegrepp/ (accessed January 6, 2022).
Swedish Film Institute (SFI) (2016). *Goal 2020: Gender Action Plan*. Stockholm: Swedish Film Institute. Available online: https://www.filminstitutet.se/globalassets/_dokument/handlingsplaner/actionplan_genderequality_eng_final.pdf (accessed January 6, 2022).
Swedish Film Institute (SFI). (2016). "Stöd till utveckling och produktion av svensk film. En nulägesbeskrivning" [Support for Development and Production of Swedish Film: A Description of the Current State]. Available online: https://www.filminstitutet.se/globalassets/filmpolitiska-dokument/stod_till_utveckling_och_produktion_av_svensk_film.pdf (accessed January 6, 2022).

Swedish Film Institute (SFI). (2018). *The Money Issue: Gender Equality Report 2018*. Available online: https://www.filminstitutet.se/globalassets/_dokument/sfi-gender-equality-report-2018---lowres.pdf (accessed September 6, 2022).

Swedish Film Institute (SFI). (2022). *406 Days: It's About Time. Gender Equality Report* for 2022/2022. Stockholm: Swedish Film Institute. Available online: https://www.filminstitutet.se/globalassets/2.-fa-kunskap-om-film/analys-och-statistik/publications/other-publications/406-days--its-about-time.-gender-equality-report-2021-2022.pdf (accessed September 6, 2022).

Sörensen, B., and Villadsen, K. (2014). "The Naked Manager: The Ethical Practice of an Anti-Establishment Boss." *Organization*, vol. 22, no. 2, 251–68.

Tasker, Y. (1993). "Dumb Movies for Dumb People: Masculinity, the Body, and the Voice in Contemporary Action Cinema." In S. Cohan and I.R. Hark (eds.), *Screening the Male: Exploring Masculinities in Hollywood Cinema*. London: Routledge.

Tasker, Y. (2010). "Vision and Visibility: Women Filmmakers, Contemporary Authorship and Feminist Film Studies." In V. Callahan (ed.), *Reclaiming the Archive: Feminism and Film History*. Detroit. MI: Wayne State University Press.

Tengroth, B. (1972). *Jag vill ha tillbaka mitt liv: Minnen*. Stockholm: Bonniers.

Terjesen, S., Sealy, R., and Singh, V. (2009). "Women Directors on Corporate Boards: A Review and Research Agenda." *Corporate Governance: An International Review*, vol. 17, 320–37.

Thompson, S. (2015). "Towards a Feminist Relational Contract Theory of Prenuptial Agreements." In *Prenuptial Agreements and the Presumption of Free Choice: Issues of Power in Theory and Practice*. London: Hart Publishing.

Thompson, S. (2018). "Feminist Relational Contract Theory: A New Model for Family Property Agreements." *Journal of Law and Society*, vol. 45, no. 4, 617–45.

Thorsen, T.S.S. (2020). "Gendered Representation in Danish Film." In S. Liddy (ed.), *Women in the International Film Industry*. London: Palgrave Macmillan.

Threedy, D. (1999). "Feminists and Contract Doctrine." *Indiana Law Review*, vol. 32, no. 4, 1247–265.

Tianqi Yu, K., and Lebow, A. (guest eds.). (2020). "Feminist Approaches in Women's First Person Documentaries from East Asia," Special issue of *Studies in Documentary Film*, vol. 14, no. 1.

Tidwell, P., and Linzer, P. (1991). "The Flesh-Colored Band Aid-Contracts, Feminism and Norms." *Houston Law Review*, vol. 28, 791–817.

Todorov, T. (1984). *Mikhail Bakhtin: The Dialogical Principle*. Minneapolis: University of Minnesota Press.

Trin T, M. (1993). "The Totalizing Quest of Meaning." In M. Renov (ed.), *Theorizing Documentary*. London: Routledge.

Truffaut, F. (1954). "Une certaine tendence du cinéma français." *Cahiers du cinéma*, vol. 6, no. 32 (January), 15–29.

Ukata, A.A. (2020). "Women and Representations in Nollywood: Questions of Production and Direction." In S. Liddy (ed.), *Women in the International Film Industry*. London: Palgrave Macmillan.

Ulin, J. (2010). *The Business of Media Distribution: Monetizing Film, TV, and Video Content*. Burlington, MA: Focal Press.

UNESCO. (2016). "Promotion of Women in Film Worldwide." Available online: https://en.unesco.org/creativity/policy-monitoring-platform/promotion-women-film-worldwide (accessed September 15, 2022).

"Vägval för filmen" (n.d.). Available online: https://lagen.nu/sou/2009:73#PS1 (accessed September 16, 2022).

Vesterlund, P. (2018). *Schein: en biografi*. Stockholm: Bonnier.

von Konow, U. (1941). *Författares och tonsättares rätt enligt gällande lagstiftning: Kommenterande utredning till Lag om rätt till litterära och konstnärliga verk den 30 maj 1919 med däri genom lag den 24 april 1931 gjorda ändringar och tillägg*. Stockholm: Natur och kultur.

Waldekranz, R. (1986). *Filmens historia: De första hundra åren*, part 1. Stockholm: Norstedts.

Wallenberg, L. (2000). "Stilleristic Women: Gender Ambivalence in the Films of Mauritz Stiller." *Aura: Filmvetenskaplig tidskrift*, vol. 6, no. 4, 39–46.

Wallenberg, L. (2008). "Moden, makar och masker. Modets funktion i två filmer av Mauritz Stiller." In D. Gindt and L. Wallenberg (eds.), *MODE: en tvärvetenskaplig introduktion*. Stockholm: Raster förlag.

Wallenberg, L. (2009). "Straight Heroes with Queer Inclinations." In S. Griffin (ed.), *Hetero: Queering Representations of Straightness*. New York: State University of New York Press.

Wallenberg, L. (2022). "Making (The) Silence Speak: Remake, Retake, Rectify." In M. Koskinen and L. Wallenberg (eds.), *Ingmar Bergman at the Crossroads between Theory and Practice*. New York: Bloomsbury.

Wallenberg, L., and Jansson, M. (2021). "On and Off Screen: Women's Work in the Screen Industries." Special Issue of *Gender, Work and Organization*, vol. 28, no. 6, 2010–025.

Wallenberg, L., and Koskinen, M. (2022). "The Politics of Gendered Work and Representation in the Nordic Screen Industries." Special Issue of *Journal of Scandinavian Cinema*.

Werner, J. (2008). *Medelvägens estetik: Sverigebilder i USA*, part 1. Hedemora: Gidlunds förlag.

Werner, G. (1979). *Herr Arnes pengar: En filmvetenskaplig studie och dokumentation av Mauritz Stillers film efter Selma Lagerlöfs berättelse*. Stockholm: Norstedts.

Werner, G. (2002). *Rött, vitt och gult: färgerna i censurens banér: den svenska filmcensurens bedömningar av Victor Sjöströms och Mauritz Stillers filmer 1912–1936*. Stockholm: Statens biografbyrå.

White, P. (1999). *Uninvited*. Bloomington: Indiana University Press.
Wiberg, C. (2018). "Filmhösten avslöjar att jämställdheten inte har gått för långt" [This Film Fall Reveals that Equality Has Not Gone too Far]. *FLM*, August 17.
Wightman, J. (2000). "Intimate Relationships, Relational Contract Theory and the Reach of Contract." *Feminist Legal Studies University Law Review*, vol. 8, 93–131.
Williams, L. (1989). "Film Bodies: Gender, Genre, and Excess." *Film Quarterly*, vol. 44, no. 4, 2–13.
Williams, L. (1991). *Hard Core*. Los Angeles: University of California Press.
Wolfers, J. (2006). "Diagnostic Discrimination: Stock Returns and CEO Gender." *Journal of the European Economic Association*, vol. 4, 531–41.
Wolodarski, P. (2013). "Sverige förenar naivitet med självgodhet" [Sweden Combines Naivety with Complacency]. *Dagens Nyheter*, May 5.
Women Film Pioneer Project. (n.d.). Available online: https://wfpp.columbia.edu/pioneers/?sort=occupation (accessed September 6, 2022).
Woodmansee, M. (1984). "The Genius and the Copyright: Economic and Legal Conditions of the Emergence of the 'Author.'" *Eighteenth-Century Studies*, vol. 17, no. 4, 425–58.
Wreyford, N. (2013). "The Real Cost of Childcare: Motherhood and Project-based Creative Labour in the UK Film Industry." *Studies in the Maternal*, vol. 5, no. 2, 1–22.
Wägner, E. (1908). *Norrtullsligan*. Stockholm: Albert Bonnier.

Newspaper Articles (Film Reviews)

Anonymous. *Dagens Nyheter*, March 28, 1954, 19.
Anonymous. *Dagens Nyheter*, May 17, 1952, 14.
Anonymous. "På lördagen 90 filmer." *Svenska Dagbladet*, May 9, 1954, 18.
Anonymous. *Svenska Dagbladet*, June 15, 1940, 8.
Björkman, C. *Dagens Nyheter*, May 6, 1953, 7.
[Björkman, C.]. "C. B-n." *Dagens Nyheter*, November 2, 1954, 12.
Brodjaga. "En duktig dekorationsmålarinna." *Stockholms-Tidningen*, October 3, 1931.
"C-a." *Svenska Dagbladet*, June 15, 1940, 8.
Casper. "Filmiska nyårsönskningar." *Svenska Dagbladet*, December 31, 1949, 11.
"Col." *Dagens Nyheter*, June 18, 1938, 13.
Dagens Nyheter, May 5, 1953, 7.
"Esq." *Svenska Dagbladet*, October 12, 1938.
Familjen Kakossaios. "Vår integritet hotas av filmen." *Dagens Nyheter*, February 9, 1983, 15.
"Filmson." *Arbetarbladet*, January 22, 1935.
Forslund, B. Svensk Filmdatabas. Available online: https://www.svenskfilmdatabas.se/sv/ (accessed September 6, 2022).

"-gram." *Svenska Dagbladet*, April 28, 1952, 20.
[Hanson, Sven], "Filmson." *Arbetarbladet* December 22, 1942.
[Idestam-Almquist, B.]. "Robin Hood." *Stockholms-Tidningen*, May 5, 1953.
[Idestam-Almquist, B.]. "Robin Hood." *Stockholms-Tidningen*, July 21, 1953, 11.
[Liliedahl, Ellen], "Lil." *Svenska Dagbladet*, April 25, 1953, 11.
[Liliedahl, Ellen], "Lil." *Svenska Dagbladet*, May 26, 1954, 15.
[Liliedahl, Ellen], "Lil." *Svenska Dagbladet*, November 2, 1954, 13.
[Liliedahl, Ellen], "Lil." *Svenska Dagbladet*, December 18, 1955, 21.
Lindberg, P. *Dagens Nyheter*, October 12, 1938, 10–11.
"Om rätten att säga nej." *Dagens Nyheter*, February 19, 1983, 42.
[Ståhle, A.G.]. "Age." *Dagens Nyheter*, May 9 1954, 20.
[Ståhle, A.G.]. "Age." *Svenska Dagbladet*, May 9, 1954, 13.
[Ståhle, A.G.]. "Age." *Dagens Nyheter*, March 3, 1954, 11.
[Ståhle, A.G.]. "Age." *Dagens Nyheter*, May 9, 1954, 20.
Svenska Dagbladet, April 28, 1937, 16.
Svenska Dagbladet, July 15, 1940, 8.
Svenska Dagbladet, February 6, 1945, 14.
Svenska Dagbladet, December 4, 1949, 18.
Svenska Dagbladet, December 31, 1949, 11.
Svenska Dagbladet, November 8, 2017.
Tirén, Sverker. "Familjens angrepp kränker Romare." *Dagens Nyheter*, Feburary 10, 1983, 20.
Veckojournalen, no. 31, 1959.

Filmography

13 Demon Street (Curt Siodmak, USA, 1959–1960)
A Question of Silence (Marleen Gorris, the Netherlands, 1982)
Amatörer/Amateurs (Gabriela Pichler, Sweden, 2018)
Apflickorna/She Monkeys (Lisa Aschan, Sweden, 2011)
Barabbas (Alf Sjöberg, Sweden, 1953)
Belleville Baby (Mia Engberg, Sweden, 2013)
Bengbulan (Suzanne Osten, Sweden, 1996)
Blott en dröm/Only a dream (Anna Hofman-Uddgren, Sweden, 1911)
Born in Flames (Lizzie Borden, USA, 1982)
Bröderna Mozart/The Mozart Brothers (Suzanne Osten, Sweden, 1987)
Bröllopsnatten (Bodil Ipsen, Sweden, 1947)
Call Me Madame Maestro (Christina Olofson, Sweden, 2021)
Charlotte Löwensköld (Gustaf Molander, Sweden, 1930)
Charter (Amanda Kernell, Sweden, 2020)
Damen i svart/The Lady in Black (Arne Mattsson, Sweden, 1958)
Den moderna suffragetten/The Modern Suffragette (Mauritz Stiller, Sweden, 1913)
Deserter USA (Lars Lambert and Olle Sjögren, Sweden, 1970)
De två saliga/The Blessed Ones (Ingmar Bergman, Sweden, 1986)
Den magiska cirkeln/The Magic circle (Pelle Berglund, Sweden, 1969)
Den vita stenen/The White Stone (Göran Graffman, Sweden, SVT, 1973)
Det sjunde inseglet/Seventh Seal (Ingmar Bergman, Sweden, 1957)
Det är aldrig för sent (Barbro Boman, Sweden, 1956)
Dirigenterna/A Woman is a Risky Bet (Christina Olofson, Sweden, 1987)
Doktor Glas (Mai Zetterling, Sweden, 1968)
Driver dagg faller regn (Gustaf Edgren, Sweden, 1946)
Dröm vidare/Dream On (Rojda Sekersöz, Sweden, 2016)
En kvinna ombord/Woman On-Board (Gunnar Skoglund, Sweden, 1941)
En lektion i kärlek/A Lesson in Love (Ingmar Bergman, Sweden, 1954)
En sjöman i frack/A Sailor in Tailcoat (Ragnar Arvedson, Sweden, 1942)
En Stockholmssilhouett/Stockholm Silhouette (Bibi Lindström, Sweden, 1943)
Eroticon (Mauritz Stiller, Sweden, 1920)
Ett besök hos Selma/On a Visit at Selma's (Raoul de Mat, Sweden, 1925)
Fadren (Anna Hofman-Uddgren, Sweden, 1912)
Fadern/The Father (Alf Sjöberg, Sweden, SVT, 1969)
Faust (F.W. Murnau, Germany, 1926)

Flicka i frack/The Girl in Tails (Karin Swanström, Sweden, 1926)
Flicka med hyacinter/Girl with Hyacinths (Hasse Ekman, Sweden, 1949)
Flickorna/The Girls (Mai Zetterling, Sweden, 1968)
Flickorna från Gamla Sta'n /The Girls from the Old Town (Schamyl Bauman, Sweden, 1934)
Fröken Julie (Anna Hofman-Uddgren, Sweden, 1912)
Fröken Julie/Miss Julie (Alf Sjöberg, Sweden, 1951)
För att inte tala om alla dessa kvinnor/All These Women (Ingmar Bergman, Sweden, 1964)
Godnatt jord/Goodnight Earth (Keve Hjelm, Sweden, SVT, 1979)
Gunnar Hedes saga/The Blizzard (Mauritz Stiller, Sweden, 1923)
Gycklarnas afton/Sawdust and Tinsel (Ingmar Bergman, Sweden, 1953)
Gösta Berlings Saga/The Story of Gösta Berling (Mauritz Stiller, Sweden, 1924)
Hemsöborna/The People of Hemsö (Arne Mattsson, Sweden, 1955)
Her (Spike Jonze, USA, 2013)
Herr Arnes pengar/The Treasure (Mauritz Stiller, Sweden, 1919)
Hets/Torment (Alf Sjöberg, Sweden, 1944)
Hon dansade en sommar/One Summer of Happiness (Arne Mattsson, Sweden, 1951)
Hotell/Hotel (Lisa Langseth, Sweden, 2013)
Ingeborg Holm/Margret Day (Victor Sjöström, Sweden, 1913)
Intermezzo (Gustav Molander, Sweden, 1936)
I rollerna tre/Lines from the Heart (Christina Olofson, Sweden, 1996)
Jag heter Stelios (Johan Bergenstråhle, Sweden, 1972)
Jungfrukällan/Virgin Spring (Ingmar Bergman, Sweden, 1960)
Jänken (Lars Forsberg, Sweden, 1970)
Kan doktorn komma?/Can You Come, Doctor? (Rolf Husberg, Sweden, 1942)
Karin Månsdotter (Alf Sjöberg, Sweden, 1954)
Kvinnodröm/Dreams (Ingmar Bergman, Sweden, 1954)
Kvinnorna kring Larsson/The Women around Larsson (Schamyl Bauman, Sweden, 1934)
Kvinnors väntan (Ingmar Bergman, Sweden, 1958)
Kärlek och anarki/Love and Anarchy (Lisa Langseth, Netflix/Sweden, 2020–2022)
Kärlekens bröd/The Bread of Love (Arne Mattsson, Sweden, 1953)
Körkarlen/The Phantom Carriage (Victor Sjöström, Sweden, 1921)
Landskamp (Gunnar Skoglund, Sweden, 1932)
Lucky One (Mia Engberg, Sweden, 2019)
Långt borta och nära/Near and Far Away (Marianne Ahrne, Sweden, 1977)
Made in Sweden (Johan Bergenstråhle, Sweden, 1969)
Mamma/Mother (Suzanne Osten, Sweden, 1982)
Mamma, flickan och demonerna/The Mother, the Girl and the Demons (Suzanne Osten, Sweden, 2016)
Manhood (Mia Engberg, Sweden, 1999)

Mannekäng i rött/Mannequin in Red (Arne Mattsson, Sweden, 1958)
Mannekängen/The Mannequin (Mauritz Stiller, Sweden, 1913)
Min skäggiga mamma/My Bearded Mum (Maria Hedman Hvitfeldt, Sweden, 2003)
Misshandlingen (Lars Lennart Forsberg, Sweden, 1969)
Mod att leva: en film till Pia/The Courage to Live: A Film to Pia (Ingela Romare, Sweden, 1983)
Muntra musikanter/Jolly Musicians (Weyler Hilebrand, Sweden, 1932)
Musik i mörker/Music in Darkness (Ingmar Bergman, Sweden, 1948)
Människor i stad/City People (Arne Sucksdorff, Sweden, 1947)
Nattlek/The Night Game (Mai Zetterling, Sweden, 1966)
Ni ljuger (Vilgot Sjöman, Sweden, 1969)
The Nile Hilton Incident (Tarik Saleh, Sweden/Germany, 2017)
Norrtullsligan/The Nortull Gang (Per Lindberg, Sweden, 1923)
Nära livet/Brink of Life (Ingmar Bergman, Sweden, 1958)
Paradistorg/Summer Paradise (Gunnel Lindblom, Sweden, 1977)
Pelle Svanslös på äventyr/Peter-No-Tail in an Adventure (Stig Lasseby, Sweden, 1981)
Persona (Ingmar Bergman, Sweden, 1966)
Play (Ruben Östlund, Sweden, 2011)
Pleasure (Ninja Thyberg, Sweden, 2021)
Regissören: en film om Mai Zetterling (Lena Jordebro, Sweden, 2015)
Ryttare i blått/Rider in Blue (Arne Mattsson, Sweden, 1959)
Rätten att älska (Mimi Pollack, Sweden, 1956)
Salka Valka (Arne Mattsson, Sweden, 1954)
Sameblod/Sami Blood (Amanda Kernell, Sweden, 2017)
Selma och Sofie/Selma and Sofie (Mia Engberg, Sweden, 2002)
She Must Be Seeing Things (Sheila McLaughlin, USA, 1987)
Sjunde inseglet/The Seventh Seal (Ingmar Bergman, Sweden, 1957)
Skyddsängeln/The Guardian Angel (Suzanne Osten, Sweden, 1990)
Smultronstället/Wild Strawberries (Ingmar Bergman, Sweden, 1957)
Sommaren med Monika/Summer with Monika (Ingmar Bergman, Sweden, 1953)
Sommarnattens leende/Smiles of A Summer Night (Ingmar Bergman, Sweden, 1955)
The Square (Ruben Östlund, Sweden, 2017)
The Stars We Are (Mia Engberg, Sweden, 1998)
Stockholmsdamernas älskling/The Darling of the Stockholm Ladies (Anna Hofman-Uddgren, Sweden, 1911)
Stockholmsfrestelser/Stockholm Temptations (Anna Hofman-Uddgren, Sweden, 1911)
Surname Nam, Given name Vet (Trin T. Minh-ha, USA, 1989)
Systrarna (Anna Hofman-Uddgren, Sweden, 1912)
Till Österland (Gustaf Molander, Sweden, 1926)
Tomas Graals bästa film/Tomas Graal's Best Film (Mauritz Stiller, Sweden, 1917)
Tomas Graals bästa barn/Tomas Graal's Best Child (Mauritz Stiller, Sweden, 1918)

Ture Sventon – privatdetektiv/Ture Sventon – The Private Detective (Pelle Berglund, Sweden, 1972)

Tösen från Stormyrtorpet/The Lass from the Stormy Croft (Victor Sjöström, Sweden, 1917)

Valborgsmässoafton/Walpurgis Night (Gustaf Edgren, Sweden, 1935)

Vägen till Klockrike/The Road to Klockrike (Arne Mattsson, Sweden, 1953)

The War Game (Mai Zetterling, UK, 1962)

The Woman Who Cleaned the World (Fia-Stina Strandlund, Sweden, forthcoming)

Tystnaden/The Silence (Ingmar Bergman, Sweden, 1963)

X & Y (Anna Odell, Sweden, 2018)

Återträffen/The Reunion (Anna Odell, Sweden, 2013)

Älskande par/Loving Couples (Mai Zetterling, Sweden, 1964)

Äta sova dö/Eat, Sleep, Die (Gabriela Pichler, Sweden, 2012)

Biographies

Louise Wallenberg is Professor in Fashion Studies at Stockholm University, Sweden. She holds a Ph.D. in Film Studies (2002) and she was the establishing director of the Centre for Fashion Studies between 2007 and 2013. Among her publications are the collections *MODE* (2009), *Nordic Fashion Studies* (2011), *Mode och modernism* (2014), *Harry bit för bit* (2017), *Fashion, Film, and the 1960s* (2017), *Fashion and Modernism* (2018), and *Ingmar Bergman at the Crossroads* (2022).

Frantzeska Papadopoulou is Professor of Intellectual Property Rights in the Law Faculty at Stockholm University. She is the editor-in-chief of the *Stockholm Intellectual Property Law Review* and a member of the Advisory Board of the National Library of Sweden. She is the author of several books and articles including *Evergreening Patent Exclusivity in Pharmaceutical Products* (2021) and *The Protection of Traditional Knowledge in Genetic Resources* (2017).

Maaret Koskinen is Professor Emeritus in Film Studies at Stockholm University. She was also a film critic in Sweden's largest daily *Dagens Nyheter* (1981–2011) and a board member of the Swedish Film Institute (2011–2016). Her latest publication is "Involuntary Dogme Restrictions: *Orca* and COVID-19 Screen Culture" (2021). Other publications include *Ingmar Bergman's The Silence: Pictures in the Typewriter, Writings on the Screen* (2010), *Ingmar Bergman y sus primeros escritos: En el principio era la palabra* (2017), and *Ingmar Bergman at the Crossroads* (2022).

Tytti Soila is Professor Emeritus in Film Studies at Stockholm University, and former Vice Dean at the Faculty of Humanities Stockholm University. She is the editor of *The Cinema of Scandinavia* (2005) and *Stellar Encounters: Stardom in European Film* (2009). Her most recent publications include "Ingrid Bergman" (2019), "Activism, Ideals and Film Criticism in 70s Sweden" (2019), and "Featuring Monica Zetterlund: Jazz in early Swedish Television" (2021).

Index

Abbasi, Ali 192
Ackerman, Chantel 97
Adolphson, Edvin 152
Ahrne, Marianne 9, 41–2, 110, 126–7
Åkermark, Arne 164
All These Women (film) 2
Älskande par (film) 98, 110
Alw, Gabriel 144, 147
Amateurs (film) 79
Amatörer (film) 79
Andersson, Bibi 108, 110, 129, 130
Andersson, Harriet 108, 109, 110, 129, 147
Andersson's Kalle (film) 155
Anderssonskans Kalle (film) 155
Another Round (film) 86, 192
Apflickorna (film) 79
Arvedson, Ragnar 169
Aschan, Lisa 79
Äta sova dö (film) 9, 79
Återträffen (film) 79, 188, 192

Barabbas (film) 159, 170–1
Barklind, Carl 154
Bauman, Schamyl 148, 152, 153, 165, 166, 168
Beck, Lili 100
Beckman, Anders 167
Belleville Baby (film) 79, 121, 133
Bengbulan (film) 128
Berg, Stina 100
Bergenstråhle, Marie-Louise De Geer 127
Berglund, Erik "Bullen" 153
Berglund, Harald 165
Berglund, Pelle 178
Bergman, Hjalmar 102, 103
Bergman, Ingmar 2, 40, 108–9, 112, 123, 147, 159, 166, 169, 170, 178–9, 194
Bergman, Ingrid 106, 143, 154
Bergquist, Britta 170
Bier, Susanne 127
Bigelow, Kathryn 9

Björkman, Carl 168
Bladh, Hilding 165, 166, 174
The Blessed Ones (film) 109
The Blizzard (film) 55
Blott en dröm (film) 99
Bock-Tammelin, Bertha 147
Boman, Barbro 6, 108
Borden, Lizzie 97
Border (film) 192
Borgström, Hilda 100, 101, 152
Born in Flames (film) 97
The Bread of Love (film) 159
Breien, Anja 97
Brink of Life (film) 108, 112, 121
Bröderna Mozart (film) 128
Bröllopsnatten (film) 108
Broström, Gunnel 172
Brunaeus, Olle 164
Brunius, Pauline 6, 100
Bryde, Vilhelm 163

Cæsar, Julia 106, 146
Call Me Madame Maestro (film) 129
Campion, Jane 9
Can You Come, Doctor? (film) 169–70
Career (film) 148
Carlsson, Sickan 152, 154
Chaney, Lon Jr 177
Charlotte Löwensköld (film) 55
Charter (film) 79
City People (film) 108
Claësson, Stellan 154
The Count of Munkbron (film) 147
The Courage to Live: A Film to Pia (film) 57–9

Dahlbeck, Eva 108
Damen i svart (film) 173
The Darling of the Stockholm Ladies (film) 99
de Mat, Raoul 54

De två saliga (film) 109
Den magiska cirkeln (film) 178
Den moderna suffragetten (film) 100
Den vita stenen (film) 178
Desguillons, Anne Marie 145
Desguillons, Joseph 145
Det är aldrig för sent (film) 108
Dirigenterna (film) 129
Doktor Glas (film) 110
Dreams (film) 109
Driver dagg faller regn (film) 108
Druk (film) 86, 192
du Rées, Göran 129
Ducournau, Julia 9, 188

Easy Money 3 (film) 188
Eat, Sleep, Die (film) 9, 79
Ebbesen, Dagmar 105–6, 151–2, 155
Edgren, Gustaf 106, 108, 154
Edqvist, Dagmar 108
Ekblad, Stina 40
Ekdahl, Hilmer 148
Ekman, Gösta 106, 148, 163
Ekman, Hasse 107–8, 173
En kvinna ombord (film) 166
En sjöman i frack (film) 169
En Stockholmssilhouett (film) 167
Engberg, Mia 79, 120, 121–2, 133–6
Ericson, Annalisa 151, 153–4
Erik XIV (play) 174
Eroticon (film) 100
Ett besök hos Selma (film) 54
Euphoria (film) 184, 188–9

Fadern (film) 178
Fadren (film) 99, 100
Fagerström-Olsson, Agneta 127
Fant, Kenne 173
Faragó, Katinka 109
The Father (film) 178
Faust (film) 106
Film Chronicle (TV show) 156
Filmkrönikan (TV show) 156
Flicka i frack (film) 103–4
Flicka med hyacinter (film) 107–8, 173
Flickorna (film) 41, 98, 99, 110–11, 112–13, 121
Flickorna från Gamla Sta'n (film) 165

Flickornas Alfred (film) 152
För att inte tala om alla dessa kvinnor (film) 2
Fredrikson, Gustaf 150
Fröken Julia Jubilerar (film) 151
Fröken Julie (film 1912) 99
Fröken Julie (film 1951) 159, 173
Fröken Krykråtta (film) 152
Fürst, Sigge 148

The Girl in Tails (film) 103–4
Girl with Hyacinths (film) 107–8, 173
The Girls (film) 41, 98, 99, 110–11, 112–13, 121
The Girls from the Old Town (film) 165
Godnatt jord (TV series) 176
Goldstein, Max 174
Goodnight Earth (TV series) 176
Göransson, Viking 167, 168
Gorris, Marleen 97
Gösta Berling's Saga (film) 55–6
Graffman, Göran 178
Gräns (film) 192
Green, Eva 184
Gripe, Maria 130
Grünewald, Isaac 162
The Guardian Angel (film) 128
Gunnar Hedes Saga (film) 55
Gycklarnas afton (film) 159, 170

Habel, Ylva 106
Hagman, Britt 106
Hagman, Gerd 155–6
Hammer, Barbara 97
Hanson, Lars 100, 105, 148
Hasso, Signe 148, 153
Hattasken (play) 178
Hedman Hvitfeldt, Maria 120, 130–2, 136
Hem från Babylon (film) 155–6
Hemsöborna (film) 171–2
Herr Arnes pengar (film) 54, 55
Herrgårdssägen (book) 55
Hets (film) 108
Hilebrand, Weyler 165
Hjelm, Keve 176
Hofman-Uddgren, Anna 99–100
Holm, Astrid 146
Holm, Magda 104

Home from Babylon (film) 155–6
Hon dansade en sommar (film) 159
Hon fick platsen (film) 102
Hotell (film) 79, 184, 187, 189
Hour of the Wolf (film) 147
Hugo, Victor 34
Hurt Locker (film) 9
Husberg, Rolf 169

I rollerna tre (film) 120, 129–32, 136
Ingeborg Holm (film) 100, 101–2, 161
Ingemar's Inheritance (film) 55
Ingmarsarvet (film) 39
Intermezzo (film) 106–7, 112, 121
International Match (film) 144
Ipsen, Bodil 108
Isaksson, Ulla 108, 109, 123

Jag heter Stelios (film) 111
Jahr, Adolf 169
Jänken (film) 111
Johnson, Mary 100
Jolly Musicians (film) 165
Jonsson, Jens 188
Josephson, Erland 109
Jungfrukällan (film) 108

Kakossaios, Pia 57–9
Kan doktorn komma? (film) 169–70
Karin Månsdotter (film) 174–5
Kärlek & anarki (Netflix series) 79, 185
Kärlekens bröd (film) 159
Karriär (film) 148
Kejsarn av Portugallien (film) 54
Kernell, Amanda 79, 88
The King of Ping Pong (film) 188
Klercker, Georg af 100
Knutsson, Gösta 59
Körkarlen (film) 55, 56, 146
Krook, Margareta 172
Kvinnodröm (film) 109
Kvinnorna kring Larsson (film) 166
Kvinnors ansikten (book) 106

Ladies' Man Alfred (film) 152
The Lady in Black (film) 173
Lagerkvist, Pär 171
Lagerlöf, Selma 39–40, 43, 50, 53–7, 130

Lagerwall, Sture 148, 152
Landskamp (film) 144
Langseth, Lisa 79, 184–94
Långt borta och nära (film) 9
The Lass from the Stormy Croft (film) 40, 54, 55
Lasseby, Stig 59
Lauridsen, Lau 151
Laxness, Halldor Kiljan 172
Lindberg, Per 102, 149
Lindblom, Gunnel 40, 97, 110, 120, 122, 123–6, 127, 129, 136, 188, 196
Lindeström, Inga 170
Lindgren, Astrid 130
Lindström, Bibi (Birgit) 109, 113, 159–80
Lines from the Heart (film) 120, 129–32, 136
Lo-Johansson, Ivar 176
Löfgren, Marianne 154
Love & Anarchy (Netflix series) 79, 185
Loving Couples (film) 98, 110
Löwenadler, Holger 154
Lucky One (film) 120, 121–2, 133–6
Lund, Richard 100
Lundin, Alva 170

McLaughlin, Sheila 97
The Magic Circle (film) 178
Mallander, Gustaf 147
Mamma (film) 120, 126–8, 132, 136
Mamma, flickan och demonerna (film) 128
Manhood (film) 133
Mannekäng i rött (film) 173–4
Mannekängen (film) 100
The Mannequin (film) 100
Mannequin in Red (film) 173–4
Människor i stad (film) 108
Manstad, Margit 146–7
Margret Day (film) 100, 101–2, 161
Markelius, Sven 163, 167
Marmstedt, Lorens 168
Mattsson, Arne 159, 169, 171, 172, 173–4
Milano, Alyssa 11
Min skäggiga mamma (film) 120, 130–2, 136
Miss Church-Mouse (film) 152
Miss Julia's Anniversary (film) 151
Miss Julie (film) 159, 173

Mod att leva:
  en film till Pia (film) 57–9
Modéen, Thor 105, 151
The Modern Suffragette (film) 100
Molander, Gustaf 39, 106–7
Molander, Karin 100
Molander, Olof 152, 169
Moodysson, Lukas 193
Mother (film) 120, 126–8, 132, 136
The Mother, the Girl and the Demons (film) 128
The Mozart Brothers (film) 128
Munkbrogreven (film) 147
Muntra musikanter (film) 165
Murnau, F.W. 106
Music in Darkness (film) 108
Musik i mörker (film) 108
My Bearded Mum (film) 120, 130–2, 136

Nära livet (film) 108, 112, 121
Nattlek (film) 98, 110
Near and Far Away (film) 9
Ni ljuger (film) 111
Night Game (film) 98, 110
The Nile Hilton Incident (film) 68, 88
Nilson, Alice "Babs" 153
Nomadland (film) 9
Norrtullsligan (film) 102–3, 112, 121
The Norrtull Gang (film) 102–3, 112, 121
Now About All These Women (film) 2
Nykvist, Sven 166–7
Nyman, Lena 178

Odell, Anna 79, 188
O'Fredericks, Alice 151
Ohlin, Lisa 42, 122–3
Olofson, Christina 110, 120, 127, 129–32, 136
Olsson, Lotten 104
On a Visit at Selma's (film) 54
One Summer of Happiness (film) 159
Only a Dream (film) 99
Osten, Gerd 127
Osten, Suzanne 120, 126–8, 132
Östlund, Ruben 70, 88

Paddock, Sven 145
Palme, Ulf 159
Paradistorg (film) 120, 122, 123–6, 136

Pehrsson, Emil A. 164
Pelle Svanslös (film) 50, 59–61
The People of Hemsö (film) 171–2
The People of Värmland (film) 154
Persona (film) 109, 166
Persson, Edvard 105, 153
Peter-No-Tail (film) 50, 59–61
Petersson, Birgitta 172
The Phantom Carriage (film) 55, 56, 146
The Piano (film) 9
Pichler, Gabriela 9, 79
Ping-pongkingen (film) 188
Play (film) 70
Pleasure (film) 79, 86, 190
Pollack, Mimi 108
Potter, Sally 97
Pramm, Birgitta 170
Pure (film) 184, 187

A Question of Silence (film) 97

Rampling, Charlotte 184, 194
Rapace, Noomi 186
Rätten att älska (film) 108
Ravinen (book) 42
The Reunion (film) 79, 188
Rhudin, Fridolf 146
Rider in Blue (film) 173–4
The Road to Klockrike (film) 172
Rolfsen, Katie 151
Romare, Ingela 57, 58, 109
Rosengren, Birgit 147
Ruud, Sif 124
Ryghe, Ulla 109
Ryttare i blått (film) 173–4

A Sailor in Tailcoat (film) 169
Saleh, Tarik 68, 88
Salka Valka (film) 172–3
Sameblod (film) 79, 88
Sami Blood (film) 79, 88
Sawdust and Tinsel (film) 159, 170
Scenes from a Marriage (TV series) 123
Selma and Sofie (film) 133, 135
Serner, Anna 7, 67–88, 196
The Seventh Seal (film) 108, 172
She Monkeys (film) 79
She Must be Seeing Things (film) 97, 121
The Silence (film) 109, 123

Silverman, Kaja 98
Siodmak, Curt 176–7
Sjöberg, Alf 108, 155–6, 159, 169, 170–1, 174, 178
Sjöman, Vilgot 178
Sjöström, Victor 54, 55, 56–7, 100, 102, 105, 146, 148, 161
Sjunde inseglet (film) 108, 172
Skoglund, Gunnar 144, 166
Skyddsängeln (film) 128
Smiles of A Summer Night (film) 108
Smultronstället (film) 108
Snabba Cash 3 (film) 188
Söderblom, Åke 146, 151
Söderholm, Margit 108
Södrans revy (film) 145
Soila, Tytti 106
Sommaren med Monika (film) 108
Sommarnattens leende (film) 108
The Sons of Ingmar (film) 39
The South Theatre Revue (film) 145
Spjuth, Arthur 169
The Square (film) 88
Stacey, Jackie 13
Stanislavsky, Konstantin 147
Star Gazing (film) 13
The Stars We Are (film) 133
Stevens, Ruth 148
Stiller, Mauritz 54–6, 100–1, 105
Stockholm Silhouette (film) 167
Stockholm Temptations (film) 99
Stockholmsdamernas älskling (film) 99
Stockholmsfrestelser (film) 99
The Story of Gösta Berling (film) 55–6
Strand, Marianne 131
Strindberg, August 99, 145, 161, 172, 174
Sucksdorff, Arne 108
Summer Paradise (film) 120, 122, 123–6, 136
Summer with Monika (film) 108
Surname Nam, Given Name Vet (film) 121
Swanström, Karin 6, 100, 102, 103–4, 105, 147, 148, 154
Swing it, Magistern! (film) 153
Swing it, Teacher! (film) 153
Systrar (film) 102
Systrarna (film) 99

The Tale of the Manor (book) 55
Teje, Tora 100, 102

Tengroth, Birgit 147, 154
13 Demon Street (TV series) 176–7
Thulin, Ingrid 108
Thyberg, Ninja 79, 86, 190
Tidblad, Inga 102, 106
Till det som är vackert (film) 184, 187
Till Österland (film) 55
Tillsammans (film) 193
Titane (film) 9, 188, 191
Together (film) 193
Tomas Graals bästa barn (film) 100
Tomas Graals bästa film (film) 100
Tomas Graal's Best Child (film) 100
Tomas Graal's Best Film (film) 100
Torment (film) 108
Tösen från Stormyrtorpet (film) 40, 54, 55
Tower of Lies (film) 54
The Treasure (film) 54, 55
Trin T., Minh-ha 97
Ture Sventon – privatdetektiv (film) 178
Ture Sventon – The Private Detective (film) 178
Tystnaden (film) 109, 123

Ullman, Liv 109
Unger, Bertil 177
Unger, Gustaf 177

Vägen till Klockrike (film) 172
Valberg, Britta 124
Valborgsmässoafton (film) 106
Varda, Agnès 97
Vargtimmen (film) 147
Värmlänningarna (film) 154
Vikander, Alicia 184
Vinterberg, Thomas 192
Virgin Spring (film) 108
Vos, Marik 109

Wägner, Elin 99, 102
Waldekranz, Rune 168, 170
Walk with Me (film) 42
Wallén, Sigurd 146, 147, 155
Walpurgis Night (film) 106
Wechselmann, Mai 110
The White Stone (film) 178
Wiby, Marguerite 152
Widgren, Olof 148
Wifstrand, Naima 145, 147

Wild Strawberries (film) 108
The Wind (film) 148
Winterstein, Franz 148
A Woman is a Risky Bet (film) 129
Woman On-Board (film) 166
The Women around Larsson (film) 166

X & Y (film) 79

Zellman, Tollie 148, 154
Zetterling, Mai 40, 98, 99, 108, 109–11, 121, 129, 147, 169, 194
Zhao, Chloé 9
Ziedner, Lili 100, 102–3